Buy with the Sun in Capricorn. Se
Buy after planets conjunct the S
conjunct the Nu. ...
Sell at any Solar Conjunction. Buy after.
Buy gold in Aquarius and Libra. Sell in Aries and Leo.
Sell towards the Full Moon or the Moon conjunct the North node. Buy
at the New Moon or conjunct the South Node.

This Book Is for You

• **Students of astrology** will find much in these pages to help them understand not only financial and economic analysis, but also principles of mundane astrology. Economics is a view of world events, not something separate or special.

• **Investors, market analysts and students of cycles** will find much to apply to their own knowledge of fundamental and technical analysis of the financial markets, timings that can be enhanced by simple references to ephemerides and astrological charts.

• **Anyone concerned or curious about the future** will find not only forecasts, but astrology's basic tenets of good and bad money practices to help you care for your own economic health and judge the demands and practices of your government. You will be able to spot the differences between slogans, solutions, and common sense.

Our present perspective on economics revolves solely around our materialist, money-centered economies. Today's financial theories and projections have an even shorter perspective of the ebb and flow of wealth, seldom reaching beyond the crash of the Twenties and the depression of the Thirties. *Time and Money* goes deeper, far beyond the short perspectives of today, to demonstrate patterns of economic activity that enable the average person to dig through the hysteria that is seeping into our consciousness as we try to correct the Eighties in the Nineties.

"The field of financial astrology has needed a book like Barbara Koval's for some time. If you've been intrigued by financial astrology but intimidated by all the technical journals and "insider" techniques, there's no better place to start than with *Time & Money*. Barbara Koval knows her subject. She is an excellent teacher, drawing you in so you can learn on your own. Nowhere else can the beginner get such a pleasant, expert, and practical text on the subject. Which is not to say that you pros out there won't find a lot too! You will. *Time & Money* is packed with good, sound astrology all around. I recommend it."

—Michael Erlewine
Director, Matrix Software

About the Author

Barbara Koval has practiced as a professional astrologer for more than twenty years. She has a diploma from the Faculty of Astrological Studies in London, and certification from the Astrologers' Guild of New York. Koval has published articles in almost all the major popular and serious astrology magazines over the last fifteen years, among them *Dell Horoscope, American Astrology, True Astrology Forecast, Astrology Today, CAO Times, Astrological Review,* and *Mercury Hour.* She is the author of *The Lively Circle: Astrology and Science in our Modern Age.* A popular lecturer, Koval has appeared on many radio and TV shows. Her academic background includes a B.A. and a M.A. in English Literature.

To Write to the Author

We cannot guarantee that every letter written to the author can be answered, but all will be forwarded. Both the author and the publisher appreciate hearing from readers, learning of your enjoyment and benefit from this book. Llewellyn also publishes a bimonthly news magazine with news and reviews of practical esoteric studies and articles helpful to the student, and some readers' questions and comments to the author may be answered through this magazine's columns if permission to do so is included in the original letter. The author sometimes participates in seminars and workshops, and dates and places are announced in Llewellyn's New Worlds. To write to the author, or to ask a question, write to:

Barbara Koval
c/o LLEWELLYN'S NEW WORLDS
P.O. Box 64383-364, St. Paul, MN 55164-0383, U.S.A.
Please enclose a self-addressed, stamped envelope for reply, or $1.00 to cover costs.
If outside U.S.A., enclose international postal reply coupon.

Free Catalog from Llewellyn

For more than 90 years Llewellyn has brought its readers knowledge in the fields of metaphysics and human potential. Learn about the newest books in spiritual guidance, natural healing, astrology, occult philosophy and more. Enjoy book reviews, New Age articles, a calendar of events, plus current advertised products and services. To get your free copy of *Llewellyn's New Worlds,* send your name and address to:

Llewellyn's New Worlds
P.O. Box 64383, St. Paul, MN 55164-0383, U.S.A.

TIME & MONEY

The Astrology of Wealth

Barbara Koval

1993
Llewellyn Publications
St. Paul, Minnesota, 55164-0383, U.S.A.

FIRST EDITION 1993

Cover design by Christopher Wells
Cover art by Randy Asplund-Faith
Book design and layout by Susan Van Sant
Astrological charts courtesy of Matrix Software, Inc.
Transit graphs and financial charts by Susan Van Sant

Library of Congress Cataloging-in-Publication Data

Koval, Barbara
    Time & Money : astrology and wealth / Barbara Koval.
      p.   cm.
    Includes index.
    ISBN 0-87542-364-7
    1. Astrology and personal finance. 2. Astrology and business.
    I. Title II. Title: Time and money
    BF1729.F48K68 1992
    133.5'833—dc20   92–34572
                                                          CIP

Llewellyn Publications
A Division of Llewellyn Worldwide, Ltd.
P.O. Box 64383, St. Paul, MN 55164–0383

To My Father

John Paczosa

Who Gave Me the Courage of My Convictions

Acknowledgements

My thanks to Michael Erlewine of Matrix for the use of the Cycles Program while it was in development, to Michael Munkasey for his helpful comments on the manuscript, to Susan Van Sant for her considerate editing, to John O'Connor for the space and encouragement to research and write this book, and to all who participated in bringing it to materialization.

Other Books by Barbara Koval

The Lively Circle: Astrology and Science in our Modern Age

Video Tape

"How to Communicate When You're Not Communicating"

TABLE OF CONTENTS

Charts and Graphs

A WORD ABOUT OLD KNOWLEDGE

Every civilization stores its knowledge. Before hi-tech and throw-away paper, the ancient Mayans, Egyptians, Babylonians and Greeks mastered internal computer design. Instead of loading data into machines, they compressed wisdom into symbols. Instead of turning on a machine for answers, they turned on their minds. We can duplicate their processes. We can retrieve the megabytes of history and observation that pulse in ancient pictures. Astrology began as a calendar and a diary. It became a record of the cycles of human affairs and a philosophy of human impulse and need. Whatever one feels about the validity of this ancient art, it requires no stretch of the imagination or belief to see how the facts of planetary design position themselves against the facts of times present and past.

We are where we have been. If we understand our position we need not go where we went.

STELLAR ECONOMICS

E very day we hear scare stories about the huge debt, the burgeoning deficits, how we are mortgaging our children's futures, about greed and homelessness. Should I buy a house? Should I buy stocks? Is the money in my bank account safe? Will I be able to keep my job? Will I go hungry? Will I survive?

We ignore yesterday. We dwell on tomorrow. We want to know what is to be. We want more to know what will happen to us and what we can do about it, if our children can be better off than we and how to make that happen.

Observation, analysis, and history help us make informed decisions. Observation enables us to view today's reality without pre-judgment. History enables us to view yesterday's reality with the bonus of knowing past problems, past solutions, and past results. Analysis enables us to correlate present observations with past history to make wise and educated guesses about tomorrow.

By shining the wisdom of the past on the problems of today *Time and Money* helps us understand the personal impact of inevitable and unavoidable economic shifts, when to expect them, what to do, how to build wealth in spite of conditions, and how to time investments and sales.

Economics[1]

Economy is the art of making wise provisions for the future. Economics is the study of how it is done. Economy has

1. A very clear and readable treatise on economics: Carson, Clarence B., *Basic Economics,* American Textbook Committee, Wadley, Alabama, 1988.

been a fact of life since the first cave man planted the first seed. Economics has been studied for less than three hundred years. Trade, the fast track to wealth, has been around since the first rock was traded for a shell.

Our present perspective on economics revolves solely around our materialist, money-centered economies. Today's financial theories and projections have an even shorter perspective on the ebb and flow of wealth, seldom reaching beyond the crash of the 1920s and the depression of the 1930s. *Time and Money* goes deeper, far beyond the short perspectives of today to demonstrate patterns of economic activity that will enable the average person to dig through the hysteria that is sure to befall us when the next great correction occurs.

Unlike many modern astrological works, which attempt to fit astrology into current methodologies and knowledge, *Time and Money* is based on the premise that astrology and its symbols form a theoretical model that contains almost everything one needs to know about economic principles and trends. Astrology counters and compensates for the errors of modern mindsets, not the other way around.

In these fading years of the 20th century we are constantly beset by statistics designed to create fear, awe, panic, and excitement in order to sell books, sell advertising space, in order to get votes. Scratch any expert, you find a different pot of gold. Scrape an economic theory, you discover a political point of view.

We are always victims of our age, blinded by a fashionable consensus. Facts alone speak truth.

The Value of Astrology

The science of economics is at best adolescent, with all the impulse of discovery of things new only to itself. Astrology was a calendar long before it became a cult, a diary before it was twisted into cosmic cause and effect. Astrology is and has always been a condensation of knowledge that enables us to compare the painstaking observations and calculations of today to the records of thousands of years before us to see ourselves as a sage of 50 A.D. might see.

While one might argue the validity of astrology, one cannot argue the facts of planetary positions. They, like Dow-Jones averages, population counts, and signatures on dotted lines, are part of recorded history. No system of belief or stretch of the imagination is required to see how facts position themselves against facts.

Technical Analysis

Is a cycle a mathematical, numerical repetition, as scientific analysts would have us believe? Of course not. Simple addition will tell you that any given period is not a constant measurable interval.

The intervals are not time periods but planetary periods that coincide with changing human attitudes, impulses, and actions. Astrology, the art of meaningful coincidence, plots those changes. Though planetary periods seem to follow measurable time intervals, they are, in fact, exact only to themselves and the charts with which they interact. Strictly mathematical calculations of human events are usually off by a year or more. A year may create a gigantic hole in the pocket if one relies on numbers alone.

Technical analysis has value. Technical analysis without content is like an engine without fuel. The design is wonderful, but the vehicle never moves. We do not live in a mathematically prescribed universe, modern science notwithstanding. We live in a near mathematical universe, with an irregular periodicity that correlates to the dance of the celestial spheres.

Astrological timings correlate to accumulations of cyclic forces. They are not cyclic in themselves. Though many repetitions seem mathematically precise, they are the result of convergences not repetitions. The many attempts by technical analysts to establish market predictability inevitably work for a number of years, then falter badly when new long term cycles kick in. The parade of temporary genius millionaires is endless.

The second problem of cycle analysis is its disaster orientation. This is both a result of its mathematical nature and its lack of content. Astrological cycles, while periodic, reflect discernible trends. They have content. Steadiness in a market is not the result of inaction in a cycle, but of one set of trends balancing off another set. You have to understand what is going on between the points to understand the timing.

The great desire of mankind in this scientific age is to be able to reduce all considerations to neat mathematical formulae that can be put into a machine so nobody will have to think or analyze or make a judgment call. The same dream invades most astrological researches, especially in the market sphere. We will always have to interpret and use our judgement. Even the most exact planetary timing will be amenable to interpretation for EFFECT. Effect is always the result of decision making and free will.

Though people and governments often facilitate prediction by following the path of least resistance, we know that wise decisions make the good better and the bad tolerable. Wise decisions are grounded in reality and observation, not theory. Astrology, as a tool of observation that removes us from the fashions of the day, enables us to see ourselves outside ourselves and beyond our fears, our politics, and our doubts.

Impact

All countries do not share equally the fate of universal indicators. Every stock market will not crash at the same hour, nor every government go to war. Individuals are not hit equally in bad times. The greatest fortunes, like that of the Kennedys, were made in the worst of times, not the best. Planetary cycles mark the turning points and the options. They do not always describe the action. What happens correlates to the signs and to the houses of the appropriate charts. What happens is the result of an informed will, the courage to act in spite of.

Not only will *Time and Money* make sense of the multitude of parallels in our history, it will show how and when they repeat, and it will elucidate the underlying problems without reference to the political and the contradictory wisdoms of today. We need every bit of insight we can get if we are to avoid the threat of economic dislocation that is ripening for the 1990s. Astrology gives us old eyes for new viewpoints.

Organization

Time and Money is a book of common history and common sense for people who cannot take the time to sort whether economist A or politician B or media analyst C is right about our financial future. It is divided into three parts: DEFINITIONS, CYCLES, and DESIGNS.

DEFINITIONS describes money, what it is, what it is not, and how it functions in the three fundamental economic modes. When we understand the astrological symbols we know the truth about money and how to preserve, protect, and expand our wealth.

CYCLES covers: Astrological correlations to known cycles: Kitchin and Juglar Cycles; the Kondratieff Wave; the 60-Year Cycle; the Mutation Cycle, a classic astrological cycle, which forms the basis for most economic forecasting; and the Solar Field, all new research on short and medium length movements.

DESIGNS addresses various world, national, and individual charts[2] that mesh global events with specific geographical locations, their impact on specific people, organizations of people, commodities, and trade.

The final chapter is about tomorrow, what it could bring, signs and signals to watch for, that we may position ourselves and our offspring for the real New World Order with a minimum of pain.

Value

If you are a student of astrology you will find much in these pages to help you understand not only financial and economic analysis, but also principles of mundane astrology. Economics is a view of world events, not something separate or special. If you are worried or curious about the future, you will find not only forecasts, but astrology's basic tenets of good and bad money practices to help you care for your own economic health and judge the demands and practices of your government. In an age driven by media hype, the best ideas always succumb to the most exciting presentation of ideas, both good and bad. You will be able to spot the difference between slogans, solutions, and common sense.

If you are a student of cycles, an investor, or a market analyst, you will find much that can be applied to your own knowledge of fundamental and technical analysis of the financial markets, timings that can be enhanced by simple references to ephemerides and astrological charts.

Time and Money provides all the information we need to evaluate the decisions of government in the new crisis so we can protect ourselves from ignorant panics, self-serving blame, and unnecessary loss.

---

2. For those individuals who are not familiar with the symbols used in astrological charts, a list of symbols is supplied in Appendix I, page 285.

Remember the story of Hansel and Gretel? Abandoned in the dark forest by their impoverished parents, the unfortunate brother and sister dropped crumbs in the hope of finding a way back home. Animals of the night gobbled away their foresight. Hungry and frightened, they stumbled onto a gingerbread house owned by an evil witch, whose favorite meal was plump little boys.

We, too, have stumbled into a gingerbread party, hosted by bankers, ordered by politicians, and paid for by an entry at the Federal Reserve. The activists blame greed and cry for a redistribution of the wealth. The politicians blame deficits and cry for more taxes. The crumbs left by those who saw it all before suggest eternal cycles of repetition, eternal impulses of human nature, and universal truths that play themselves out in the unique economies of a person, a country, or an era's inclination and taste.

The ovens are fired. Though trussed and stuffed by faddish theories promoted for political ends, we can break the momentum and pull our fingers from the fire if we but look beyond our narrow perspectives. We cannot change human nature. We can protect ourselves from foolish repetitions when we identify the history that repeats.

Everything we need to know we have. As above, so below. Time is the master of money. The stars are the master of time.

Part I

DEFINITIONS

Serpents in the Sky

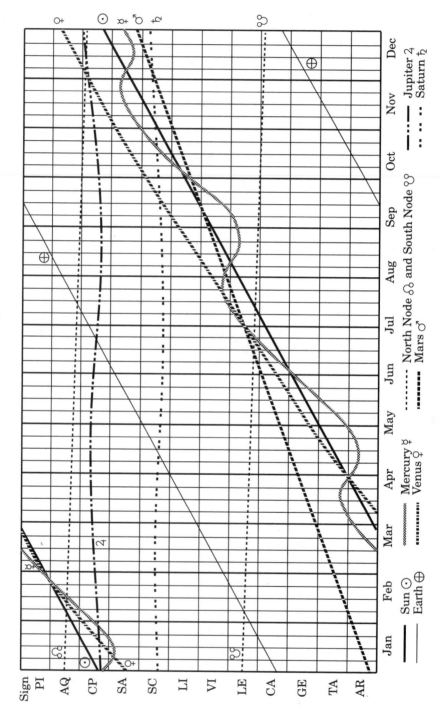

8

Chapter One

FUNDAMENTALS AND MULTIPLES

Everybody talks about the economy. Nobody knows what it means. Ask the experts. They all have answers. They all have different answers. We swim in a world of indiscriminate information—truth entangled with lies. To separate the lie from the real, best we go back to what our forefathers and their forefathers knew. They knew that love and money spring from the same human urge: the urge to be whole, to be complete, to be safe. The Prince kisses Sleeping Beauty and ends up a king. The knight slays the dragon, gains a treasure and a wife.

The basic impulses of money are the same as the basic impulses of love: getting, exchanging, multiplying. The problems of money, like love, are getting, competing, and being deceived.

What Is Money?

Money is a piece of paper, an accounting of assets, labor, and debt. The paper has no value except as a medium of exchange. The more important question is: What is wealth? Wealth is a storehouse of value, what we have to trade. Wealth is the power that creates trading value. Wealth was gold, a commodity of mutually agreed upon intrinsic value. Gold in the ground had no value. Gold in circulation did.

The sages who observed love and money back in the shadows of man's distant past identified love and money with the planet Venus. They created meanings for Venus, both from her position relative to the other "wandering stars," as the planets were called, and from observed events that correlated to her changing position relative to the Sun, to Mercury and to the other creatures that danced along the solar highway we call the Zodiac. Because the orbit of Venus is between the Earth and Sun, we see her only briefly as a morning or evening star. Both she and her elfin companion, Mercury, lead the parade of the rising Sun or, like camp followers, straggle into a sky gone black.

In the astrological tradition the Sun is associated with gold, Venus with copper. Mercury, the messenger of the Sun, is the symbol of paper. The Moon, the Earth satellite that fills our nights with its cool sheen, represents silver. Together they make up what civilized man has used for money, once he gave up beads and shells.

Wealth is not money. Wealth is Venus, what money can buy.

The Standard of Value

The Sun (gold) is the fundamental storehouse of energy (value), and the fundamental regulator (standard) of all planetary interaction (trade). In real terms, the gold standard is impersonal and the least subject to the manipulation of politicians, princes, and wheeler-dealers, from the rug merchants in ancient Persia to the junk-bond profiteers of New York and L. A. Just as the Sun does not protect us from droughts and monsoons, neither does a gold standard eliminate cycles of up and down. The gold standard is only a means of keeping money (our value accounting system) out of the grasp of those who place immediate profit before long term stability or fail to connect public power with public service.

The Dollar Bill

Mercury, the satellite of the Sun, is a speedy accountant that gives us a slip of paper that assures us we have gold in the bank or value in our accounts. Paper is a dollar bill. A dollar bill is the word of the powers that be that we do indeed own our assets. Mercury disappears into the Sun every few months and is consumed. Paper is merely paper, after all. Paper must be turned back into gold periodically to keep the system stable. In 1873 and 1933 we restabilized our inflated currency against the gold standard to counter the depressions that followed orgies of economic growth and debt. Since we removed ourselves from the gold standard in 1971, we have allowed our currency to fluctuate against other currencies as a measure of our relative strength in the world economy. As measured against gold, our currency has depreciated by a factor of 10. Today a dollar buys what 10 cents bought 60 years ago. Today's dollar is barely worth a dime and falling.

Tangible Assets

Venus follows the same pattern as Mercury on a longer time scale. In addition to copper, the substance of our pennies, Venus represents land and tangible assets. Gold into paper is a short term transaction. Gold into property of all kinds creates long term wealth. Venus, too, falls back into the Sun to be revalued against the norm.

Barter is the primary mode of Venus—value for value apart from any arbitrary human standard. Though barter is subject to the dictates of nature, the seasons of earth and men, Venus stabilizes. When our money is orderly, prices rise and fall in a relatively predictable sequence. The Dow-Jones Industrial Average rose and fell in a range of 500 to 1,000 from 1960 to 1982. This was not a sluggish market, it was a stable market. In a balanced economy, you earn your money from dividends, not from speculating on how high the price of stock will rise. Trading and investing are fraternal twins at best. Trading is Mercurial, a paper transaction. Venus is investing in vehicles of intrinsic worth. Venus is a planet of saving. How many of us have a penny jar? For many, copper is the only thing we save. Coppers are the only coins that both rich and poor can hoard.

Consumables

The Moon is the planet of the consumer and of consumables, that is, commodities. We see its cycle very clearly every month from New Moon to Full, growing, failing, and being eaten on occasion by eclipses, just as we eat up our non-durable goods. Like the constantly changing Moon, silver, its metal, has a history of wild fluctuations—overproduction, underproduction, in the currency and out. The Moon is the planet of public taste and public interest, homes, and consumables, what must be constantly replenished, is eaten up, what dances to the whims of the market, what enters the market only to disappear. The Moon is the satellite of the Earth and all its moods and desires. The people of the earth are always trying to substitute silver for gold.

The Serpent in the Sky

The illustration at the beginning of this chapter shows the paths of the Sun, Venus, and Mercury on a 360° graph. It is the modern manifestation of the caduceus, two serpents twined about a central sheaf of wheat, a symbol of knowledge and health, and the planetary version of the double helix, the carrier of genetic information. Sun, Venus, Mercury, and the binding Moon are the basic symbols of human commerce. They compose the fundamental trade cycle and are responsible for all short and medium term fluctuations. They are the serpent in the sky, the fundamental knowledge of what we are, the dynamics of human interaction.

Interest and Debt

The real spoiler in the neat little balancing act achieved by the Sun, Moon, Venus, and Mercury is the planet Mars. Mars is the twin of Venus on our far side, the planet that connects Earth wealth to the planetary indicators of authority and law: Saturn and Jupiter. Saturn and Jupiter also represent the universal law of supply and demand, but for now we will use them as indicators of governments and markets. Venus and Mercury give us the wealth of the Sun. The Moon consumes it. Mars takes it away to the government in the form of taxes. Mars takes it to financial agents in the form of interest and fees.

Mars rules other people's money or value that is shared or used without having full control. Mars is a loan. Mars is debt. Mars is getting something for nothing or making the attempt. In an inflationary economy such as we have had since 1933, and even more intensely since 1970 when we went on floating exchange rates, Mars buys goods with borrowed money and pays back with cheaper dollars thereby beating the inflation and paying no effective interest. Not only was the price cheaper to start with, but a locked-in interest rate at a time of rising interest rates driven by rising inflation made it more profitable to borrow than save. If you saved, your purchasing power did not increase, but diminished.

Mars is the planet of iron. Steel production in our technological economy has always been a major factor in modern economic health. Iron and steel are weapons of war, both industrial and real, and of cuts. Mars always represents those transactions that are represented as "cuts." A percentage is a cut out of the price or the value. Interest rates and taxes are always represented in percentages. Mars is the planet that represents interest rates. An interest rate does not determine a price level, only percentages (interest, taxes, and profits) of price levels. When these percentages rise too high, the value of markets declines. Industry prices itself out of the market. The rising price of steel throughout the 1970s eventually priced the United States out of the world markets and destroyed steel production at home. In a service economy, Mars is no longer steel, but iron-fisted debt.

Mars is the planet of speculation. The speculator anticipates a cut and tries to get in and out of the market as fast as he can. Short selling is the province of Mars as is buying items on sale, at auction, and profiting on disasters and crises. Mars is the attack. Mars is self-defense.

Mars makes you a profit or gets you a deal, but it does not create or multiply wealth. It only creates and multiplies money.

Mars goes for the bargain. Venus buys and sells fair. The Sun stabilizes. Mercury connects and trades. The Moon consumes.

Definitions

At this point we have two planets that create wealth, two that destroy it, and one that facilitates trade. From this we can deduce the basic meanings of these planets and how they relate to economic analysis.

SUN Gold and substances of intrinsic value. Gold is the final authority and limiter of price rises and falls. When currency values measured against gold or trading media and commodities reflect gold prices, they send signals of intrinsic value or market adjustment.

MERCURY Paper money and media of exchange. Mercury is the trader who records the value of goods and services against the universal standard. Mercury is the active buyer and seller as opposed to the relatively inactive investor. Its transactions give us instantaneous feedback on the current state of financial affairs.

Mercury creates market statistics. Mercury creates the market itself.

VENUS Venus is copper and barter, value given and value received. Venus looks for long term appreciation; land, raw materials, durable goods, and objects that give pleasure apart from their cost, such as art. In market terms, Venus is the great stabilizer. She always tries to achieve a price level she held before. If Venus ruled the market it would always rise and fall within a predictable range.

MOON The Moon represents the consumer, the instincts and needs of people *en masse*. It represents short term fluctuations, inclinations, market ups and downs and mindless urges driven by fundamental need and public propaganda. Its metal is silver. What it buys disappears.

MARS Mars is the planet of the quick buck, interest rates, taxes, debt, cuts, losses, speculation, and crisis. It represents the desire to get something for nothing. It is the planet of iron and war.

The Money Economy

A money economy solves the major problem of barter: Joe has a motorcycle I want to buy, but he doesn't want my riding lawn mower in exchange. Fred wants my lawn mower, but I don't want his skimobile. On the other hand, Joe might like the skimobile, but I don't want to trade and risk getting stuck with a skimobile I don't want, minus a motorcycle I do. We all end up with something we want to sell and nothing we want to buy. With gold or some other standard of exchange, we trade the standard for the product and everyone gets what he wants—if he has the money. If the standard of exchange is barter, no one gets to trade unless he has a surplus and is prepared to take a risk.

If the standard of exchange is unstable, we never know if we get what we bargain for. The following example illustrates the complexity of any standard trade.

The Family Home

To understand how these planets operate in action, we can use the example with which most of us are familiar, the purchase of the family home.

Solar Value

Suppose you buy a house. The intrinsic value of the house would be the price it would fetch in gold. This is the only way one could reasonably assess the value of the goods and labor that went into its creation *vis-á-vis* the value of goods and labor that went into a comparable house. In an inflating economy or one without a gold standard, the Sun value would be calculated by the cost of goods and labor in a new home and the relative selling prices of other houses in a neighborhood of comparable homes.

Mercurial Price

Mercury represents the actual selling price of the house regardless of the value received by either buyer or seller: the accounting of the trade.

Venusian Exchange

The owner value of the house, Venus, is what the buyer is willing to pay and what the seller is willing to accept. The Venus value of a property is its barter value: not only what the seller and buyer agree to as a purchase price, but what the seller can get for the money he receives. In determining true equity, one must determine if the money received can buy a property of equal size, equal appointments, and comparable location.

Lunar Satisfaction

Lunar factors in a trade are very personal and specialized. They range from social aspirations because of the neighborhood, to flower gardens, and a room with a spectacular view. They represent the old real estate saw: Location. Location. Location.

Martian Cuts

Costs beyond the transaction itself reduce value for both buyer and seller: fees for title searches, lawyers, points and commissions.

All the above are factored, consciously or unconsciously, into the purchase price. Because the price is based on so many imponderables, it can go above or below the true value of the Sun. In soft real estate markets or with a distressed seller, you get a deal. In sellers' markets you may have to settle for less than you desire or pay more than you planned. Venus is barter value, which may be higher or lower than intrinsic value or even market value.

Unlike a standard of value (the Sun), a selling price is individually determined. In a stable economy, houses would sell

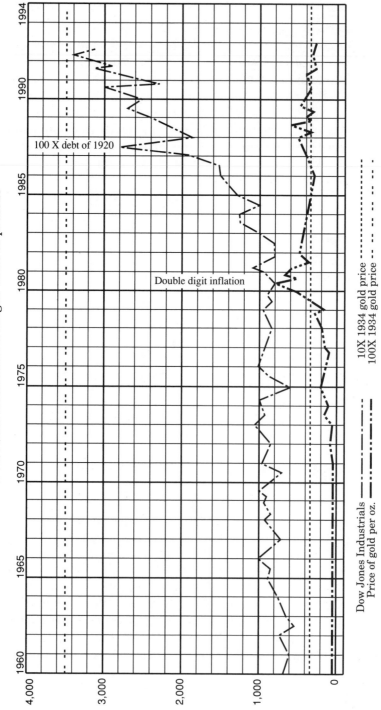

Gold and the Dow

Dow Jones Industrial Averages 1960 to present

100 X debt of 1920

Double digit inflation

Dow Jones Industrials ————
Price of gold per oz. —··—··—

10X 1934 gold price ··········
100X 1934 gold price ·· ·· ··

over and over at approximately the same price, fluctuations determined only by the negotiations of sellers and buyers. Everyone would have a very clear idea of what a house is worth. In an unstable economy, or one with unstable currency, it is impossible to determine either intrinsic or trading value.

A deflating economy, which is characterized by either a shrinking of the money supply or a growth in population in a stable economy, produces falling prices. An inflating economy with a growth in money supply or a shrinking population with a stable money supply produces a rise in prices. The value of the house as a "living machine" is unaffected. Price does not determine the "live-ability" of a home. The Solar value is there no matter what the price. If a house is "consumed," that is, it is a once in a lifetime purchase; any valuation beyond the original purchase price is irrelevant. It will hold its value for the owner as a home for the rest of his life.

Martian Loss

When homes become a tradable commodity, rather than a consumable, brokers and Mars enter the picture. Mars always represents a "cut," it can be a cut in the financial return for the seller, or an added expense for the buyer. Mars activity tends to increase the selling price, without increasing the value received. Mars is always a drop in value. It is often followed by a drop in price. Once you drive your car off the lot, you have already lost 20% or more of its value. Once you buy a home you have already lost the broker's fee.

When you pay a broker a 6% commission on a $100,000 house ($6,000), the seller actually receives $94,000 for the house. This is the actual trading value received. The person who bought the house for $100,000 will have to sell it for $106,000 if he is to get his purchase price back using a broker. He will have to sell the house for $12,000 more than the first seller received, an approximate increase of 12% in trading value.

Brokers may argue they get better prices than sellers alone. They have to earn their fees. In a speculative market real estate must appreciate over the time the property is held to support two commissions. The broker raises the price of the house without raising its intrinsic value. Thus, the buyer always experiences a loss in value after purchase—particularly if the selling price remains the same.

Martian Taxes

In the dark ages before property taxes, the cost of the house was the cost of the house. At its best Mars represents co-ownership. It represents any claims to a property that restrict your ability to do with it totally as you please. Mars is also the arm of the law that extends from Jupiter and Saturn to Earth, law enforcement. It is the flow of money from the Earth back to Jupiter and Saturn in the form of taxes.

Property taxes, fees, and assessments all add cost to owning and maintaining one's property. Burglaries, vandalism, expenses for trash removal, well-digging, and sanitation can also add cost and therefore subtract value from your home if you do not have a government that provides adequate service. Taxes are necessary. Taxes are Mars. As Mars they always represent a loss.

How To Determine Value

Although many pooh-pooh the role of gold in modern economies, only two planetary symbols enable us to judge the real value and the equitable price of any transaction. One is Venus, the barter trade. If you paid $50,000 for a house you sell for $150,000, will a new home purchased for the recent selling price have the same space and amenities? Price is not the determinant. The barter trade is.

Since we do not want to have to sell our house in order to find its true worth, we can judge relative value, before we buy or sell, by the relative price of gold. The relative price of gold is the key to the loss of value of our currency due to inflation.

History of Multiples

The Gold Multiple

If we look at our own brief history we know that gold began at $20.67 an ounce when the value of our dollar was first established in 1837. In 1933, it was revalued to $35 an ounce, which it held until it was further devalued to $40 and $45 in the early 1970s. When it could not hold that figure, we went off the gold standard *de jure*. *De facto* it still exists. A revaluation does not mean that the price of gold is going up, though that is what it appears to do. The truth is that the value of our currency is going down. *When the price of gold goes up the value of the currency goes down.*

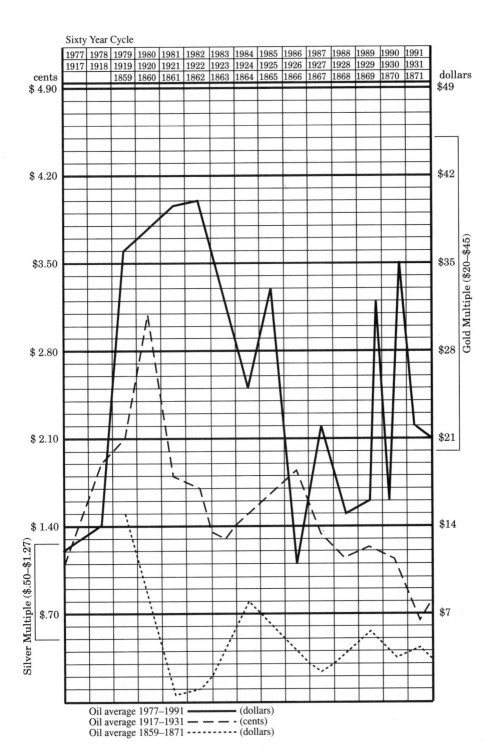

Sixty Year Cycle

	1977	1978	1979	1980	1981	1982	1983	1984	1985	1986	1987	1988	1989	1990	1991
	1917	1918	1919	1920	1921	1922	1923	1924	1925	1926	1927	1928	1929	1930	1931
cents		1859	1860	1861	1862	1863	1864	1865	1866	1867	1868	1869	1870	1871	dollars

Oil average 1977–1991 ————— (dollars)
Oil average 1917–1931 — — — — (cents)
Oil average 1859–1871 ·········· (dollars)

Multiples—Solar Field Oil Averages

19

The intrinsic value of the Sun never changes. Nor does the intrinsic value of gold. Market price and intrinsic value are not the same. Market price is Mercury, what the accounting system determines the value of our currency to be. Market value is Venus, the equitable trade. All price levels are a function of the interaction of the Moon, Mercury, Venus, and the Sun. This is not only true from an interpretational stance, but as will be demonstrated later in the discussion of the Solar Field, the primary indicator of medium and short term market cycles.

During the Civil War, though the dollar was still pegged to $20 an ounce, inflation pushed greenbacks up to $200 per ounce of gold. Though we had no Dow-Jones Industrial Average at that time, the general stock price levels fell into the $20 to $40 range. The trading average reached a high just before the economic debacle of 1874 when the banking system failed. What we see in these figures is that the greenbacks used to finance the Civil War reached an upper limit that was 10 times the price of gold. *Multiples of gold are always indicators of upper and lower limits.*

Likewise, limits on the price of durable goods and financial instruments (Venus) stated in dollars (Mercury) are also a multiple of gold (Sun).

In 1929, the DJIA peaked at $380, very close to the revalued dollar of 1933. The market crashed as it overreached its multiple of gold. The price of gold today fluctuates between 10 times the prices of gold in 1933 and 1971. The value of our dollar has fallen in the same ratio as the dollar value to gold. That is, our prices have risen by a factor of 10. The price of gold has risen by a factor of 10. The price of gold is an indicator of the cost of inflation. To put it a slightly different way, if you pay more than 10 times the cost of anything 60 years ago you are paying too much.

The Silver Multiple

Silver, our secondary storehouse of value, is the trading medium of consumables and housing. In astrology the Moon rules home. Although a home is a piece of durable property, in most cases it is not a marketable commodity. Once bought, in stable times, it goes out of the market indefinitely. It is "consumed." (Art and raw land are technically always up for sale.) The price of silver was established at the same time as gold at $1.27 an ounce. In the history of the United States it rarely achieved this level and mostly hovered in a *de facto* area of $.50

to $.75 an ounce, on rare occasions rising with government manipulation as high as $2. Today's price factored by the multiple of 10 to account for our inflated currency, should produce a silver price of $5 an ounce. At this writing, it is closer to $4, undervalued, and a good buy. $4 is a gold multiple and a sign of distress in the silver market.

In the 1920s, housing peaked in the vicinity of $11,000, the median price for a single family home. Today the multiple is still a factor of the silver range ($50,000 to $160,000—100,000 times the price of silver) and 10 times higher than it was 60 years ago.

Any look at selected prices on the commodities market shows that most of them fall into the silver multiple area. Commodities with government price supports fall in the gold multiple area. Gold and the Sun are authoritarian symbols. Government supported prices for consumables are authoritarian, not market driven.

The Debt Multiple

The federal debt is the source of inflationary price levels in the economy. The federal debt will be discussed more clearly in the chapter on Neptune, but the limits of the growth of public debt (not to be confused with ongoing budget deficits) seems to reach a critical mass at multiples of 10 to the period approximately 60 years earlier. Our current debt is now more than 100 times the debt of 1919, the high reached prior to the 1929 crash. The system has more than enough money to support gold, silver, and Dow multiples that are 10 to 100 times the price levels of the 1920s.

Application

Scarcity, panic, and mass mania often drive the prices of consumables into the durable price area. Always anticipate hardship when you see a gold price multiple on a consumable or a gold price on an investment vehicle, such as the DJIA. When money is invested it acts like a consumable, it goes out of circulation and therefore carries a silver multiple, 5 to 12. When money is spent on speculation it is a tradable, and carries a gold multiple, 2 to 4.

Illustration

The most telling statistics come from the great oil, silver, gold mania circa 1980. In previous years as a consumable, oil always followed the silver pricing. Sixty years ago it was $1.25 *a barrel*. After the great run-up, which was an adjustment for inflation, oil held in the silver range, around $11 to $19, until Iraq took over Kuwait. At $19 a barrel oil is slightly overpriced. Oil in the $30 to $40 range puts it at a gold multiple and therefore unstable. The price has to crash.

At the turn of the decade metals frenzy, silver reached $17 an ounce. Historically high but not really overvalued. A $5 range is far more comfortable. Silver is perennially overproduced which militates against its ever becoming a standard of currency. It is especially overproduced in this country, a factor which will become more clear in the chapter on economic styles.

When oil went over $30 a barrel it moved into the gold pricing area. In fact, oil was called the new gold as OPEC gathered together and drove up the price. They were able to drive up the price, not simply because they formed a cartel, but because our inflated currency demanded such a price. The Arabs have always had a healthy respect for gold. They were not fooled by floating dollars and international deals to maintain stable prices. When gold moved into a silver range, trading at $900 an ounce, it became a commodity. Oil became "gold." Gold became "silver." Since oil cannot by its nature as a consumable ever take the place of gold, which as jewelry and ornament, not to mention coins, is always up for sale, the situation could be temporary at best. Oil at $20 is tolerable. Oil at $12 is an appropriate range. Oil at $5 a barrel is a probability, depending ultimately on stability in the Middle East and the state of the federal debt.

Investment vs. Speculation

To repeat, in 1929 the Dow-Jones Industrial Average peaked at $380, a close multiple of the 1933 valuation of gold. (Since the value of gold was fixed by law in 1929, we do not know what its real value was at the time.)

The relation of the Dow pricing to multiples of either gold or silver reflect whether the market is a speculative or an investing market. When the Dow is trading in a silver range, the previous 500 to 1,200 levels, stocks are a consumable. That is, people buy and hold like true investors. When the market is in a speculative phase, the gold range, people buy to resell at a higher price. When the Dow-Jones overreached 1,200 in 1982 (the top multiple of silver), it moved into a speculating phase. For the Dow to restabilize as an investment rather than a trading vehicle it will have to return to 1,200 or climb to 5,000.

Gold multiple markets are trading and speculating vehicles: gold, art, jewelry, stocks, and raw land. Speculative markets are always dangerous in the long run. For stocks, the danger of collapse comes when speculative fever drives the Dow to a multiple of gold: anything from 2,500 up.

Whether or not the Dow-Jones is a true stock market indicator, its price levels have accurately reflected the true value of our trade, when measured against the value of gold. With gold at $350 to $400 an ounce and the Dow hovering between 3,000 and 3,400 we are at a critical point. When the Dow tickled 3,000 and gold slid to $350 an ounce we came very close to a major correction.

Today and Tomorrow

The current Dow trades in a gold range and is, therefore, unstable. To determine the limits of that instability we have to measure the market against the price of gold. The adjustment point of the Dow will be a multiple of the current price of gold to the original price of gold, which it has already surpassed, or 10 times its price level in 1929 ($3500 to $4,000). The problem here is more complex than simple multiples. We have already seen that there is more than enough money in circulation to support the high Dow figures, but the trade deficits have exported much of this money, and the collapse of the junk-bond market, the decline of real estate values, and the S&L failures have removed much that circulated internally.

In terms of the real inflation in our economy, the Dow would have to reach 5,000 to 10,000 to restabilize on the upside or fall below 1,300 on the downside. Because we have exported much of our inflation, we do not see the multiples in our own economy. The DJIA should reach at least 3,500 in order to absorb the money created by our federal debt. Since much of our currency is being "exported," that is, it is buying foreign goods, and because the U.S. currency for many years has substituted for gold as the international medium of exchange, we can expect to see multiples of the price of gold in U.S. dollars showing up in other national trade figures.

It is no coincidence when Japan's Nikkei Index reached 40,000 it reflected a multiple of gold priced around $400 an ounce. When the price of gold and the Nikkei shared the same integer, the Nikkei fell just as the Dow did in 1929. In 1992 it was 17,000.

The undervalued Dow suggests either that the stock market is the best place to invest, or the state of our industry is declining and on the verge of collapse. Certainly on a global scale our stock market is underpriced relative to an accurate financial adjustment. The Nikkei trading average indicates unequivocally where much of our inflation went. The United States inflation drove the Japanese stock market to all time highs. From our perspective that should be viewed as good news. The Nikkei took the big hit. The trade imbalance kept our consumer inflation down.

Crisis and Change

When the prices in any market or commodity begin to converge with the price of gold, in fact, or as a multiple of 10 (or whatever the differentiation in foreign currency), we can expect to see at the very best a limit. A major economic adjustment is in play. The dollar can absorb no more inflation without going out of control. Our danger is not the trade imbalance but the debt and tax increases that could lead to recession, depression, or runaway inflation.

In the 1950s we made a safe adjustment to 10 times the level of the 1890s with only a mild recession. Whether we can achieve that outstanding feat again depends much on the choices and decisions made by the government and the Federal Reserve. As will be shown in the cycles segment, we do not have the same protections we had in the 1950s and considerably more negative pressures than we had either in the 1930s, 1950s, or 1870s, all of which had similar transits and mutual configurations.

The price multiples of gold (Sun) and silver (Moon) indicate whether the commodity is a consumable, a tradable, an investment, or a speculation. This knowledge combined with astrological technique enables a more quantitative level of interpretation than simply the cyclic calculations or qualitative interpretations of planets and their motions.

The role of Venus and copper in our more recent economic events are also instructive. Our copper trading medium, pennies, are the fine tuners of balance. When pennies cost more to mint than their value, Venus is not doing her job.

Debt and the Future

In ancient astrology there were only seven bodies: Sun, Mercury, Venus, Moon, Mars, Jupiter, and Saturn. They are the fundamental significators of human impulse and organization. Jupiter and Saturn are the government planets, how the social order is maintained, how it impacts the natural movements and motivations for trade. The more recently discovered planets— Uranus (1781), Neptune (1849), and Pluto (1930)—are more relevant to the global economy and mass psychology, particularly on a generational level. What these planets represent and how they impact the economy will be discussed later.

Mars, as the taxing planet, not only binds us to government, it puts us at the mercy of our creditors. Taxes, likewise, limit ownership. Debt demands a benevolent future—Scorpio, Sagittarius, and Pisces ever spiraling into the clouds. When the future does not cooperate, if the fundamentals are out of whack, we risk losing everything we have. In times of prosperity and inflation, indebtedness circumvents the currency's falling value. In stable or deflating times, debt is a shaft in the heart.

The fundamental rules of money always assert themselves in the long run. The long run is knocking at the door.

Precautions, Patterns, and Profits

- Sun equals gold equals intrinsic value. Multiples of the gold price (2–4) represent speculative markets and upper and lower limits of growth.

- The Moon equals silver equals consumables. Multiples of the silver price (5–12) reflect the normal range of real estate, investment vehicles, and commodities.

- Venus equals the barter trade, replacement value apart from apparent jumps in price, whether you can replace what you sell.

- Mercury equals selling price, the impersonal accounting of any transaction in terms of the currency, not always what you get.

- Mars equals cuts and off the book costs: fees, commissions, taxes, etc. These reduce the value of your trade.

- The multiple of 10 reflects a normal adjustment point in all financial transactions, tops and bottoms. Do not pay more than 10 times the price of silver or gold on any trade. Do not buy when consumables carry a gold multiple or tradables a silver multiple. Sell.

Chapter Two

THE LAWS OF WEALTH

Forget what you know about money. Even the truisms contradict. *Play it safe. Land is the best investment. It takes
money to make money. The more you have the more you
get. A penny saved is a penny earned. Neither a borrower nor a
lender be.* If you had followed most of this advice over the last
ten years, you would have lost money, not gained.

Put aside your politics. Greed is a non-working explanation
for economics. The basic definition of greed is: "You go after
money in ways I don't like and make more than I do in the
process." Greed, in fact, is the inability to be satisfied with what
you have no matter how much, coupled with an inability to
share or spend for fear of personal loss. The greed of the rich is
never being satisfied with what they have and grabbing more,
no matter whom it hurts. The greed of the poor is trying to get
something for nothing and giving back even less. The rich man's
love of money is self-indulgent. The poor man's is parasitical.

Astrological interpretation is a matter of understanding
what is going on in real life and connecting that to the patterns
of the planets and stars. Trying to derive everything from an
analysis of numbers and symbols is like living in the plan of a
house before it is built.

The Nature of Money

Astrology is both a system of analysis and a philosophy of
life. The dignities and rulerships of houses and signs tell a tale
of money practices, good and bad.

The Dignities of Venus:

1. Venus is the natural ruler of Taurus, the sign of holding on, slow and steady growth, intrinsic value, land, art, and personal satisfaction. Its sin is greed. Its excess is hoarding.

BASIC LAW: Money is made by saving. A penny saved is a penny earned.

2. Venus is also the natural ruler of Libra, the sign of barter and fair exchange. By trading fairly the exchange of goods and services satisfies both parties. Its excess is trying to get the best deal for the sake of winning.

BASIC LAW: In the best deal, both sides win. No one gets anything for nothing.

3. Venus is exalted in Pisces. Money multiplies when it is spent. Once spent, it distributes itself through the economy and seeks an even level like water, the element of Pisces. The sin of Pisces is envy, the victim's view that one has somehow been excluded from wealth, the millionaire's anger that someone else has a million more. Without wealth there is no spending. Without spending there is no distribution. Without distribution the impoverished have no chance at wealth. Money is an illusion. Excesses are inflation and scams, the ability to play on peoples' envy and greed.

BASIC LAW: It takes money to make money. The more you spend the more you have.

We can conclude that a stable economy requires a solid financial base (Taurus), a system of fair and balanced trade (Libra), and a system of distribution that allows money to seek its own level in the economy. Elementary, you say? Of course. We tell ourselves this is what we do. In fact, it is not. Redistribution of wealth, a government's taking from the rich to give to the poor, goes against the fundamental principle. Money trickles down if the playing field is equal. In a manipulated economy those with the most influence stop the flow.

Improper Uses of Wealth

Let's look at the improper uses of wealth.

The Debilities of Venus:

1. Venus in Scorpio represents debt, death, and taxes, which destroy intrinsic value, even as they support multiplication and distribution (Scorpio trine Pisces). Scorpio represents one's ability to use other people's resources on behalf of one's financial goals, both sides engaged in a high risk venture. Borrowing and lending require a growing economy in order to work. By their nature they help the economy grow, at least by the numbers. Usury, exorbitant interest rates, destroys the value of a loan. An interest rate equal or lower than the inflation rate equals no interest at all. Debt and taxes are crisis payments. They should be nothing more.

   BASIC LAW: Loans and taxes discourage saving and negate ownership.

2. Venus in detriment in Aries indicates a high risk high stakes player who must always win in a deal and usually ends up wealthy and alone. He who gets the most for himself takes the greatest risks. Eventually he loses it all. How many entrepreneurs have lost and won more fortunes than most of us see only in the movies? One might call this the King of the Hill syndrome. If you claw your way to the top, you need only look down to see new claws clutching your muddy feet.

   BASIC LAW: Easy come easy go. He who grabs eventually gets taken.

3. Venus is in its fall in Virgo. The money schemer never makes as much as he could because he never takes a risk. One might call him the intrinsic technical analyst. You do not make money by working hard. Money is made by being prudent or by sacrificing one's immediate desires for success in the future. Money is made by trading it (Libra) and spending it (Pisces). Money goes beyond working hard for it. Just working or thinking

about it never gets us more than the pain required to get it. Wealth is dependent on saving, trade, and distribution—not work, a concept hard to understand in a nation founded on the work ethic.

BASIC LAW: Working hard is wage slavery. Too much analysis kills opportunity.

The worker-induced prosperity of American consumerism, required a worker income that enabled the working man to spend *and* save. Low wages eventually stifle economic growth. High wages create prosperity. Japan's wealth is dependent on American markets. They have neglected their own consumer needs.

We have money with love: by investing in value, by making honest deals, and by spending our largesse to enable it to spread through all levels of society, creating jobs, which create more earnings which create more sales and multiplies. We have money without love: wheeling and dealing, working hard, and going into debt. The benefits of the latter are temporary or sparse.

Start-up Wealth

Mars is enterprise, start-up wealth, the ability to use resources you did not create and do not own, debt. Debt gets you into trouble when you do not pay back, when you do not keep it under control.

The Dignities of Mars.

1. Mars is the ruler of Aries, the 1st house and the start of all activity. All things start with aggressive/assertive confidence. Aries is prior to money, Taurus. It is the self-absorbed need to survive, to take what one needs no matter how it impinges on others. The essence of all enterprise is risk. The excess of enterprise is rapacity and cut-throat competition.

BASIC LAW: No risk, no gain. The winner gets there first.

2. Mars is exalted in Scorpio, the sign of debt and other people's money. Debt is useful in helping you through a crisis. Joint enterprises spread the risk. The capitalist

system is basically a means where money is raised by selling ownership in the company and in its future profits. The excess of Scorpio is robbery.

BASIC LAW: Spread the risk. Sell the future.

3. Mars is exalted in Capricorn, the sign of goals, objectives, and discipline. Debt is useful in helping you achieve specific goals and objectives. Debt and joint ownership can help you take advantage of low prices and enhance the prestige and the survival of your company. The excess of Capricorn is government abetted self-interest, manipulating political power for personal gain.

BASIC LAW: Don't get carried away.

Mars (debt) works best when it works fast (Aries), when it is controlled (Capricorn), and when it is attached to a low interest loan that spreads the risk over a number of people (Scorpio). The joint stock company, the essence of the American way, is a essentially debt structured system of doing business. Companies do not own themselves, they are owned by other people, the stock holders. Mars in Scorpio says, "I don't want to do the job myself, so I'll give you money to start a business. Pay me back, not at a fixed rate, but as a percentage of your profits."

To understand the difference between Venus and Mars is to grasp the difference between asset-creating Martian activity and genuine asset growth. When Mars enterprise is balanced by Venus value, there is no debt. A loan backed by collateral is a convenience, not a debt. A loan tendered on promises of future growth may be a fast track to bankruptcy.

The Sun is exalted in Aries, which suggests that speed and enterprise will prosper if it is tied to intrinsic value and integrity. Martian activity prospers only against an arbitrary standard of value—gold or some other form of financial integrity.

BASIC LAW: Buy value not percentages. Gold enhances the barter trade.

The Safer Side of Mars

A Mars dominated economy encourages speculation, high interest rates, high taxes, inequitable distributions of wealth, cutthroat competition, and ultimately government controls. If you stay outside the flow, you lose. But, there are milder, safer versions of Mars.

The Debilities of Mars.

1. Mars is in its fall in Cancer. Perhaps the most inoffensive form of debt is the home mortgage. While it negates the security of home ownership, the odiousness of the mortgage leads people to pay it off quickly, or steadily for fear of losing both their investment and their home. If you buy debt, buy the home mortgage. Home "owners" have the most to lose and are the least speculative of all debt holders.

BASIC LAW: Invest where people have the most to lose by default.

While debt can help you buy your home, it lessens your security. Home equity loans are the most risky investment you can make as an abstract astrological concept. The money created by debt is *never* under your control. You are at the mercy of the whim of man and fate.

SAFETY RULE: Own your own home as quickly as possible (the Moon exalted in Taurus).

2. Mars is in its detriment in Libra, the sign of partners and enemies. The risk of debt is lessened by partnerships. Debt is useful in creating the speed that can beat the competition.

BASIC LAW: If in need get help. If in danger buy now, pay later.

Mars in Libra tells us that debt kills relationships. If you want to lose a friend, lend him money. If you want to lose a friend, borrow from him. There is no love in a debt transaction. Everyone is Shylock when in need.

SAFETY RULE: If you lend or borrow, make sure the contract is legal and enforceable. Get it in writing so you can litigate if you must. If not, be willing to lose it and the person to whom you lent it.

3. Mars is debilitated in Taurus. If you own what you borrow, the risk is lessened. Borrow against collateral. Only borrow when you do not need to.

BASIC LAW: Own the debt. Don't owe it.

Debt ultimately kills ownership. On the other hand, there is a form of money from another person that can contribute to having a financial stake—inheritance. The only good lender is a dead one.

SAFETY RULE: Don't lend unless you have collateral. Don't borrow unless you have collateral.

Debt is always of value in getting started, Mars in Aries. If you have not saved to create assets, you double your risk. If you have assets and borrow against them, your assets either appreciate against the cost of your debt or at least keep pace with the face amount, enabling you to pay off at any given moment. In reality, you carry no debt at all. If a company uses money from the stock sale to purchase materials that will enable it to produce goods that make a profit, it, too, carries no debt at all, because investors do not "call in the loan" by selling their stocks back to the company. They sell to each other. If a company could liquidate its assets at any given time and pay off the debt, they would have only their management skill and the market to worry over.

BASIC LAW: Debt must always be balanced by assets. Scorpio opposite Taurus, Venus in harmony with Mars.

Laissez-Faire

We hear much talk about free markets and getting the government out of the business of business—*laissez-faire*. A *laissez-faire* economy is not a fair economy. A healthy economy is a Venus balanced economy. A *laissez-faire* economy is ruled by

Mars. He who can grab the most by any means fair or foul gets the most. In addition to fair trade, Venus represents equality before the law. A Venus economy demands that *everyone,* rich or poor, play by the same rules.

The remedy of Mars is not Capricorn, the government, it is Venus, *fair* trade. Saturn is exalted in Libra. The government does not control trade, it is subordinate to it. It establishes equity. It does not redistribute the income. Taxation, as it relates to Mars in Capricorn, means only one thing: government established inequity. The Libertarians and the Humanitarians are both wrong and both right. More government is not the answer. Equitable trade is. *Laissez-faire* is not equitable trade. Level playing fields spread prosperity better than government control. Government must control Martian impulses: Mars in Capricorn. That is appropriate. It should be controlled by Venus: Saturn in Libra, fair exchange.

Government Intervention

Just as government distorts on the side of the poor with transfer payments, it distorts on the side the wealthy with subsidies, such as building roads to facilitate the auto industry or regulating air traffic for the airlines. Both skew the economy towards special interests, no matter how deserving or "economical".

Human beings do not choose naturally to follow sound economic principles. However, the basic rules of economy and Venus assert themselves over time. Money always seeks its true value.

Japan's economy is dependent on our buying their products. In an economic collapse, in a surge of protectionism, American industry might draw on a whole "new" market of American consumers. In a worldwide economic collapse, where is Japan going to find the foreign wealth it needs to keep its industry alive?

Japan's government encourages the creation of wealth. Ours has perpetually sought to tax away legitimate wealth with personal and corporate income taxes. When the income tax was first established in 1913, the first $20,000 of income was excluded. The aim and the justification was to tax those with excessively high annual incomes. If that principle were still active today, based on a 10 times inflation multiple, we would exclude the first $200,000 of income. The government is not taxing the rich—it is taxing everybody. Every dollar that the government takes from the middle and lower classes means fewer dollars trickling down or back to support American industry and American jobs. In order for Americans to enjoy the full benefits of their incomes and get around the tax bite, they buy cheaper foreign products. Likewise, to avoid the corporate income tax, companies borrow money rather than issue stock or pay dividends. If that does not work, they move to foreign countries and more hospitable economic spheres. Mars, as heavy taxation, leads to a loss of markets. Mars *always* leads to loss.

> **WARNING SIGN:** When borrowing becomes the smart thing to do you know the economy is heading for trouble.

The Fundamental Truths of Wealth

1. *Only material goods have lasting value.* Our tangible possessions serve us regardless of the price. Value tends to increase with time. Saving is important to wealth. Taurus.

2. *Money in vehicles of intrinsic value can either stabilize or stagnate the economy.* Tangible assets promote a sense of personal value and security, but do not expand the money supply, nor do they spread prosperity through the economy. Once you've purchased everything you need, you stop buying. Taurus.

3. *All business transactions are a matter of exchanging wealth for wealth,* the win-win situation. You cannot exchange your wealth without someone to buy. You do not have the price of your house until you sell it. Libra.

4. *Money in circulation flows to all levels.* The more money is spent the more it expands—the famed multiplier effect. Pisces.

Most people look at the partnership or transactional side of trade as either a contest to get the better of the other person, or as an attempt to use other people to provide money they cannot raise themselves.

We see the same competitive mentality operating with the hysteria about the trade deficit. Trade means value for value. The Japanese may have more of our dollars, but we have more of their goods. They buy our real estate—if the market fails, who loses? You throw your trading partner into bankruptcy, money goes out of the system. Take on too much debt, you put yourself at risk of someone else's whim.

On a personal level, Mars and Venus—money and joint money—are usually matters of a temporary nature. You buy a mortgage. Within a specific amount of time, you pay it off or default. This is not true in government.

Government debt is a universal mortgage which creates an illusion of great wealth. It is like the person with a million dollar home, who drives a Rolls, wears tailor made suits, has a mountain chalet in Switzerland, and a cottage on the Riviera, most all of it owned by a consortium of banks. If he is doing everything so wrong how come he is living so right? Like debt, the rewards are temporary. You can rape the system. Eventually the system fights back. Excessive government debt encourages speculation and inequities. The money manipulators win—at least, for awhile.

Venus in Virgo: you do not make money by working hard.

Venus in Scorpio: you do not own money by being in debt.

Venus in Aries: you do not keep money by looking out for number one.

On a personal level hold enough in reserve to assure that your assets are secure. Save enough to have money to trade. Spend to keep others working thereby creating more money to spend.

Some individuals have charts that show an ability to amass wealth no matter what they do. They are as rare as being born a prince. Most charts show some difficulty with money, especially from attitudes and expectations that deny prosperity. Anyone who violates the fundamental planetary strictures of good money management fails in the long run, fails to amass or fails to enjoy. Love and money are one. You can have money instead of love. You cannot enjoy your wealth without it.

The Four Cornerstones of Wealth

Venus, wealth, is a balance of opposing forces. Great wealth is a combination of spending and saving, trading and dealing, going it alone and interacting with others. If you wonder why economists are confused, it is because wealth is confusing.

The four elements, Fire, Earth, Air, and Water and their respective succedent houses, 2nd, 5th, 8th and 11th, show an individual's or nation's ability to accumulate wealth. They show what is native and local in wealth creation. They show what countries and individuals substitute for wealth. The United States' stellium of planets in the 8th, shows wealth created by debt, the capitalist joint stock company.

The cornerstones of wealth accumulation are as follows:

Taurus, Second House—Intrinsic Value

Land, raw materials, and man-made products all have intrinsic value. If it exists in material form, it has trade value. Money, insofar as it represents a firm and dependable relationship to a commodity, would also fall in this category. Consumables do *not* fall into this category. Taurus and the 2nd house refer to what you can possess. All possessions that support your life and security, including the produce of the land—minerals. For the purpose of economic analysis, what is *not* consumed. Thus in a manufacturing context, raw materials that are transformed to create a new product still retain their basic value. You can remelt the gold in your bracelet to create a pair of earrings, a coin, or a microcircuit on a computer chip. You cannot reconstitute a gourmet dinner, except to fertilize your crops.

> **CORNERSTONE #1.** Wealth accumulates and endures in material goods.

Leo, Fifth House—Speculation and Power

Leo is the planet of gold, the most stable non-perishable commodity there is. Gold is solidified fire, man's attempt to create an arbitrary standard against which the value of consumables and tradables can be measured. Leo is the value sector of the house of consumables, their promotion of life through a transfer of energy. We must eat for health and strength. We must put energy into our manufacturing so that value will not be lost in manufacturing costs. Thus, Leo is energy and the power to maintain quality and impeccable standards. Leo and gold enable buyers and sellers to judge their trades against an arbitrary, impartial, and unmanipulated standard. Leo is the power to attract buyers through pride in the product to be sold, which excites the buyer to be.

Leo and Taurus create wealth: the application of labor-power to durable materials produces goods to trade. Labor and energy are intrinsic to product creation. Confidence and pride are intrinsic to wealth creation.

CORNERSTONE #2. Wealth is power. Wealth is gold and the ability to excite.

Scorpio, Eighth House—Risk and Shared Resources

Scorpio is how the trading partner values his goods, what it will take to part him from his money or his product. In risky ventures, who will put up the money, share the win and the loss? Scorpio as joint ownership and as short term venture capital promotes wealth. Scorpio as taxes and long term debt destroys or postpones it. Scorpio as restoration of what is apparently dead and useless creates wealth. Scorpio as price cutting and bargain hunting, denies the seller a fair trade and lessens his ability to spend towards greater wealth in the community.

CORNERSTONE #3. Share the risk. Share the wealth. Restore, repair.

Aquarius, Eleventh House—Customers

You cannot sell to a market that has no interest or no money. Do you have what the public wants? Is the price right? In an inflating economy the pool is always sufficient to support the price. In a deflating economy it is not. Aquarius is the new and unusual, the innovative and foresighted. Anticipate people's needs before they know them themselves, wealth is yours.

CORNERSTONE #4. Wealth is foresight and insight into human needs.

The Basics of Buying and Selling

- Have a product of innate value and know its market price. Shop around, look for quality, beauty and durability. The ugly and run down is cheaper, but unless rehabbed, is resold cheaper still.

- Buy and sell what you are most proud of. If you love your purchase you will put a higher value on it when it is time to sell. Expensive quality is more satisfying than cheap junk.

- If the venture is risky, use other people's money. Share the ownership and spread the risk.

- Follow the fashions and the trends. Know what the market wants and needs. Ask a price the market will bear.

The Cornerstones in Today's Economy

Scorpio—Waste

Many people in their zeal for a bargain violate all these rules. They buy a run down house in an undesirable neighborhood with a mortgage they cannot afford, just because the price seemed right. If they do nothing but live in it until they can afford the house of their dreams, they will sell at a loss. The impulse to take on debt is similar. Soon all problems are being solved by resorting to debt, not by restoring and repairing companies, products, and systems. It may appear that a throwaway society creates more jobs by having constantly to replace what breaks. If you understand that wealth resides in the product, a throwaway product is throwaway wealth. We could put people to work for a century just cleaning up after ourselves. Wealth never dies, it just goes to the dump. The ecology and recycling movements are Scorpio attempts to preserve assets and wealth. Better the waste was not created at all.

Aquarius—The Money Pool

When pricing an asset, the availability of money impacts the selling price as much as public fashion and desire. Without inflation, prices cannot rise indefinitely. Growth always corrects itself. Price levels eventually break, because more and more goods tie up ever larger portions of money. People who buy before the boom can take a lower resale price than people who enter a buying boom at its peak.

If the total income available among ten buyers is $100,000 per person—10 houses equal in value and each valued at 100,000 will not necessarily bring $100,000 on the market. The first sale may bring $75,000 because buyer #1 and seller #1 are not sure of the market and the buyer is more cautious with his money because of it. Buyer #2 and seller #2 feel a little better about trading at $80,000 because that is not too far off precedent. By the time the transactions reach buyer #5 or #6 we may be up into the $125,000 range. At this point the money left available for the last few houses may be down to $90,000 per capita. The last few houses may not sell at all, because buyer #1 knows he can still make a profit if he undercuts buyer #5's price. In fact, he can cut it by one third and still break even.

As will become apparent in later chapters, we are already selling to buyer #7. We have obvious non-technical parallels to the 1930s. Rising technical indicators, whether it be for a market average or an individual company, will mean growth if the money is available in the economy. Good technical indicators and prosperous transits mean that a company or a country will do better than most if the economy declines.

Aquarius also represents people organized into groups: corporations, associations, cartels, unions, and clubs. The pool of money available for trade markets is always dominated by special groups. In the 1920s a small number of men controlled the stock market on behalf of themselves and their enterprises. Today the small number of men who control huge pension, investment, and insurance funds do the same. Watch the market makers. The price of a stock does not indicate the health of an economy or a corporation, only of the money available to buy it.

Taurus—Banks

Venus, Taurus, and the 2nd house represent banks, the storehouses of wealth. We have always looked at banks as the epitome of financial stability and good management. We think we are protected by the FDIC and the FSLIC. Both these agencies have about 2.5% assets to the deposits they are supposed to cover in the event of failure. The Fed cannot save the thrifts. It cannot save the regular banks when their loan structures fail. From 1920 up to 1933 more than 50% of the banks in this country failed. We travel the same road today. Mars dominated the markets and the thinking in the 1920s. It dominates the thinking today. Borrow and tax. The philosophy is equally entrenched in government, in industry, and in political points of view. Mars kills.

Most people think the Federal Reserve System is a guarantee against disaster. The Federal Reserve System was created in 1912. It did not prevent the Great Depression. The Federal Reserve System is basically a machine to assure that the federal government will be able to borrow so it can spend beyond its means. The Federal Reserve System was created so that the government could manipulate the economy. It was not created to mandate sound financial standards. The Federal Reserve System is Mars in Capricorn, not Saturn in Libra.

The safety of our banking system depends entirely on the faith of the depositors. The current spate of bank failures, despite all the finger pointing, is not simply the result of greedy speculators and venal bankers. It is the result of a total distortion of the proper uses of money and the destruction of the value of our currency through inflation. Our society and our government have valued Mars above Venus. Mars always gets revenge. Venus always gets even. The current legislation enabling banks to cross state lines, sell insurance and stocks, means only that they will be able to perpetrate their bad practices over a larger territory. Banks are supposed to be stable and stuffy. They should be the antithesis of speculation, not the vehicle.

Leo—Integrity

While gold is too inflexible a medium of exchange for growing populations and productivity, any currency must maintain its value in order to facilitate trade. The falling value of our dollar represents both a lack of integrity in our government's manipulation of the money supply and the cheating of people who took our currency in exchange for their goods. The falling value of our dollar also represents the market cutting our overvalued dollar down to size.

Most of the financial difficulties in the United States today have at their root the lack of integrity in our money supply. Too high a price on our dollar denied us markets abroad and made our industry non-competitive. Our movement towards a service economy is not a new stage of growth but an indication of declining productivity and value in our industry.

In the 1930s the Saturn transit of the U.S. 2nd house produced a depression and a shrinking of purchasing power. In the late 1980s and early 1990s the shrinkage of purchasing power was clouded by the simultaneous appearance of Neptune and Uranus. Continued inflation and the influx of foreign money gave us the illusion of continued wealth and kept the prices high. Even so, profits continued to decline, unemployment rose, and everything retail is on sale.

The United States has the wealth (Taurus), the markets (Aquarius), and shared capital (Scorpio) that should keep us as the number one producer in the world. What we lack is a sound currency, Leo, that creates trust that the value of what we spend will not deteriorate before the buyer can realize its true value. If the dollar collapses, so will our economy. In earlier times we revalued against a standard of gold. We can restabilize without a gold standard if we pass a balanced budget amendment with teeth and stick to it. A stable dollar is an honest dollar.

Third World economies never got off the ground because they did not operate on a sound financial base with currencies of integrity. All wealth comes from the ground, Taurus. Wealth is not created by loans. It is created by using "borrowed" tools (Scorpio) to pull from the Earth (Taurus) with the sweat of one's brow (Leo) goods desired by people (Aquarius). Borrowed money is a tool to be returned as soon as you manufacture your own.

Our society has confused money with the value it represents. Money is of no value. Material substances, natural or manufactured, have value. Possession, trade, and distribution create wealth. Money is simply a facilitator of trade. The price is merely a reference that enables you to compare your trade to other similar ones. Money is a way to translate your labor into wealth. Wealth is the value you derive from the trade.

Precautions, Patterns and Profits

- Put your money in real estate and tangible goods.
- Buy quality at a fair market price.
- Share ownership of what you cannot afford to buy.
- Sell to fads and fashions.
- Invest contrarian in sound, well managed companies.
- Use short term debt to build assets.
- Hold the long term debt of those who fear default.
- Vote for the integrity of the money supply.
- Hold silver and gold as protections against runaway inflation.

Chapter Three

SUPPLY AND DEMAND

S upply and demand seem simple. The harvest is wonderful, prices fall because everybody has more than they need. The harvest is poor, prices rise, everybody has less. Too many grab for a very small pie.

Jupiter and Saturn represent supply and demand. On a cyclic level Jupiter and Saturn operate in a rather simple way. On an interpretational level, they are as complex as the notion itself. Even in a subsistence economy supply and demand is not simple. In a luxury economy, demand is as much a whim as it is a need. Oversupply is the rule. Oversupply once meant falling prices because purchases were driven by need, not desire. Now an oversupply may command high prices because of the persuasiveness of the seller. In an inflated economy (chapter four), prices rise no matter what the state of the harvest or the level of production.

Market Behavior

Leaving out the factors that distort an economy, the basic astrology suggests that the market has four corners.

The fundamental assignments of buy and sell are:

	The Price 10th	
The Buyer 1st	Angular Houses	The Seller 7th
	The Goods 4th	

As a market phenomenon, as opposed to an economic phenomenon, discussed in chapter five, the 10th house is the market, and the 4th, the land and its produce. Roughly speaking, demand is the 10th house, which determines the price and the marketability. Supply is the 4th house, what is available to sell. The 1st house is also a demand house, the buyers. The 7th house is also a supply house, the sellers who control the goods. Demand defines the price that the market will bear relative to the supply of goods. It is both a function of the amount of goods and the willingness of the controllers of those goods to take the price offered.

Buying and Selling

The following may be a bit technical for the non-astrologically inclined reader. If so, skip the text and read the points.

The 4th house is ruled by Cancer. Cancer is need and desire. It is survival need and desire, whether it is satisfied in the marketplace or at home. Demand is what is demanded in the marketplace, Capricorn, the 10th house, as opposed to what people need and may be able to produce for themselves.

> **POINT 1.** Not all supply and demand goes through the market.

Cancerian commodities are consumed. They must be constantly replenished, particularly foodstuffs. Cancer, as a marketable commodity, represents the goods *before* they reach the market place. The goods in the marketplace then become the 10th or Capricorn, the goods relative to the demand for them in public.

> **POINT 2.** Supply has two tiers: goods before they reach the market and goods in the marketplace.

Keep the above in the back of your mind for a moment while we examine the exaltations that are involved with these two signs. Jupiter is exalted in Cancer. Therefore, Jupiter as abundance is also a planet of supply.

Mars is exalted in Capricorn. Mars, the ruler of the 1st house, the buyer, is the ultimate demander. Mars is exalted in Capricorn, the demand of the marketplace. The Moon, of need and desire, rules Cancer, the 4th house of non-market supply, therefore, there is a constant need to replenish the bounty, Jupiter, of supply because of consumer Lunar demand.

> **POINT 3.** Demand has two tiers: consumer demand, which grows perpetually, regardless of availability; and market demand, which is dependent on the willingness of people to buy.

The 10th as the 4th of the seller, 7th house, represents the goods controlled by the seller. Jupiter is the supply of the 4th. The Moon is the demand (consumer need) of the 4th, *both* as the seller's 10th determine whether a seller has goods to sell. Saturn is the supply of the 10th and Mars is the demand of the 10th, both of which are satisfied by the willingness of the seller to sell.

> **POINT 4.** Sellers determine which goods are available in the market.

A market dominated economy accommodates both buyers and sellers. First house buyers (demanders) vie for the goods against their 7th house competitors or bargain with sellers. Because the 1st house controls the 4th house of supply, speculators generally try to get the pre-market materials to control the price. Who arrives first gets the goods. In a *laissez-faire* economy Mars gets there first every time.

> **POINT 5.** Control of the supply affects the ability of goods to reach the market.

Since Mars is exalted in the 10th, buyers set the price. Mars rules cuts. Prices always tend to fall. Because the ruler of the price, Saturn, is exalted in Libra, sellers control the sale. Though the market ultimately finds a balance, sellers always feel they are taking a loss.

> **POINT 6.** Sellers control the sale. Buyers determine the price.

To extend this even further, the astrological wheel also tells us that the cost of the goods in the market or the profit made will be the 2nd house from the 10th, which is the 11th and also

Saturn-ruled. Saturn is a planet of restriction and lack and the primary indicator of price levels. Those levels are subordinated to Libra which is ruled by Venus, which means the price is a factor of a balance or a barter exchange between buyer and seller.

POINT 7. The real price is the barter exchange.

We have already seen that the most likely buyers are going to be ruled by Mars. Mars' ability to buy is determined by the 2nd house, Taurus, ruled by Venus. The price Venus/Libra will accept for her goods is the 2nd house from the 7th, or Scorpio. What Mars is forced to pay is determined by Venusian wealth or lack of it. With Mars as ruler of the seller second, (the 8th) the seller usually takes a loss. With Mars as previously mentioned ruler of the 10th, prices always fall.

POINT 8. Falling prices are the rule, not the exception.

On the other hand, Scorpio is what Mars/Aries/1st house borrows. Aries' impatience and desire is satisfied by borrowing. Borrowing drives prices up because it creates money that is not there and enables the Libran seller to get a higher price. The 8th is also the house of death. Borrowing eventually kills the market and the people who trade.

POINT 9. Borrowing reverses the norm and raises prices.

The Sun is exalted in Aries. Kings buy anything they want. In a despotic economy the price is determined by what the king or the central authority determines. The governing power as either Capricorn or Leo produces the same result. When the arbitrary standard of financial value is held firmly in place or if gold is the bedrock of a medium of exchange, then control of the gold will not only create the value in the system, but it will control the system itself.

POINT 10. The economy is kept in bounds by an arbitrary standard of exchange. Who controls the standard controls the economy.

We can easily see why speculators through history have periodically tried to corner the market on gold. The stock market crash of 1869 followed Jay Gould's attempt to corner the market on gold. Government as the 10th house has the potential either to control or encourage speculation. The Sun/Aries connection encourages speculation and aggressive self-interest. One can easily see where government intervention and the gold standard itself have their pitfalls.

POINT 11. Power inclines towards speculation.

Accounting

As we have seen in chapter one, Mercury is the messenger, the go-between, the trader. Mercury is neutral. It is the messenger of the Sun, which makes it the accountant of the price levels of any market as opposed to the apparent or even the bartering value. Mercury is associated with two signs, Gemini and Virgo. Gemini follows Taurus and totes up the result of the trade. Virgo follows Leo, which gives us an accounting of the actual value of gold. Mercury does not create any value. It simply makes an accounting or creates the conditions for the process of trade as opposed to the place of trading, the desire to trade, or the demand for trade. Mercury tries to put buyers and sellers together. Mercury gets stuck with the goods (Virgo) if there is too much lag time between buying on speculation and finding someone who is willing to buy. The intention of Mercury is not to buy to hold. *Mercury simply facilitates trade.*

Buying and Selling Styles

Now lets see what we can make of this in terms of the people and their motivations in the marketplace. To understand the interpretation, remember that any 2nd house is the wealth of the previous house, the 3rd is the trade or the reason for the activity, and the 4th is the result.

Venus

Venus buys to accumulate. Taurus is a holding sign. Libra has an empty coffer with Scorpio on its 2nd. Venus/Pisces/12th house has an Aries/Mars/2nd house (money troubles) and wants to stabilize, Taurus.

Venus always feels empty. Only when she holds on to what she has does she feel full and safe. Venus sells only out of necessity. Venus can be persuaded (Gemini on the Taurus 2nd) to part with its goods if the trade will bring a significant increase or satisfy a pressing need (Jupiter and Moon in Cancer). Otherwise, Venus is patient in her trading. If Venus is strong on your chart by position or sign, you want to amass money and goods, not simply gamble and trade. Venus buys, rarely sells.

Venus wants a fair price when she buys. She wants a profit when she sells. Venus does not like to buy "dirty." If the price is too low, she does not see a bargain but a threat. Venus is slow. She will not buy at the bottom. She often sells after the top, if at all.

Mars

Mars buys to sell. Taurus is on the 2nd of Aries, Gemini on the 3rd. Aquarius is on the 2nd of Capricorn, Pisces on the 3rd. In short trading, Martian types sell before they buy. Scorpio buys all it can (Sagittarius on 2nd) to control the market (Capricorn 3rd). Mars is a percentage player. He only looks for a cut. He looks for a low price so he can sell high. He is not interested in long term value or in holding assets, only in speed. Mars thrives on the adversity of others. He creates the adversity if he must. Mars likes high prices when he has to sell. He likes low prices when he has to buy. Because he is impatient, he will sell before the top and buy at the bottom or just before. If you have strong Martian indicators, you love the thrill of outsmarting the markets and getting something for less.

Mars does not stay in long enough to accumulate. He will make millions and lose millions on a gamble or a hunch.

Sun

The Sun is on the side of Mars. Unlike Mars, who will buy anything if he sees a potential profit, the Sun buys only what he likes. Profit is secondary to enjoyment. The Sun waits for the best opportunity. Though the Sun is exalted in Aries, which loves risk and speed, the Fire triad is completed by Jupiter in Sagittarius, great confidence in the future and a knack for anticipating trends. The Sun follows what is popular at the time. The Sun buys what he likes at the bottom, goes along with the crowd in the middle and sells what he does not want at the top.

If you have strong solar tendencies, you play the market carefully and take occasional risks. Over time you will do very well.

Moon

The Moon is on the side of Venus. (Moon exalted in Taurus). She buys what she needs and is cautious about the price. She is always worried that she has paid the wrong price so she follows the crowd—Jupiter (Jupiter exalted in Cancer). If everybody else is doing it, she does it too. She sells at the bottom and buys at the top. Lunar types should stay away from all speculative endeavors, including the stock market. They make their money by accumulating, not by trading. They have no stomach for risk.

Mercury

Mercury keeps running back and forth trying to keep everybody satisfied. Mercurial types are technical analysts who publish newsletters but do not trade themselves. They are brokers who make a profit on every trade or arbitragers who try to make a profit either way. They are not interested in the goods so much as ideas and patterns of trade. They are the ultimate schemers. They find loopholes. They figure the odds.

Mercury is paper money. Without it a money economy is unable to put buyers and sellers together. While Mercury, strictly speaking, does not participate in the market price, prices do rise and fall relative to its activity or inactivity. You do not sell your goods until you exchange them (Gemini). The exchange itself is neutral, since in a barter situation each party theoretically receives equal value. If equal value is not exchanged, it is not the fault of Mercury, but the sharpness of Mars *vis-a-vis* the sense of fairness of Venus.

If you are a Mercurial type, chances are the mechanisms of the market interest you more than the profit or loss. Publish a newsletter. Breaking even is more your style.

Jupiter

Jupiter is the *what's wonderful* consensus. It is the bounty of the harvest in Cancer. Jupiter is confidence in the future and the confidence of the crowd. Jupiter is the herding instinct of Cancer, Pisces, and Sagittarius. It represents salesmen, who show you the upward price movements stocks they want to sell. They sell at the top.

Lucky Jupiter types buy when everyone else has given up hope, Pisces. They sell when the rage is on. Unlucky Jupiter types do the opposite. Jupiter usually travels light. It buys to sell or simply sells, the perennial salesman. Like Mercury, Jupiter wants it both ways. Unlike Mercury, Jupiter does not scheme so much as it inspires. Jupiter types are lucky. The people they deal with are not.

A strong Jupiter is necessary for amassing wealth through financial dealings. The only caution is knowing when to stop. Jupiter can get carried away with its own success and drown in Piscean swamps.

Saturn

Saturn is the great limiter. Saturn is cautious. Saturn buys at a low price or a fair price. It sells at a high price or a fair price. Saturn enters the market at tops and bottoms. Saturn has the instincts of both Venus and Mars. Being ruler of an Earth sign, it holds and is more patient than Mars. Being co-ruler of excitable Aquarius, it buys because everyone is buying and sells for the same reason. Being exalted in Libra, it wants to trade for a fair profit, which may not be the seller's idea of a fair price. Though Saturn and Mars often trade the same way, Saturn ultimately dominates Mars just as Venus dominates Saturn. The Saturnian market ultimately limits the rapaciousness of Mars and returns it to Venusian balance. Everything that goes up will come down. Everything that went down will rise.

A strong Saturn indicates that you will be cautious in money matters and have a very good sense of the tradable value of any commodity or stock. Play the fundamentals. You cannot go wrong.

Trading Styles

- SUN Gambles on sure things. Follows trends. Buys after the bottom and before the top.

- MOON Uncertainty. Follows the crowd. Sells at the bottom and buys at the top.

- MERCURY Facilitates and analyzes trade. The technical trader who breaks even. The arbitrager who tries to have it both ways.

- VENUS The true investor who buys and holds on.

- MARS The wheeler-dealer. The profit taker and the short-seller.

- JUPITER The salesman. He profits whether the buyer wins or loses. He has a knack for spotting trends and getting tips.

- SATURN He trades on fundamentals, holds on through difficult times, misses out on short term leaps, picks the winners overall.

Principles of Supply and Demand

Demand is a function of perceived scarcity, Saturn; Jupiter popularity; Cancer need; Mars speculation; and Venus desire.

Supply is a function of a bountiful harvest (Jupiter in Cancer), market availability (Saturn in Capricorn), Venusian sellers, and Martian buyers.

Supply inevitably exceeds demand. While this is not apparent to civilized minds, consider that life in the wild has supported man for centuries without running out. Famine is a matter of being in the wrong place at the wrong time. Somewhere on Earth there is simultaneous bounty.

Price is Capricorn. The low price is Mars in Capricorn, what the buyer wants to pay. The level or limiting price is Saturn in Capricorn, what the market will bear. The high price is Jupiter in Capricorn, a configuration that means constriction in supply. The fair price is Saturn, the ruler of Capricorn in Libra. Supply and demand work primarily through the 4th and 10th houses, Moon and Saturn, and the mutual configurations of Jupiter and Saturn.

Moon in Cancer—Saturn in Capricorn

A harvest or an availability of goods that satisfies consumer needs, Moon in Cancer, results in a stable market, Saturn in Capricorn. Prices seem low if you are looking to make a profit. They seem high on the buying end. When you must buy necessities you have little choice. You must bid for what is offered to stay alive. If the supply is only sufficient to satisfy need, the Saturn/Libran sellers have no surplus to sell. Mars cannot speculate (it is under the control of Capricorn) because the prices are not high enough to sell or low enough to buy if Mars is to make his kind of killing, unless he corners the market. Then he can charge what he will. A balanced state of affairs is production to need. In a fair trading economy, prices stay level. Since we all tend to see prices as demanding and restrictive and a steady trading range as stagnation, we do not view the situation with enthusiasm. There is no surplus here. We cannot buy more than we need. We must try to get the best value for what we buy.

If we understand that the Moon in Cancer/Saturn in Capricorn dynamic is the fundamental condition of life, we will not be fooled by booms and busts.

> **PRINCIPLE #1.** Production to need equals stable prices and low market activity.

Jupiter in Cancer—Saturn in Capricorn

With Jupiter in Cancer, we have a bountiful harvest. Because consumer demand for non-consumables rises with it, we are likely to perceive either shortages in the marketplace or falling prices (Saturn in Capricorn). If Saturn represents shortages in the marketplace, retailers or sellers do not have the goods to satisfy rising prices. If they have an oversupply of goods, prices fall. Either way their profit is limited. Jupiter in Cancer may drive commodity prices down and drive other goods up, because of the level of increasing wealth in the community. If everybody has a good harvest, no one needs another's surplus. Prices fall. Prices for things farmers cannot produce rise. Prices also fall with Jupiter in Cancer because everyone is content and feels no pressure to buy. The key to understanding Jupiter in Cancer is not so much a function of price but of a shift in market interest. If everyone's consumer/life-giving needs are satisfied with increased wealth, the market interest will shift. Commodity prices will fall. Manufactured goods may rise.

> **PRINCIPLE #2.** Oversupply equals falling prices. Over-demand equals market shortages. Low profits either way.

While the present discussion is designed for a better understanding of the mechanisms of supply and demand, it is also useful in applying the planetary meaning to fixed positions on natal and mundane charts and transits to the same. If a progressed Moon transits the 4th house of a national chart, subsistence harvests may be the rule. Saturn transiting the 10th would then indicate scarcity in the marketplace and high prices. If Jupiter transits the 4th while Saturn transits the 10th, Saturn in the 10th may indicate falling prices because of supply surpluses. In the abstract, Saturn means constriction. Whether it means a narrowing of price or a shortage in supply depends primarily on the condition of Jupiter at the same time.

Saturn in Cancer—Jupiter in Capricorn

If we switch we see that a bad harvest (Saturn in Cancer) is matched by rising prices (Jupiter in Capricorn). This creates rising commodity prices, and falling prices for manufactured goods. Jupiter in Capricorn produces a surplus of manufactured goods. Demand for manufactured goods fall because there is no surplus money/assets with which to purchase them. To put it another way, the abundance of manufactured goods in the market place is not matched by purchasing power. Jupiter in Capricorn does not produce high prices for manufactured goods, because that price is determined by the Saturn in Cancer as the 10th of the 7th house seller.

> **PRINCIPLE #3.** Low supply equals rising prices. Low demand equals market surpluses of manufactured goods.

This is how supply and demand operate on a very simple level. If we take Jupiter and Saturn and insert them in their normal movement through the Zodiac and through the supply and demand houses, we get a better picture of the cyclic complexities of supply and demand.

Remember that simple and permanent meanings cannot be assigned to astrological symbols, except for their core meanings, because their meanings shift relative to one another. Yes, Saturn means scarcity and Jupiter means bounty. The real question is, does it mean scarcity of profit or scarcity of supply? Bounty of profit or bounty of supply? If we assign Capricorn as significator of manufactured goods and Cancer as commodities, we get a very clear picture of what Saturn and Jupiter do.

The Progress of Bounty and Scarcity

The real cycle of supply and demand is a function of the progress of Jupiter and Saturn through the signs and their relation to one another. Before we delineate the movement of these two planets let us examine what they do when they are functioning in the four corners of the market. The four corners (squares or angles) are the important turning points. Soft

aspects between Jupiter and Saturn, when there is no movement of Saturn relative to itself, create a neutral market.

Saturn is the ultimate determiner of the market and price
levels. Jupiter is a primary marker of confidence and supply.
Since the Jupiter and Saturn conjunction is the key factor of the
Mutation cycle, to be discussed in chapter six, they are the
appropriate place to begin.

Jupiter and Saturn in Capricorn

Short supply and big demand, but no capacity to supply it.
Demand cannot be satisfied because there is no capacity for purchasing. This occurred at the Great Mutation in 1842, when the
Earth-materialist economy began. In the United States there
were few banks and the only specie coins were minted elsewhere.

Jupiter and Saturn in Cancer

This represents the same thing on the demand side. Big
supply, no demand. Thus Jupiter and Saturn conjunctions are
always poor markets. Saturn is stronger than Jupiter. When the
two are in conjunction, expansion and wealth are limited. You
cannot expand a rock. You can smother fire. Jupiter-Saturn conjunctions in Cancer occurred during the Renaissance when
wealth was highly concentrated in families, like the Medicis,
and, of course, Mother Church. The relatively impoverished producers, traders, and craftsmen were captive to the relatively
small market of the wealthy and the churchmen.

Jupiter and Saturn in Aries

Every man for himself. The general market conditions that
preceded our present materialist system.

Jupiter and Saturn in Libra

Buyers in collusion. Combines and cartels. The general
market conditions that will follow us and the condition of the
world at the 1980-81 preview.

Jupiter in Aries—Saturn in Capricorn

Low prices or short supply of manufactured goods, plenty of
buyers.

Jupiter in Aries—Saturn in Libra

Eager buyers, reluctant sellers. A sellers' market.

Jupiter in Aries—Saturn in Cancer

Plenty of buyers, no supply, much speculation.

Saturn in Aries—Jupiter in Capricorn

High prices, no buyers, therefore an excess of goods in the market place.

Saturn in Aries—Jupiter in Cancer

No buyers, lots of supply. Prices fall.

Saturn in Aries—Jupiter in Libra

Eager sellers, reluctant buyers. A buyers' market.

Jupiter in Cancer—Saturn in Libra

Plentiful supply, sellers take a hit or try to control the marketplace. Cartel time.

Saturn in Cancer—Jupiter in Libra

Short supply, sellers profit.

Jupiter in Capricorn—Saturn in Libra

High prices, nobody can sell or an abundance of manufactured goods and heavy competition.

Saturn in Capricorn—Jupiter in Libra

Plenty of sellers, low prices or shortages of manufactured goods and high profits for sellers

Remember, the marketplace is two tiered: manufactured goods and commodities. They do not operate in tandem. Surpluses in the one are often matched by dearths in the other. The availability and price of manufactured goods can and often are modified by the availability and cost of the raw materials with which they are manufactured. As a rule of thumb, prices of commodities perform in an inverse ratio to prices of non-commodities. Each situation must, however, be analyzed separately.

When you see the complexity you can understand why it is so difficult to buy low and sell high. You see why a short supply can also equate to low prices. If buyers do not have the money to buy, nothing can be sold at any price. When there are limitations of Jupiter and Saturn, particularly during their hard aspects, you see a falling market regardless of the amount of goods available. During the Great Depression, Saturn in the 2nd house of the U.S. chart indicated that people simply did not have anything to exchange for manufactured goods. The warehouses were full. This was also the period of the Dust Bowl and bad harvests. Prices cannot rise unless there is capacity to meet that rise in price. The model also suggests it is far easier to buy than to sell. People seldom advertise to buy something. They always advertise to sell.

Buyer and Seller Psychology

In a society such as our where there is always overproduction, it is almost never a seller's market, *even though prices continue to rise.* They rise because of inflation, not because of increasing value. Mars and Venus tell us why.

Venus in Libra—Seventh House

Venus wants a fair price or profit and hates to sell unless she gets what she wants.

Mars in Aries—First House

Mars won't buy unless he has a deal. Result: no sale

Venus in Aries—First House

Buyers see value everywhere and want to get in fast to capture the rise.

Mars in Libra—Seventh House

Sellers are afraid of losses if they do not take profits. Result: plenty of sales and rising prices.

Venus in Cancer

Plenty of money and lots of desire.

Mars in Capricorn

Falling prices. Result: lots of sales and price cutting to beat the competition.

Venus in Capricorn

High prices.

Mars in Cancer

No demand or no money to buy. Result: no sales and rising prices to try to stay in business.

Of course, these do not always happen the same way, but you can see a fundamental market psychology emerge. If your sales are down, you may have to raise prices in order to stay in business. That cuts further into your sales. Either way you lose. With a lot of money in the economy, prices fall as the need for a large profit margin decreases. The drive to cut the competition drives the prices lower.

What you also see in all models is that a large supply or a large demand is no guarantee that prices will either rise or fall, particularly in the middle levels. Competition and the buyer/seller dynamic have a large impact on whether supply and demand is simple or complex.

A harvest model is quite simple. Either there is a surplus or there is not. A harvest and its market coincide in time. The recovery period is the time lag until the next harvest. Two bad harvests in a row create great deprivation. This happens rarely. Under normal conditions it is much harder for prices to rise than it is for prices to fall. Prices rise slow, Venus, and fall fast, Mars. The faster they rise, the faster they fall when the turning point is reached.

The time lag on an industrial model in some cases may be shorter than the agricultural, but from start-up to finish it is generally longer. A factory can go into production when the demand for the product is extremely high. By the time it gets to market, there may be no demand at all.

Sector Growth and Decline

The general concept of supply and demand is difficult, if not impossible, to apply in practice. Astrology enables us to separate out sector growth and decline. Jupiter is where the discretionary money goes. Saturn is where the necessity money goes. Jupiter is purchasing power. Saturn is product availability. When Saturn and Jupiter conjoin, there is high demand because of scarcity, but no purchasing power. Everything falls. In a non-inflationary economy, prices rise in the sign or house sector and fall everywhere else. In an inflationary economy, prices may rise wildly in the sector and rise slower everywhere else.

Saturn and Jupiter through the signs give a long range idea of what will sell and what will be in short supply on a one to two and a half year basis. The general rule of thumb is to take one action in the first half of the sign and the opposite action in the other half. For instance, if prices are going to rise in the computer sector, buy computer stocks in the first half and sell them in the second half of Jupiter's transit of Gemini or Aquarius. If prices are going to fall in the computer sector, sell in the first half and buy in the second.

Jupiter in Aries

The most profit will be made in new issues, iron and steel, and all products that involve iron, such as automobiles and heavy machinery. Jupiter in Aries is bullish for gold and energy, although surpluses may drive the price down. Own the commodity, don't gamble on it. Highly speculative market. High risk ventures and new issues make the most money.

Saturn in Aries

Falling prices, increasing costs, or shortages in the above. The speculators are out of the market. Steel shortages may drive the price of the commodity up.

Jupiter in Taurus

Bullish for raw materials, land, banks, and all financial instruments. Rising prices for land and art. Prices try to keep stable everywhere else. No large growth, but still room for profit in things you have held for a long time.

Saturn in Taurus

This transit indicates very conservative banking practices and a constriction in the money supply. Banks fail. Good buys in all of the above. No sales.

Jupiter in Gemini

Unstable. Wide price fluctuations. Good for all communications stocks, computers, software, and motor vehicles. Jupiter in Gemini does not give great profits. Prices are simply better in these sectors than they will be elsewhere.

Saturn in Gemini

Expect shortages in the above, poor workmanship, low profit margins despite rising prices on the retail level.

Jupiter in Cancer

Increased food supply and good market value, a peak and fall in real estate, especially homes. Profit for all products that cater to public taste and public whim, and for women's products and liquids.

Saturn in Cancer

Commodity shortages, rising real estate prices or a shortage of homes. Consumer needs are not satisfied because of high prices or a lowered ability to pay. Cost of living rises.

Jupiter in Leo

All entertainment and sports vehicles. Speculative market. Good for art, toys, movies, etc. Conspicuous consumption. Abundance can make gold a good long term investment or raise gold speculation to unrealistic highs. The key is the stability of the money standard and supply, rather than the value of gold *per se.*

Saturn in Leo

No interest in the above or no money to buy. Shortages in gold can drive the price up. Because Saturn is weak in Leo, the market does not dominate the psychology. Intrinsic value asserts itself. Saturn in Leo equated to the great price adjustments in the 1970s that revolved around oil price manipulations. Market forces raised the price of oil to its true value relative to U.S. inflation. The same happened in the precious metals market. During the transit of Saturn in Leo prices rose to match true value. In the Jupiter in Leo era they rose way out of proportion because of the feverish and speculative frenzy in both precious metals and oil.

Jupiter in Virgo

Good for medical and service industries, particularly health and hygiene. Prices and confidence fall, because of Jupiter's detriment in Virgo. Neutral for agriculture and crops. Prices stay low.

Saturn in Virgo

Marked by losses of productivity, worker unrest, increasing health and service costs, and declining profits in agriculture and manufacture.

Since Jupiter and Saturn are often in conjunction in the Earth sector, we get a double loss of confidence when both are in this sign. The conjunction is a great buying opportunity. It usually equates to the start of the speculation fever of the Mutable Mutation and the bottom of a previous seven to nine year drop in the markets.

Jupiter in Libra

This shows good buying opportunities in general. An abundance of sellers and a tendency for both sides to feel satisfied. Good for beauty, social/service corporations, all arbitration and litigation. Invest in your lawyer. Weddings and all vehicles that cater to public receptions and social events. Also good for consulting firms.

Saturn in Libra

Saturn through Libra, a sign of Saturn strength, reduces the number of sellers, and puts most transactions under market conditions. Where there is scarcity there will be a sellers market. Otherwise there will be little interest. When the mutation occurs in Libra, as it did in 1980, we see a great adjustment in the social order and a shift in values. Since the combination of Jupiter and Saturn always produces a lack, there is a sharp fall in trading during this period as nobody has any funds. When the next mutation occurs in 2020, it will mark the beginning of the Air era, and may well be the most disruptive economic state of affairs since the "Hungry Forties" (1840's), the first great depression of our materialist era.

Jupiter in Scorpio

This transit indicates rising interest rates. Great demand for loans therefore higher costs of getting loans. Good for insurance companies, mortuaries, and businesses that have to do with handling crisis and repair. Good for people and businesses that work off percentages: agents, brokers, etc. Good for nuclear power industries.

Saturn in Scorpio

Interest rates fall as demand for loans decline. Bad for the above. This is a period of maximum belt-tightening and reorganization. Declining tax revenues can create more general economic problems and the danger of more inflation through deficit financing.

Jupiter in Sagittarius

Generally confident, optimistic, and rising prices because of growth and increasing sales. Wonderful for all travel vehicles, especially international, and the ships and planes that are part of that industry. High growth in schools and colleges, advertising vehicles, and all broadcast media and publishing.

Saturn in Sagittarius

This transit puts few limits on natural market processes. Demand rises in all of the above, creating limitations, and restrictions in the second half of the sign. Expect a reversal of general price trends some time in the second half of the sign.

Jupiter in Capricorn

When Jupiter is in Capricorn, growth is severely curtailed and limited. Government takes greater command and control of prices through regulation. Market prices rise. Good for high retail prices with decreasing profit margins. Good for old-age homes and all products that have to do with the elderly or with wearing out in general.

Saturn in Capricorn

General limitation and restrictions. Shortages of goods and money. High prices for necessities.

Since these occur at the start of the 60-Year Cycle, severe economic upheavals occur at the Jupiter-Saturn conjunctions and oppositions in Capricorn.

Jupiter in Aquarius

Good for electronics and all the products that have to do with the cutting edge of technology. Excellent for all foreign markets and for overseas travel. High time for mergers and diversification/acquisitions. Since Aquarius is contrarian, there can be unexpected swings in many areas, mostly up.

Saturn in Aquarius

Restrictions or shortages in the above. Prices fall to a low and start up, the opposite of Saturn in Capricorn. Saturn in Aquarius is usually the low/low of any period of severe downturn, just as the constellation Aquarius is in the coldest part of the celestial sphere.

Jupiter in Pisces

This transit is wonderful for hospitals, drugs, and getaways. Excellent for all sorts of institutions, health spas, rehabilitation centers, nursing and old-age homes. Wonderful for foreign markets. Jupiter is a trickster in Pisces. It can take the markets to all time highs, but being a Mutable sign the high will not hold. Bullish for established corporations and service industries, in general.

Saturn in Pisces

Huge demand for the above, but short supply. Expect drastic price reversals. These are potential times for trade wars and restrictions of foreign products. Bearish for blue chips. After the shakeout, we get back to Aries and new products and new speculative fever asserts itself.

What we can see is that there are no clear cut interpretations for Jupiter and Saturn. Falling prices on a retail level, which could equate with Saturn, could mean an avid buying of stocks that capture the public fancy. If the profits of a company rise because of Saturn, that could trigger an interest in other stocks of the same sector. If the huge market supply on a retail or wholesale level triggers lower prices and profit margins, the sector stocks may be widely available and prices could decline. You must know the market to determine which way Saturn and Jupiter will operate. As a rule Jupiter increases the supply of commodities and therefore drops the price. It often increases the commodity because of the profits made in the first half of the sign. If the price of silver rises, more silver will be mined. If the commodity can be stored, such as silver and gold, it is an excellent buying opportunity. Jupiter raises the price of manufactured goods because it increases buyer desire. Saturn restricts the supply of commodities and therefore raises the price. It can indicate either supply constriction or profit constriction in manufactured goods.

In this way Jupiter is a good *buy* sign for commodities and a good sell sign for marketplace goods. Saturn is a good sell sign for commodities, but bad for selling in general.

If uncertain, watch sign changes. What sells early in the period will sell even better and vice versa until the next change.

Market Activity

In *Cardinal signs*—Aries, Libra, Cancer, Capricorn—the market dominates. Expect more speculative and herd activity than at other times.

In *Fixed signs*—Taurus, Scorpio, Leo, Aquarius—there is a tendency to hold and put off purchases. True value dominates as the currency tries to re-establish itself against arbitrary standards of value.

In *Mutable signs*—Gemini, Sagittarius, Virgo, Pisces—the market makes major corrections. If the prices are too high relative to market or intrinsic value, the sector will fall. If the prices are too low, they will rise.

Jupiter is the great enthusiast and teacher. Saturn is the great limiter and corrector. The difference between Jupiter and Saturn can be seen in teaching styles. Jupiter gives you the answers before it gives you the test. Saturn gives you the test then tells you what you did wrong.

Jupiter sweeps in on Sagittarian confidence. It rises or it picks itself up after disaster. It ends in Piscean despair, having flown beyond all reason to lose everything it gained. If it does not lose immediately, it loses in time. All the price gains of

Jupiter in Pisces in 1986 were lost in the crash of 1987. Saturn creeps in on Capricorn shrewdness and blasts out with Aquarian contrariness. Saturn in Capricorn rises then falls. Saturn in Aquarius falls then rises.

Government Intervention

Because the government is Capricorn and Capricorn is the market, governments get caught up in economics and try to control the economic flow. In trying to assure a level playing field and a fair market, governments impose taxes and manipulate the money supply through federal debt and interest rates, both Scorpio, 8th house, and Mars-Pluto entities—Mars against Mars. Mars against Mars is war. War destroys. Mars, like *laissez-faire*, is never fair. Mars-run governments eventually destroy both free trade and fair trade.

In the long run a market cannot be manipulated. Saturn rules. Short term prizes go to those who enter fast and fearless and who get out in the same decisive way. The market is not a place for investors, except for the very long term. Taurus is the investor. Patience equals profit.

The Jupiter-Saturn oppositions of 1989, 1990, and 1991 put an end to markets that rose and rose. They start the correction on the other side.

Precautions, Patterns and Profits

- The market is always a buyer's market. There is no sale without someone with money to trade.

- Prices always tend to fall.

- Money can be made in up markets and down.

- Buy early in a Jupiter sector transit. Sell late.

- Sell or hold early in a Saturn sector transit. Buy midway through.

- The enemy of the buyer is impatience.

- The strength of the seller is stubbornness.

- Markets always correct.

Chapter Four

BEYOND THE LIMITS

Inflation is the most misinterpreted and misunderstood phenomenon of modern times. Inflation is Neptune. Neptune is money multiplication carried to its extreme: Venus in Pisces in the thralls of illusion. Inflation is Venus on a roll, the flash before ground zero, the inevitability of government debt. Scorpio, debt, opposes Taurus, fiscal stability. It trines Pisces, expanding the money supply.

Rising prices do not create inflation. Inflation creates rising prices. Debt expansion, public or private, creates inflation. OPEC could have demanded $30 a barrel for oil and cut the pipelines, but the price would only have risen as long and as high as the amount of money in circulation could support the price. If there were no inflation in the economy, prices would have fallen everywhere else. If there was increasing inflation in the economy the price of oil and everything else would continue to rise. Oil would simply rise faster.

In a modern economy, inflation is created in three ways: government debt, private debt, and an influx of foreign funds. The federal debt (Neptune) is the prime fueler of inflation. Private debt (Mars and Pluto) is eventually retired either by payment or bankruptcy. Foreign funds (Uranus) flow unpredictably in and out. The Neptunian form is the most perverse because it presents itself in illusion and lies. The only antidote to Neptune is facts.

Everybody frets about mortgaging future generations, about inflation, rising prices, depression. Consider the facts of the U.S. federal debt:

Federal Debt

- In 1857.....................................$28,701,000
- By 1866..............................$2,755,764,000
  In 9 years it increased by a factor of 10.

- In 1914..............................$1,188,235,000
- By 1919............................$25,484,506,000
  In 5 years it increased by a factor of 25.

- In 1974 ....$478,000,000,000
- In 1978 ....$1,061,000,000,000
  Double 1974 in 4 years.

- By 1986........................$2,082,000,000,000
  Double 1978 in 8 years.

- In 1990 ....$3,000,000,000,000
  In 12 years (1978-1990) it increased by a factor of 3.

It took us *16 years* (1974-1990) to increase by a factor of 7. Slow, compared to previous periods. All through the 1920s the government ran budget surpluses. The federal debt was cut by a third. We had a favorable balance of trade. The 1930s followed the 1920s.

If we balance our budgets and keep the federal debt constant, our grandchildren will owe exactly the same as we. If the population grows, the *per capita* debt will decrease.

In an economy stabilized by gold, a gold rush creates rampant inflation, especially in the boom town surrounding the strike. Eventually the excess enters the wider markets and stabilizes. Gold is never put back in the ground. Government debt is supposed to go back into the ground. Government debt is bogus money. Bogus money into the economy creates inflation. Bogus money out creates depression.

Neptune is bogus. Uranus is law-breaking. Pluto is coercive. Neptune creates illusions of great wealth despite losses in real value. Uranus gangs up and cleans your clocks in the name of brotherhood. Pluto bankrupts you in the name of bailing you out.

Neptune, Inflation as Government Debt

Old fashioned Neptune was the printing of paper money without any backing in gold. Today's Neptune is the federal debt. The end result is the same. The numbers get bigger. The value gets smaller. The accounting system goes berserk.

Corporate debt borrows from future productivity, taking profits before the profit and the product is produced. It creates a bubble of activity that needs future successes to survive. If the successes are not forthcoming, the company fails. The excess money created by corporate debt returns to the system in the form of products or disappears with bankruptcy. The swings in the business cycle that result are relatively short and shallow, especially in their Martian form.

The government borrows from the future not only in great sums but over a very long period of time. The numbers rise before the genuine wealth manifests itself. Politicians point to increasing numbers in the GNP, and increasing paychecks. They blame this government-induced inflation on greedy capitalists, greedy workers, and OPEC. Inflation has one major source in a modern economy—government debt. Government debt is different from normal debt in that it is a scheme to print unbacked money without acknowledging the process and purpose and without increasing wealth. This is especially true of the United States with Neptune in the 10th house of the national chart.

Loan payoffs and bankruptcies wring excess private debt out of the economy. They create a constant economic inflow and outflow. Government debt goes only one way—up.

Prices cannot rise across the board in a non-inflationary economy. They will rise in some sectors according to perceived need and fall in others. Price rises across the board indicate inflation, Neptune at work.

Neptune's bad money seeps through the economy just as surely as good money. The great speculators of the 1980s did not take money from the mouths of babes, rather they created illusions of wealth by their own manipulations of the public and private money supply. In effect, they created their own money, cheated with it, and ultimately lost it. Unfortunately, the government through FSLIC and the FDIC guaranteed the perpetuation of their phony money. By protecting the assets of the small fry, it encouraged the money sprees of the big fries. Instead of letting this excessive debt remove itself from circulation, it simply shifted it from the private sector to the public by creating more phony money with bailout loans. Time will tell whether or not that was such a good idea.

The total money supply is stable in the long run if subject only to fluctuations in personal and corporate debt. Borrowing keeps prices up when the economic machinery falters.

As we have seen in the previous chapter, supply and demand mainly show themselves in individual sectors in the economy. It negates itself on composite price levels, because a stable economy produces self-stabilizing prices, that fluctuate only in a predictable range, as the Dow did throughout the 1960s and 1970s.

When Neptune enters a financial market or state economy there is *always* deception. The primary result of Neptune is a destruction of the accounting system (Virgo opposite Pisces— Mercury against Neptune). One cannot determine whether price and wage rises are genuine or are just an illusion of sophisticated money creation.

In an earlier chapter we saw how the only true state of one's finances was the barter trade. If you bought a house in 1965 for $29,000 and sell it today for $290,000, you do not know if you made a killing or were killed. You only find out when you try to buy something else. If the barter trade turns out to be a two bedroom condo with Jacuzzi, health club and security for a 4 bedroom colonial with basement on a half acre, no security necessary, then buying a Jacuzzi, a club membership and keeping the house would have been the more equitable trade. The point is not that you received 10 times your original price, but that your living conditions have deteriorated for the same amount of money. That is Neptune. You feel smug because the price of your property rose. You are horrified at what you get in return.

Losing One's Marbles

To understand Neptune and the effects of inflation it is best to take them down to basics: You and your playmates are playing marbles. There are three of you with five marbles each. You win the pot. You now have 15 marbles, they have none. But having indulgent parents, your two friends are given money to buy not five more marbles but 15 marbles each. This is done in the name of democracy and equality. It is not "fair" for you to have

15 marbles and they to have none. Your victory has just become meaningless. You are all back to square one. Worse still, your individual marbles are worth only one third of what they were before you began. You have lost your "superior" status. Your purchasing power has been cut by two-thirds. In order to match your previous feat of wiping out the assets of your playmates, you have to work three times harder and win at least three times more pots than you needed to before. The odds of your repeating are much worse, because the longer you play, the longer the system is likely to even itself out. In the card game of "War" many a child has seen his opponent, down to one card, suddenly start on a winning streak. The more cards you have, the more low cards you have. The high cards are all in sequence on the losing side—at least for awhile. The balance shifts, the poor become rich, and the rich become poor.

If you find yourself arguing here, what is charitable and what is fair, your politics may be influencing your astrological judgment. This is not a discussion about morality or politics, but about what happens. If we do not examine what happens, we cannot properly interpret the symbols of the effect. Should we have compassion for the unfortunate? Of course. Should we reward skill? Of course. Inflation is not the way to do it. Venus in Pisces, especially in its Neptunian, altruistic martyr form, not only multiplies itself, but multiplies the poor and needy as well.

Inflation has the appearance of evening out the economy just as it prolongs and seems to even out the marbles game. It does not make the players any better relative to one another. The skilled or the lucky still get a big slice of the action no matter what. The difference is that losers never feel totally broke. If you take all the marbles again and your playmate's parents continue to subsidize a new round of marbles, not only will you get richer after an initial dilution of your assets, but your playmates will never improve their skill or quit a losing game.

Inflation has its compassionate side, but it is destructive as an economic system, because it keeps alive many businesses that have long outlived their usefulness, it does not encourage people to learn new skills, and it not only widens the gap between the rich and the poor but it makes it difficult for the poor to make basic purchases without further subsidies.

Counterfeit Money and the Effects
of Corrections

Inflation (Neptune) is, in fact, counterfeit money. The marbles game showed us what happens when you put it into the system. Taking it out is even worse. Remember, Venus in Pisces is a fundamentally fortunate position. The removal of Venus from Pisces is the reverse.

Say you live in a very small community, Anytown. The amount of money that circulates within this community is $1,000,000 at any given time. A gang of expert counterfeiters dumps an extra $100,000 into the system. They go in and buy everything in sight at the normal prices and leave town. $100,000 dollars worth of goods has been taken out of the economy without anything substantial being added. However, the people who sold the goods have increased their monetary wealth by $100,000. Real estate is one of the first places where bogus money turns up, being one of the few markets in this country subject to bidding on the consumer level.

Storekeeper A with an extra $10,000 dollars in his pocket and a depleted inventory bids against factory worker B for a little cottage on the edge of town with a picket fence and an acre of grass, all Kentucky blue. Who's going to get the house? The storekeeper, of course. The house seller receives $5,000 of the bogus money with which A outbid B. Everybody is happy except the factory worker. Because of the purchases made by the counterfeiters, A has a somewhat depleted inventory, and is awaiting some orders to be refilled. Because of the lag in delivery and the need to meet his overhead expenses on the smaller inventory (he's already blown $5,000 of his windfall and is reluctant to take the other $5,000 out of the bank), he raises prices just enough to keep going in case of further delays. The people grumble, but the beneficiaries of the bogus money are able to handle the prices without too much damage to their pocketbooks. The other storekeepers follow suit. A few more houses are sold and everybody is feeling very prosperous, except the factory worker, so he goes on strike for a cost-of-living increase. Prices continue to rise across the board. The teachers go on strike, followed by the firemen and police, taxes go up to meet the costs, and we're all spiraling up.

If the counterfeiters had not dumped the money into the town, storekeeper A might still have outbid the factory worker, but if he had tried to raise his prices to make up for the expenditure, only the person from whom he bought the house would have been able to accommodate the price rises. If, because he was the only grocery store in town, they had to pay the price, they would not have been able either to buy new homes or pay a price comparable to his original transaction. Real estate would either stagnate or fall. Seeing the price of vegetables rise, many would grow their own next year. Although his volume might drop, the storekeeper would at best maintain his old profit level with his new high prices.

Now suppose the FBI nabbed the counterfeiting ring and learned that Anytown had been one of their targets. In come the Feds and take back all that money. All of a sudden, people who were involved in the first wave of prosperity, if they still have the cash, experience a great loss. In fact, they are only losing something they didn't have to start with, so they should be back to square one. In fact, these people have all the goods they purchased with their windfalls, and the second level of prosperity people will be stuck with the counterfeit bills and cash. These people not only lose the cash—they sold homes and bought new homes at higher prices so they now have no money to pay for them. The bank took a bath on this withdrawal, so they are reluctant to extend any more credit. The bank has a bunch of houses to be auctioned off. Not only is the real estate market glutted, it is glutted with fire sale houses. The price of real estate goes through the floor. The people who have taken a loss on the reclaim of the counterfeit bills cannot sell their houses for the price of the mortgage. Their credit is destroyed. They are homeless.

This is essentially the scenario of the S&L debacle and the growing economic situation of millions of people. The excess money created by the Fed and leveraged by the likes of Silverado Savings, and Drexel, Burnham, Lambert made huge profits for people in on the ground floor, money they spent on personal perks and investments, money that skyrocketed the price of real estate, eventually paid by the little guy for a home. Now that billions have been taken out of the economy, the little guy is standing in line to get his money from the purses of the aggregate little guys who make up the taxpayers.

Putting counterfeit money into a system is bad. Taking it out is worse. Suppose in the game of marbles, each of your friends were punished for staying out late by taking away their marbles. No matter how rich you are at the stage of the pullout you now have nobody to play with. The marbles you do have are worthless except to look at and gloat over. In fact, your marbles are just as worthless as they were when you won them all. A market, like any game, needs more than one to play.

To go back to the prescripts of an earlier chapter, your wealth lies in its tradability, not in its numbers. It is not wealth unless you have it in your hand, no matter what the numbers say.

If the value of your assets, real estate and otherwise, rises dramatically on paper, you can be sure in an inflating economy only that you are not a total loser. Whether you have stayed even depends on what you can barter your assets for. Numbers do not lie in a closed economy. They always do with Neptune.

Neptune and Pisces have always been known as symbols of illusion and delusion. The price gouging associated with the run-up in oil prices in the 1970s did not create inflation, though it was blamed for it.

Neptune is the planet of oil. A rise in the price of oil is reflective of the need or value of oil to an economy. If the economy of the 1970s had been non-inflationary, the price of oil could have risen drastically *only* if prices *fell* elsewhere.

Inflation is usually blamed on things that create rises in sector prices, not rises in the general price level. Let's look at the 1920s and the progress from high jinks and high living to the pits.

Lag Time

The total Federal Debt in 1919 reached a peak of $25,485,000,000. That's roughly twenty-five and a half *billion* dollars. Most of this was due to the cost of World War I. As we have seen from our small town model, and from our examination of Venus in Pisces, money spreads throughout the economy. In fact, it doesn't spread, it seeps. It takes seven to ten years to seep and find its place of rest. These are Saturn-cycle numbers. Saturn is the limiter, it always tells us when something has been stopped or a realistic level has been reached.

In our small town model, if the counterfeit money had never been discovered, it would have been seven to nine years before everyone had partaken of the windfall of the counterfeiter's gift. Of course, that is much too long for the people who get their share last, but that is one of the evils of doctoring the system.

From World War I the money in the system increased by a factor of 25 in four short years. That money would start to show in all the markets between 1921 and 1929 (the increase started in 1914. Seven years later the economy showed the major part of the increase). As you will see later, all cycles have a lag time. War spending is a peculiar phenomenon, particularly as the United States has practiced it over the last 70 odd years. The initial spending is directed towards certain sectors of the economy and directed away from others. Initially there are shortages and a lack of disposable income that results from men being drafted and certain industries failing. Within a short period of time, the money stabilizes, but tons of equipment are made—not to enter the economy of the nation but to be destroyed. So everybody is working and making money but there is no place to spend it and no products to spend it on.

Because our industrial base was still strong after all our trading partners had their economies destroyed after World War I as well as World War II, instead of having a major post war decline, our economic endeavors shifted, not only to satisfy our own pent-up consumer demand but to serve the foreign demand our once devastated allies and enemies had for our products, which they bought with money we lent them. We had a very favorable balance of trade in the 1920s as we did in the 1950s, a similar period of absorption of inflationary growth. Both periods are typical of Neptunian activity.

The Federal Debt		Stock Prices	
1866	$2,756,000,000	1874	20 to 40
1919	$25,485,000,000	1929	380 Peak—1932, 42
1946	$270,991,000,000	1954	404
1986	$2,082,000,000,000	1990	3,000 peak

Being a purely discretionary market, the stock market is usually the last place to get its share of excess money. The lag time is seven to nine years after the initial injection. The federal debt in 1919 was 10 times the federal debt in 1866. In 1929 stock prices were 10 times the price level of 1874, the year of the previous great debacle. By 1932 it bottomed at the same price as the 1874 peak. In 1946 the debt was 10 times 1919. In 1954 the Dow was over 400, or 10 times the 1932 low. By 1990 the debt had grown by another factor of 10. The Dow tried to as well. The question is: Will it make 4,000 or 400?

If we apply scientific analysis to these apparent recurrent observed repetitions, we will conclude that the Dow has a long way to go.

If we apply astrological cycles to this data, as we will in a later chapter, we will understand not only the timing, but why it is happening and the significance. We cannot make a good judgment on the significance if we do not understand inflation, i.e., money that enters a system that was not part of barter value.

The high inflation in Japan is due mainly to our buying their goods for more money than their economy could sustain on its own. This is why they put it back into our real estate and our government debt.

The Twenties

All during the 1920s the government, in an attempt to reduce the federal debt, ran budget surpluses. They did this, incidentally, by cutting taxes, not raising them. Once Neptune left Cancer, and Pluto alone transited the U.S. 8th house, tax revenues were more than sufficient to meet expenses. Borrowing ceased. By 1929, the federal debt had been reduced by one third. That means that one-third of the inflationary currency had been taken out of circulation. Since it takes time for money to flow in, it also takes time for it to flow out. Don't forget a great deal of money is borrowed on inflationary money, which must be wrung out also. It does not happen all at once, but it tends to trickle out at the same pace, until a critical mass and a crash occurs. The effect of the outflow would not show till 1927 at the earliest and 1930 at the latest. Because of a favorable balance of trade during the period, foreign money took up part of the slack.

The government started to pull the rug out, before the markets fully accustomed themselves to the rug. The rug pad, money from foreign trade, slipped as well, as Germany and France repudiated their debts, and Brazil and Peru defaulted on massive loans, both Pluto activities. American banks, deprived of an inflated money supply, failed.

Had all the rugs been pulled at once, recovery would have been even slower. The high of 1930 was one-third lower than the high of 1929. The stock market was the last to absorb the input and the first to show the out-take.

Before the general price levels fell to their lowest potential, the government started pumping money back into the economy. Before the economy adjusted to the amount taken out, more started coming back in. The Dow gyrated wildly during the 1930s, eventually losing 90% of its value. General price levels dropped only 25% though the actual deflation was initially 34%.

The 1920s saw just as many mergers, just as many bankruptcies, just as many bank failures, and just as much borrowing and many defaults on international loans as today (do we never learn?). General price levels never fell below the percentage of drop in the federal debt. Discretionary stock market prices fell back to their previous levels, because the money invested in stocks was money borrowed on the borrowed money of government. The financial base evaporated before it filtered through. Stock price levels fell to their 1870s levels. Everything else decreased *only* in proportion to the decrease in the federal debt.

The Forties

In 1946 the federal debt reached its first 10 times multiple of the 1920s. Within seven years of the government's attempt to retire its World War II debt the country started to go into recession. At the same time the stock market recovered its losses and was back to 400. Again we have the same scenario, federal debt increases by a multiple of 10 due to World War II. Stock market increases by a multiple of 10. As soon as murmurings of recession were heard, the government injected money back into the system. It has slowly inflated the currency ever since.

No bogus money has been taken out of the system since 1947. We have had no major depression in that time. Our current stock price levels are pulling towards 10 times the 1920s and 1940s. Does that mean we will never have a recession or depression again? It is likely that we have a different danger this time.

Inflation and Expansion

Charts for oil prices and gold (pages 16 and 19) show that the stock market is not the only market that rose to 10 times multiples. All prices have risen at 10 or 10 times 10, whether or not the stock market was able to sustain the rise along with the rest of the economy.

In the 1840s, the beginning of our major economic era, the country was in a depression the likes of which had never been seen. All through the 1820s the government ran surpluses and was carrying almost no debt at all. In 1835 and 1836 the federal debt was $38,000, down from a high of $127,000,000 in 1816. Keep this in perspective, $38,000 was not a lot of money even in those years. Most of that $38,000 was short term debt, paid off as it accumulated. In other words, the money supply had not only shrunk, but there was no money to fund necessary economic and industrial expansion. Andrew Jackson had destroyed the U.S. Bank. Financial institutions still in their infancy had little means of creating money in the private sector.

The "Hungry Forties" as this depression was called, did not end until the gold strike and gold rushes in 1849. A gold rush is nature's version of inflation. Without some inflation or new sources of money or gold, an expanding population does not have enough currency to manage its economy. An expanding population and an expanding economy must have an expanding money supply to keep prices level and to fund future expansion. The problem is where to get it. In an earlier chapter we found that the foundations of wealth are material goods and the bounty of the earth. The United States certainly had the raw materials on which to create capital for future industrial growth. At the time, the capitalist system had not been fully developed. Stocks, shares in future productivity, is the best, if not the only way to finance growth because the expansion is always tied to productivity and the investor never demands his money back from the company. Like gold, shareholder debt is never put back into the ground.

Booms sponsored by government debt and by private debt that has to be paid back is money created in advance of any productivity which has to be repaid at the peak of productivity. Thus the 1920s, like the 1980s, borrowed money from the future to create financial bubbles that could not be sustained. If you take your profits before you produce, you have no profit when you produce and no funds to finance future production except by going perpetually into debt.

What is significant about the 1840s and the gold rush, is that new gold also creates inflation, if inflation is defined as sweeping increases in prices across the board. A gold rush town has the same frenzy and inflation as any economy that experiences sudden or large increases in its tradable medium. If new dollars are injected into an economy, prices rise. If new gold or new sea shells or bones because a tribal war brings booty into the economy, you spend more for what you want. Once gold goes into the economy, it never leaves. Once value created by stock certificates goes into the economy it never leaves. Once the money generated by the federal debt goes into the economy it should never leave. When it does, a depression is assured.

A depression, as we know it, is really a deflation. If the economic adjustment is one of deflation, prices will fall across the board and everyone gets less and needs less with which to purchase things which now cost less. Although the adjustment is difficult on the way down, it is only the reverse of the upswing. The upswing is easier to manage. Up always looks better than down.

A corporation has lag times between purchases of raw materials, payment of wages and receipts from sales. If it is to make a profit, it must have a selling price higher than its costs. Inflation guarantees that the books will always look good.

The wage earner, on the other hand, has to pay the higher costs before he gets the raise in pay.

In a deflating economy, the company buys the goods, pays the wages high, and sells lower. In the deflationary time lag, lower costs devolve into even lower selling prices. Many companies go out of business. Workers lose jobs or are forced to accept lower wages. Thus, slow inflation is much more accommodating to the economy as a whole than deflation.

It is obvious that one of the prime reasons for the depression of the 1930s was a matter of the U.S. government's pulling money out of the economy. It was not the only reason. Speculation and margin buying created tons of illusory money. International defaults on loans and bank failures shrank our money supply, and tariffs killed our international trade, a typical Pluto aftermath.

On a purely technical level it appears that the 10 times multiple is the point where the influx should stop to take a breather as it coincides with the natural turning points of economic movement, which will be much more apparent in the cycles chapters.

Inflation Multiplication

The problem is not simply the multiple of 10 as a function of the federal debt but of the money created as a result of the federal debt. Again we have a trickle down effect, but this time with the multiplying of bogus money. With Neptune the trickle grows into a flood. Suppose the government borrows $10,000,000 and pays one thousand people $100,000. Those thousand people pay $10,000 more each than they should to buy a house. That means that prices of homes will rise by a similar percentage. Suppose each takes out a loan for $200,000 to cover the cost of the house and uses $25,000 of that $100,000 to purchase the house. We now have another $20,000,000 in circulation. The $25,000 taken out was partially negated by the $10,000 more the original seller had to spend and is almost totally nullified by the fact that there is still $75,000 left to spend both on necessities and on luxuries. For all practical purposes the amount of money in circulation did not increase by the $10,000,000 the government borrowed, but by $30,000,000. Federal debt is worse than coat hangers multiplying in your closet. This is Neptune.

One might argue that the money lent was savings, which had been taken out of circulation and was now being put back in. Fractional Reserve banking is a system of money expansion that assumes everyone will not default or withdraw their savings all at once, therefore, one needs only a percentage of the total amount of money loaned in reserve to cover possible withdrawals. Two and a half per cent is on the high side. In other words, you can loan someone $10 if you have only $.25 in your account. No, it does not make sense, but you can see how unbacked government money can double and triple by the time it reaches the man in the street.

Neptune and Oil

Neptune represents oil. Think back on 1970s hysteria about running out of oil. There is always a lie or a poison with Neptune. Always. The lies of the oil panic and OPEC in the 1970s were:

1. There was a shortage of oil. There was not.

2. Oil caused the double digit inflation. It did not. Government debt did.

An astrologer who does not understand Neptune and inflation is likely to be swayed in his interpretations by the demagoguery of politicians and analysts who give as bogus an explanation for Neptunian conditions as the money that creates them. Until the Iraqi invasion of Kuwait, we had an oil glut and an oil price moving in its appropriate range, the 10 times variable price of silver, and just over 10 times the price of oil 60 years ago. Oil is high because the cartel is still nominally operating and the oil suppliers and distributors like things just the way they are, not to mention the overindebted countries that are depending on oil revenues to pay their interest. Oil should eventually sit in the $5 to $12 a barrel range when the world economy achieves a balance. If we continue to over-inflate our currency, it could restabilize at $50 to $120. More likely, our economy will collapse first.

The price of oil could never have achieved present levels solely on the basis of an oil cartel. It and the precious metals run-up of the late 1970s and early 1980s were only adjusting to the 10 times multiple of our excess money creation. Gold was $35 an ounce; silver, $.50 to $1.25; oil, $1.25 *a barrel*. The truth is that they took 20 years to catch up to what was happening in the rest of the economy.

When you are dealing with Neptune in an economic sense you know:

1. Expansion is limited only by self-destruction.

2. Things always seem more wonderful than they are.

3. Artificial purchasing power is being created outside the normal flow of commerce.

Debt Exportation

One of the reasons the U.S. has been slow to reach price levels comparable to the level of the inflationary debt is that the money is not spent entirely inside the country. Goods, purchased with inflationary dollars, were distributed to Europe and Japan or destroyed in Korea and Vietnam. When Europeans complained in the 1950s and 1960s that we were exporting our inflation to them we felt insulted that they would not be thankful for our largesse. What we did was borrow to lend to them so they could purchase from us. We did not give them real money based on a share of our productivity, but debt based on the government's power to issue bonds.

Our economy tends to overproduce—why will become clear in chapter five. In war time our overproduction is destroyed as fast as it is made. In the Cold War it was simply put out of commission in the nuclear weapons stockpile. While the process did create jobs and an increasing wage pool, which ordinarily would drive the cost of available goods up, rebuilding battle-torn countries took up the excess.

When European production became competitive, Americans, attracted by the lower prices of foreign goods, started to import. By importing foreign goods, paid for with inflated dollars, we continued to export our inflation. Now our inflation is coming back as foreigners invest in our stock market and in our real estate. The world is no longer our safety valve. When the government turned its spending from guns to butter and domestic programs, we started to experience the double digit inflation our economy had been manufacturing all along. The stock market absorbed the excess in the 1950s. The consumers got soaked in the 1970s and early 1980s. Politicians blamed OPEC, the Uranian vehicle that drove our Neptune home.

Foreign Money as Inflation

Both Neptune and Uranus are planets of foreign money. Another form of artificial purchasing power comes from foreigners buying our goods. Neptune and Uranus transiting the U.S. 2nd house give us our inflation back. We buy from Japan with our inflated currency, they buy back our land with the profits our imports afforded them. If we had no trade deficit, the price of our real estate would have risen without the intervention of the Japanese or English middleman.

There is good and bad on both sides. Japan's high cost of living is a direct result of the American money that has over-heated its economy. The low rate of consumer inflation in this country is a direct result of our purchasing goods abroad at costs lower than our own. If our economy were a closed system, that is, if we were not able to export our inflation by buying cheaper abroad, our price levels could conceivably be 10 times what they are now. Our federal debt has reached banana republic propor-tions. Our actual rise in prices is still at a level that is tolerable and safe, if the 1940s and 1950s are any indication.

Japan has also given us back our inflation by purchasing government securities and corporate stocks and bonds. The only reason that many of our markets have not collapsed is because of foreign investment. Despite the hysteria about the trade deficit, we actually have much of that money coming back, some of it is even coming back in the form of foreign companies that hire Americans. While we may not like the idea of "resident aliens" telling our workers what to do, from a purely economic standpoint it is merely reestablishing a balance.

If our economy fails, it will be the "foreigners" who will lose the most. Japan is dependent on American markets to maintain its high level of employment and prosperity. All the United States has to do is go back to buying its own goods. Of course, Neptune in the 2nd will create all kinds of hysteria about foreign devils and the impoverished American that will be far worse than the reality.

Neptunian hysteria tells us that we are in great danger from trade deficits, and budget deficits, and greedy foreigners buying up our assets. The reality is, as it always is, that things are always in balance. As long as the balance is maintained, the system will correct itself over the long term. Over the short term we may not be so fortunate.

Uranus

Uranus contributes to inflation and market distortions in the form of foreign money, and of groups of people acting in con-cert to produce a certain effect. It is also a planet of reversals and upsets. Though considered democratic and humanitarian, it is equally a symbol of democratic despotism. With Saturn, the planet of government and control, it co-rules Aquarius. OPEC is a Uranian-Saturnian cartel that totally turned the flow of the world economy by its unilateral, and high-handed actions. The action of Uranus is always arbitrary and despotic, the result of groups, organized activities, or actions based on altruism and brotherly love. Uranus always breaks rules, breaks tradition, or starts a new trend. Despite its connections with rebellion and individual eccentricity, Uranus represents the herd instinct. It can be the murderous rebellion of the mob or the panic of three-piece suits on the trading floor. The programmed trading of the crash of 1987 is a perfect example of a Uranian event. Hundreds of institutional money managers all punching the electronic button to trigger instant calamity.

Uranus, a planet of international impact, represents a sudden influx or outflow of international funds. Foreign money is inflationary because it is not created in the economy. The inability of the market to recover after October of 1987 was due to the flight of foreign capital from our markets. The international herding instinct decided property was a better buy.

Uranus is a planet of fads and political fancies, aggravated by the actions of groups and cartels. While the ability to bid stocks higher and higher is dependent on public and private debt, the translation of that debt into the market is accomplished by trading cartels. If pension fund and mutual fund managers all trade by using the same computer program, or similar ones, they have *de facto* formed an electronic cartel that times purchases to a formula adhered to by all. In the 1920s a few wealthy men who traded in their own interest dominated the market and formed a cartel to save it when it failed. Today, trading is still done by a small number of men, albeit on behalf of millions.

As a planet of modern technology and electronics, Uranus creates economic log jams in sophisticated ways, particularly by control of communications systems. Uranus believes everything can be done in a computer. Uranus would have a credit card economy, with everyone on a universal balance sheet. If we never get to hold even the paper proof of our toil in our fat little hands, just think of the Uranian potential for unlimited and unjustified creation of "wealth."

Uranus is a planet of the expropriation of goods by fiat. If a government takes over an industry, it empowers itself to use the industry as a source and base of money creation. A boycott produces a similar effect for different reasons. By denying the flow of goods out of a company or into a country, the money available to purchase existing goods is far in excess of the goods available for purchase. Prices rise everywhere. This is the classic definition of too many dollars chasing too few goods.

The boycott of South Africa is typical of the mass movements that generate economic turmoil. Instead of achieving the abolition of apartheid by increasing the prosperity and clout of the blacks, the boycott constrained the economy and threw many blacks back into poverty. It also enabled wealthy whites, who were already holding most of the money, to buy international corporations at bargain prices. Although there is great and often honorable conviction in the actions of Uranus and great intellectual certainty, there is little foresight, and fewer facts.

Uranus and Neptune both equate with panic and euphoria. Both are mob planets. Both are driven by feeling. Neither thinks things through. Uranus acts quickly, without warning. Neptune creeps along. The dawning is slow and deadly. You never think of the consequences with Uranus. With Neptune the consequences are never what you think.

Pluto

Pluto is the planet of total disaster, bankruptcies, impossible debt, starting all over from scratch. The great run-up in the stock market and in real estate in the 1980s was largely a function of the junk-bond market. It had little to do with real money in circulation or value derived from productivity of any kind. The Pluto version of inflation is leverage, excessive borrowing against assets, excessive borrowing against the future, excessive borrowing to manipulate and control. Mars takes a reasonable percentage of assets, Pluto tries to take it all.

Pluto is exorbitant interest rates, once known as usury. It is the hidden interest you pay for the federal debt without even suspecting. At the present writing, Neptune and Uranus are ahead of Pluto in the Zodiac, which means that Pluto will sweep through the signs they have already passed. Pluto is particularly adept at gouging out the negatives of both these outer planets. At the present time it is passing over the position of

Neptune during the Vietnam war. Money created by the federal
government during that period and subsequently multiplied by
the banks is being destroyed. Neptune is the generational illusion. Neptune in Scorpio is piggyback debt. Pluto in Scorpio
forces a debt crisis as it illuminates the damaging effect of policies perpetrated in those guns and butter years.

Pluto always kills the market. The degree of damage
depends on the degree of distortion. We may think of death as a
distortion, just as we think of severe market adjustments as distortions in the nicely flowing upward curve. A Pluto market
event is a correction back to reality and a statement about
proper price levels. *When the market corrected in 1987, it corrected down to 10 times the level it held 60 years before.*

Pluto brings depression and fear. The market dies. Everybody is afraid to trade. Pluto, being the pits, is the best place to
buy, but it takes massive courage to go contrary to world wide
despondency and terror.

Pluto steals. Pluto is the bankruptcy that steals from creditors. Pluto is the hostile takeover. Pluto is totally lawless, with
a potential for execution and bloodthirsty revenge. If in a hostile
takeover Pluto pursues a purpose of getting rid of the deadwood,
the takeover will be successful. Most takeovers have been an
attempt to steal assets that can be turned into cash for a quick
and dirty profit.

We will see in the next chapter that the economic style of
the United States denies property ownership. A company does
not own its assets, stockholders do, yet the takeover artists buy
sufficiently into the company to get control. When they get control they sell it all.

Pluto, like Mars, is no caretaker—it is a percentage
player. Its purpose is always to buy to sell or to get control to
make a profit.

Pluto is also oppressive taxation. Pluto takes whatever it
needs or wants. It does not leave enough to live on if that inter-
feres with what it wants. Pluto in action is even worse, not only
does it take, but it sells back what it took after the profit. Conceivably, the government may one day, if it gets control of
industry, be not only the taxer but the chief and only employer
as well. We need only look at the events of the 1930s to see the
operation of Pluto from the moment it was discovered in 1930:
Hitler through fascist means controlled the German economy,

relocated and murdered millions of people, and started a war; Stalin took food from Ukrainian Kulaks and let 15 million people starve to death so Russians could eat; Roosevelt confiscated the gold of U.S. citizens and denied them the ownership of their property.

Pluto makes arbitrary decisions over who can live or die. Pluto takes what it wants and gives back what it wants and when it feels like doing so.

Internationality

Uranus, Neptune, and Pluto are all mass movements of people—international fads and movements, regardless of race, creed, or nationality. These are generational planets, millions of people drawn to the same illusions, ideologies and hatreds all at the same time. These are the apocalyptic horseman of democracy and globalism. They have the capacity to destroy all tradition, all law, and all sanity.

On an economic level they can be as harmless as the Cabbage Patch Doll craze or as necessary as the price adjustment of oil to the level of inflation. They can be as deadly as the total destruction of a nuclear war, terrorist blackmail, the inevitable consequences of money spent on death and destruction, the toxic waste of a nuclear power plant, the pesticide residue in food, or the foul air generated by the internal combustion engine in our cars. They can be as beneficent as heart transplants and CAT scans.

Uranus is the exciting, technological, new, and innovation. Neptune is the waste generated by the exciting, technological, and new. Pluto is the death generated by the waste of the exciting, technological and new, and also side effects and fallout.

The market is no different.

Prospects

As we have seen in previous chapters, the median price of housing is roughly 10 times what it was in the 1920s and 1940s. The price of gold, silver, and oil are all at 10 times their prices 60 years ago or less. All indicate that these markets have adjusted to inflation. The debt level has surpassed its 10 times multiple, a warning that a major adjustment is in play.

Only the stock market has failed to absorb its full share. Because the Jupiter-Saturn opposition, the termination point of the 1980s frenetic growth, completed itself between September 1989 and June 1991, it is dubious that the Dow will reach the 10 times multiple of 1929 at its top—3,800. Historically, the 60 year shift points to 1992 as a point of maximum market expansion. Saturn in Aquarius and Jupiter in Virgo,the placement of 1932, usually mark an economy's low point. In the United States' chart, Saturn in the 2nd contracted the money supply before the Dow had a chance to reach its maximum, so a Dow beyond 3,800 seems unlikely, except under the possibility of runaway inflation. If the federal debt and budget deficits continue to balloon, if the government tries to spend itself out of job losses and business failures, our money could become worthless. In that case a Dow reaching 4,000 is a sign of potential disaster.

The government bailout of S&L and bank depositors, transfers bad private debt (Pluto) into public debt (Neptune) and postpones the necessary and inevitable correction (Uranus). The higher the numbers, the longer the postponement, the more dangerous the effects.

Prosperity does not reside in numbers. To survive the 1990s, pay off your debts, put your wealth in tradable goods, a loss is better than a wipeout, and believe only what you can see, taste, touch, and feel. We are at a crossroads. We can go up. We can go down. We have surpassed the level of money needed to stay stable. If our productivity declines, our exports increase, or our imports decrease, expect consumer inflation. In the best of all possible worlds, we will adjust to a new level of inflation with a Dow at 5,000, an average income of $200,000 and the median price of a home at $1.2 million.

The key is the federal debt. If it escalates towards any multiple of 10 before the economy adjusts to its present levels, we could have runaway inflation, the unimaginable worst. We had it during the American Revolution. The South had it during the Civil War. Hold tight, it will be some kind of ride. Don't even think of the downside.

Precautions, Patterns, and Profits

- Debt creates inflation.

- Government debt underlies long term inflation and major run-ups in across the board price rises.

- The DJIA run-up of the 1950s and the 1980s signalled the market's absorption of its share of the federal debt.

- Injecting bogus money into the system is not as bad as pulling it out.

- Anticipate major upheaval if any portion of the federal debt is retired. Anticipate the same if the rate of money creation outstrips growth and temporary production demands.

- The size of the debt is of less consequence than the money needed to service it. Interest always destroys wealth.

- A favorable balance of trade will be followed by high inflation in our own economy.

- If the debt escalation of the 1990s matches that of the 1980s, we could experience runaway inflation.

- Material value, gold, silver, and paid-off property are the only protections against runaway inflation. Otherwise, they have only speculation value in today's market.

Chapter Five

ECONOMY IN ACTION

ll economies have as their goal the providing of food,
shelter and clothing. All economies achieve these basic
necessities by the transformation and exchange of
resources.

Product economies are defined by the Earth triad—Taurus,
Virgo, and Capricorn. The storehouse of value or goods correlates with Taurus. The labor or machinery needed to transform
those goods into another product is Virgo. The output and the
market price is represented by Capricorn.

The natural houses of these signs are the 2nd, Taurus;
the 6th, Virgo; and the 10th, Capricorn. Houses represent
materialization and enactment, how impulse operates in the
visible world.

In order to understand the interplay of signs and houses
the following section shows the economic meanings of the
houses and of the signs with which they naturally correspond.
Difficulties arise on individual and national charts when
signs do not correspond to their natural houses. This creates
economic practices that do not follow the natural and most
productive order.

Taurus is the natural sign of the 2nd house. Because
the signs on the houses are determined by the rising sign,
which in turn is determined by the time of birth, specific
charts are unlikely to have the natural money signs on the
natal money houses.

Houses as Economic Sectors

1st	Buyers	Aries
2nd	Storehouse of wealth, banking system	Taurus
3rd	Exports	Gemini
4th	Supply of raw materials, consumer demand	Cancer
5th	Speculation and power	Leo
6th	Labor and manufacturing system	Virgo
7th	Sellers	Libra
8th	Debt	Scorpio
9th	Imports	Sagittarius
10th	Market demand, manufactured product supply	Capricorn
11th	Stocks, profits, and sales	Aquarius
12th	Analysis and projections	Pisces

Countries that do not have Earth signs connected to their economic sectors tend to operate financially through inappropriate or non-material means, creating satellite economies to those who make products to sell. To better delineate mundane transits and progressions we need to understand the style and viability of any given economy within its world and historical context. If we do not, we may misread the sources of a country's prosperity and misinterpret significant transits. Like many economists, we may superimpose personal and cultural biases onto an understanding of the economic machinery. Many texts use the United States as a model of proper economic practices. Unfortunately, this is not an accurate model. We have Earth signs on our money houses, which gives us an edge in a materialist phase of history. Our practices are something less than perfect. Countries with other than Earth signs on their economic houses often perform services for product economies, such as banking in Switzerland. If they do not, they may find it hard to prosper in materialist phases of history.

Scorpio on Canada's money house indicates that other people's money flows through its economy. Taurus, one's own money and natural resources, in the house of other people's money, puts Canada's economy at the mercy of other people's wealth. For other people's money substitute the United States, and you can understand why Canadians are touchy about their trading relationships with us. However, before us it was Great Britain. After us it will be somebody else until they change their birthday.

Earth economies are not necessarily prosperous, especially if the proper functions do not correlate with their appropriate houses. The notion of economy itself is Taurus, the ability to husband one's resources and create wealth. All wealth ultimately comes from the earth.

Earth economies develop in three ways, according to the sign on the 2nd house: *Taurus* on the value sector, the most balanced; *Virgo* on the value sector, the most stable; *Capricorn* on the value sector, the most dynamic.

In reverse order they represent the historic development and maturation of economic urges. The *Capricorn* economy is a primitive *hunting* economy, where little or no "economy" is practiced. The *Virgo,* or *herding* economy, is tribal and overly economic. The *Taurus,* or *agricultural* model, the economy of property, management, and foresight, is the fundamental and most prosperous model. The modern embodiments of the three economic styles: the United States is the hunting economy, free enterprise; the U.S.S.R. was the herding economy, communism; Japan, with its Sun in Taurus, functions mostly on the agricultural model, mercantilism. France, which has Taurus on the 2nd house, is one of the more stable economies of Europe, quietly and successfully, keeping its population housed, clothed, and fed with little foreign interference or help.

The Economic Standard

The economic standard is the Taurus, or agricultural model.

House 2 defines wealth. Basic wealth resides in the land: minerals, crops, and animals in the wild. Taurus is nature's bounty.

House 6 defines process or means. Labor (man and beast), design, and machinery are applied to the raw materials. Virgo is man's skill.

House 10 defines product, achievement and control. The prime determinant of product/achievement is the marketplace, Capricorn.

The market determines success, the Cancer/Capricorn dynamic of supply and demand, and the order imposed by all controlling factors, whether in nature or in government. Capricorn is market need or demand.

In the agricultural model the houses align with their natural signs. In all other economies they do not. If you understand how the general economy of a nation functions, as shown in its natal chart, you will see where it goes wrong, when it goes wrong, and why. Although we are only dealing here with Earth economies (the most functional and basic), signs of other elements on Earth houses give insights into why some economies fail to function adequately, and what they must do to improve.

Because the process of astrological interpretation is complex, please bear with the following explanation. Essentially, we are superimposing one set of data on top of another set.

The fundamental order is the agricultural economy. Put seed and land together with labor to produce a product. The houses represent these activities on the material plane. The seed/property sector is the 2nd house. The labor/animal/machinery sector is the 6th house. The product/goal/market sector is the 10th house.

All economies in the real world must work within this framework no matter how dysfunctional they might be. The dysfunctional economies confuse one commodity for another. To a child a piece of candy is a prize possession. In fact, it is a consumable that loses its value as soon as it touches the lips. Consumables must be replenished constantly. Dysfunctional economies must be replenished constantly—in our times with massive loans on which they inevitably default.

To restate these definitions more in line with modern economics:

Taurus—2nd house

Property, raw materials, value of property and raw materials, i.e., cost. In modern economic terms this would most closely equate with rent.

Virgo—6th house

Labor, which includes work animals, machinery, and human labor and their cost in salaries, upkeep and maintenance. In modern economic terms, we would generally call these wages. Though these definitions do not exactly follow the classic definitions, these are the appropriate astrological correlations. They clear away much confusion. The end result will be apparent.

Capricorn—10th house

Represents the harvest, the finished product, the supply, and therefore the market price, which determines the profit, which, in turn, becomes capital.

Capitalism is essentially a market driven system of turning profits into wages and rent to produce more profits, more wages, more rent.

Evolution of the Capricorn/Hunting Economy

To understand the flaws in our economy and to understand how we got to where we are, let's look at the natural progression of the hunting economy, the free enterprise system.

PHASE 1. Possessions, 2nd house, Capricorn. Capricorn is the sign of lack. The hunter has no possessions and no land. Sixth house: Taurus, the sign of goods is in the house of service and labor. His only possession is his labor. Tenth house: objective or harvest carries Virgo, the sign of labor, service, tools, and animals. His objective is to kill (harvest) an animal, and to find more work for himself. The success of the hunt provides, in addition to its primary purpose, food, material for clothing, shelter and significantly the bone tool/weapon, which brings us to a new level of property, the product.

PHASE 2. The second house of property now has a harvested tool/weapon. Primitive mining, and fruit gathering can also create tools/weapons: flints to cut, coconut shells for dishes, reeds for snares, etc.

The production is a tool/weapon, and the property is a product. *There is no concept of ownership until a tool has been manufactured.* The harvesting or mining of raw materials, the natural first stage objective of the agricultural model, is the first step in a hunting production process, not the last. Because the sign of property, Taurus, moves to the house of tools, tools become the prime storehouse of value, the major capital investment. Virgo on the 10th makes new tools the goal. Production becomes an end in itself.

The Capitalist/Free Enterprise System

The free enterprise American system with Capricorn on the 2nd house of property makes the finished product the main property. Because machinery is the finished product in the industrial age, machinery is the major investment, and the major start up cost.

The term capital both confuses the natural order and describes capitalism. Let's reexamine our original model as a money economy.

- The 2d house equals money and banks (rent).

- The 6th house is the cost of labor and machinery (wages).

- The 10th house represents the market, the selling price, and with it the profit or loss (capital).

With the sign of profit on the 2nd house of money, capital becomes confused with the cost of the assets you must buy to create your product—machinery and raw materials. Since the 2nd house also rules banks, a source of money, we think money is capital. The classic definition of capital is Capricorn, the product which is a source of profit. The confusion is entirely due to the U.S. 2nd house. In U.S. capitalism, the objective is always to get more money, expand profits, raise capital. The system begins with the normal end result. To put it a slightly different way, there is always a shortage (Capricorn) of money with which to begin the cycle. The heaviest burden is the start up cost, If you have to make a profit before you can start, how are you ever going to get started? (Remember in a true hunting economy everything is free and you are motivated only by your own lack.) In a modern industrial economy you have to have the tools or the capital *before* you can go into business.

How do you get those tools? You borrow. What do you borrow against? Assets? No. You don't own any assets. You borrow against a Capricorn store of value—future profits. Without going into all the astrological ramifications with respect to the U.S. chart, the stock company system is a way to get money from people based on a return on a profit to be made in the future. Because the process begins with the goal, you can see why inflation/money creation is a natural outcome of a system which needs a profit before it begins.

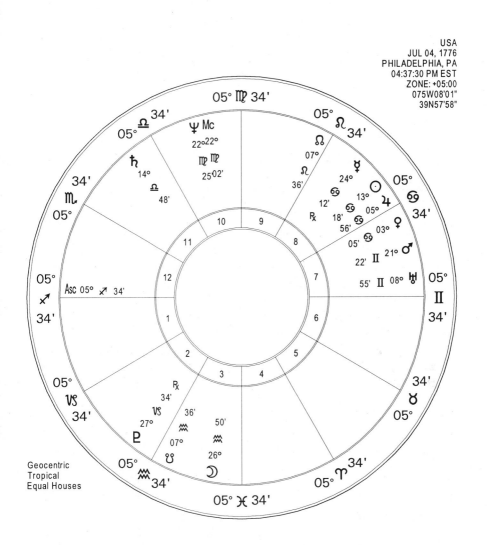

USA
JUL 04, 1776
PHILADELPHIA, PA
04:37:30 PM EST
ZONE: +05:00
075W08'01"
39N57'58"

Geocentric
Tropical
Equal Houses

U.S.A—Hunting Economy (National Chart)

97

In the United States you do not own what you have because you purchased your goods with other people's money, money from stock issues. Though you own nothing, you have the use of everything you need to achieve whatever your industry and expertise allow. You control it. Rent is the least expensive factor in this economy. In fact, it is free, because if you fail to make a profit, you pay no dividend.

As our system evolved into the 1980s, companies fell all over themselves to own even less. Because of tax policies it became more advantageous to borrow than to sell stock. The end result was that stock companies borrowed against property that they did not own in order to enhance the balance sheet. Capital assets are power whether you own them or not.

Why on earth would anyone buy stocks under such conditions? A very long look at the Dow shows that holding stocks is *not* profitable. The great bull markets were merely processes of adjusting to inflation, and mostly later than everyone else. People buy stocks to speculate on the ups and downs. If they buy for any other reason, they do no better than putting their money in a bank, and often not as well.

Not only is this system profitable, it has never gone communist because it is worker-dominated. The sign of the worker on the Virgo 10th puts labor in the governing position. Productivity, and therefore wealth, Taurus on the 6th, is at the mercy of those who do the work. There is no need for communism, when the workers control the wealth. The only aristocracy in a Capricorn economy is the aristocracy of wealth, achievement, and skill.

Lack of Ownership

While we think we own our property, we, in fact, do not in most cases.

First, in the free enterprise hunting economy, industry does not own what it uses, stockholders do. Everything is a risk and a gamble. All property, corporate and private, is heavily taxed to support government, reducing the power of ownership even more.

Second, almost every piece of farmland is mortgaged to the hilt, and almost every home. In fact, the government makes lack of ownership more profitable by inflating the currency and by allowing deductions for interest paid and none for interest earned. Why buy with expensive dollars what you can buy on time with depreciating dollars? Why pay non-deductible dividends when you can write off deductible interest? Corporations are finding it more profitable to sell off assets and rent them back, because of the more favorable tax advantage in the long run. Our system simply does not promote sound financial activity or ownership.

Capricorn on the Second

Since Capricorn is the sign of control and the 2nd house represents banks, the banks are in control of property. Thus, when the banks fail, so does everything else. The Saturn transit of the U.S. 2nd house, recently completed, correlates to the same transit in the early 1930s. Between 1922 and 1933 half the banks in the United States failed. The 1980s saw the S&L debacle and many large bank failures, the significance of which was hidden by the concurrent transit of Neptune and Uranus. While the economy could function quite well if our banks acted the stuffy way we think banks are supposed to act, the aforementioned Pluto in our natal 2nd house tends to put even the banks in hock. What they loan out are assets. What they have on deposit are liabilities. In the real world you only have what you have in your hand. Our economy is built on promises, from the home owner who promises to pay his mortgage, to the federal government who promises you everything and pays with debt.

Taurus on the Sixth

The actual wealth, Taurus, has now shifted to the 6th house of labor, services, animals and machinery. He who owns the means of production holds the keys to the kingdom. This also places a premium on labor in any form. Thus, the primary cost of doing business is the cost of labor, machinery, and maintenance.

Where does the economy stagnate? In the sign of Taurus. In the U.S. this means the production line. Taurus on the 6th also tends to monotonous jobs and one-skill workers, the kind on an assembly line. Workers become another object to move around as needed. Specialization is a hallmark of the industrial hunting economy. Like the hunter, a worker primarily does one thing. The industrial farmer plants one crop. The factory manufactures one product. It is no accident that anti-trust laws developed in our form of capitalism: nobody is supposed to control more than one thing, lest it break the overall rhythm of production.

The combination of Taurus on the 6th and Virgo on the 10th keeps production ongoing even though the goal has been reached. This tendency to overproduction aggravates the chronic unemployment and booms and busts that are natural features of free enterprise. A hunter does not hunt every day. A lucky hunter does not hunt all day. Shortening the work week was and is a necessity of the capitalist system if there is to be full employment.

Virgo on the Tenth

The 10th house price/profit-or-loss has the sign of Virgo/labor in the hunting economy. Therefore, wages are the prime component of the selling price. Since astrology defines wages as the cost of any labor—management or worker, machinery and its upkeep—we can see why:

1. We constantly replace men with machines in an effort to keep down costs.

2. We are constantly undercut in world markets by economies that have cheap labor.

Employees, on all levels, keep pricing themselves out of their jobs. Management costs are higher in this country than anywhere in the world. Is it more important to have 10 workers make $20 an hour as the unions would have it or for 20 workers to make $10? Is any manager worth $18,000,000 a year? Every dollar you remove from the cost of your product is a dollar towards making your product more competitive in the world market.

Virgo is the sign of calculation. It is also a sign of fluctuation. The United States is one of the few countries in the world and in history that does not haggle over price. It cannot afford to. Rents and wages must be covered in order to make a profit. A profit must be made to keep the machinery going. Since wages (Taurus on the 6th) tend to stay fixed, there is no mechanism for workers to accept a lower wage in response to market conditions. There is little or no provision for piece work to encourage greater productivity or to lower the overall cost.

Though we try to calculate the price against our costs, we tend to put unreasonably high prices on products, then put what we cannot sell on sale. We cannot keep our prices stable. If prices fall and a company cannot cover its costs, unemployment follows. In the final analysis, employees and machinery determine the price and a company's failure or success. Though they are not the cause of inflation as delineated in previous chapters, inflation serves the needs and compensates for the inherent difficulties in a hunting economic system.

Unless the world markets are starved for goods as they were after World War I and World War II, the United States simply cannot be competitive in terms of price. As soon as other economies become productive, we have no place to sell our glut, unless we lend others money to buy back our goods, which is what we have halfheartedly done in our generosity towards developing countries. What happens when they finally can't pay back? The same thing that happened when the 1920s ceased to roar.

The Evolution of the Herding Economy

Once hunters discovered that animals could be corralled, once they understood that cooperation with each other produced a steadier food supply, they moved to a herding economy. The source of wealth in the herding economy, the communal economy, are laborers and animals—Virgo on the 2nd house. There is no property ownership *per se* as grazing animals need free room to roam. Labor consists of controlling workers and animals (Capricorn on the 6th). To put it another way, the end result of the labor depends on the labor and stock itself. The end result of the effort is ownership, Taurus, but it is ownership of a product produced from a product you already own, the mare and sire. You own the animals produced by the animals you own. If you already own what you produce, you do not need to trade. Thus, the herding economy is one in which a group of people work to make more out of what they already own for themselves. The herding model tends to be a closed economy. Other tribes and communes are competitors for *space,* not markets. Likewise other nations. Other tribes and communes are places to buy what you cannot produce yourself. If you underproduce and still have to buy, you become excellent traders, but the trade is *external* to your own economy. Your nomadic inclinations make you middlemen for the products of other economies. The feudal system is an early analog of the herding economy when grazing land was no longer free.

Virgo on the Second

Modern notions of the feudal system falsely portray it as a kind of semi-slave society. The real money and resources of a feudal economy are the laborers (serfs), the farm animals and implements, and the soldiers. Since any implement that transforms raw materials is defined as labor, humans, too, are looked upon as chattel, which accounts for our horror at the evil plight of the serfs.

Capricorn on the Sixth

The primary work of the feudal economy is management of labor. The goal is, therefore, to create more laborers, animals, implements, and soldiers in order to achieve the true goal—stability and wealth, Taurus on the 10th of objectives and end results.

Taurus on the Tenth

Wealth accumulates in the hands of the managers (10th). Those who control the land (Taurus) control the community and are obliged to keep the peace. Serfs do not fight in wars. Soldiers and nobles do.

The feudal community grew up around the need to provide a safe environment in which farming, animal husbandry, and primitive manufacture and trade could thrive. The feudal period saw constant harassment by marauding tribes who pillaged the bounty of the land—much like hunting economies seeking perpetually new markets.

The land belonged to whoever could control it. Nobles paid their warriors with land, serfs attached, which is not the same as saying the serfs were abused or sold. The serfs were attached to the land, Virgo on 2nd, they could not be removed from it. These early communal societies were heavily governed by custom. With Capricorn on the 6th, the output of the chattel made the difference between a good harvest and a bad. If the minimum requirements of the chattel were not met: food, clothing, shelter and safety, there would be no production.

As economies became more sophisticated and external trade became a necessity, the herding economy evolved into the guild system, whereby craftsmen gathered together to control their output and increase their wealth. The Virgo workers controlled the raw materials (2nd house) and managed themselves (Capricorn on the 6th) to produce a product of high quality and

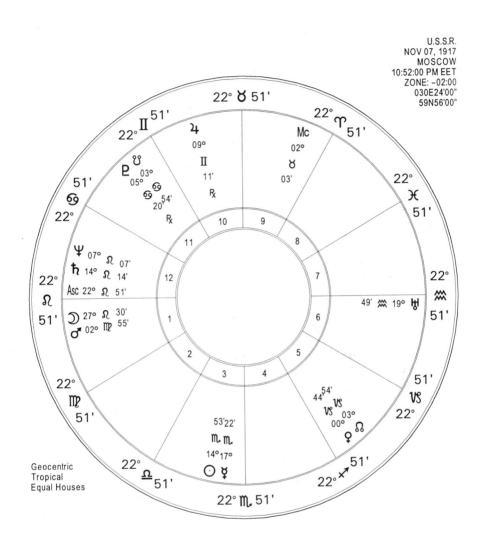

U.S.S.R.
NOV 07, 1917
MOSCOW
10:52:00 PM EET
ZONE: -02:00
030E24'00"
59N56'00"

22° ♉ 51'

22° ♊ 51'

22° ♈ 51'

♃ 09°

♇ ♉ 03°
05° ♋

Mc 02°
♉ 03'

♊ 11'
Rx

22° ♋

♋
20° 54'
Rx

51'

22°

22° ♓ 51'

10   9

11   8

♆ 07° ♌ 07'
♄ 14° ♌ 14'
Asc 22° ♌ 51'

12   7

22° ♒

☽ 27° ♌ 30'
♂ 02° ♍ 55'

1   6

49' ♒ 19° ♅

22° ♒ 51'

22° ♌ 51'

2   5

3   4

22° ♍ 51'

44° 54'
♑ ♑
♑ 00° 03°
♀ ♌

51' ♑

22° ♑

Geocentric
Tropical
Equal Houses

53'22'
♏ ♏
14° 17°
☉ ☿

51' ♐

22° ♎ 51'

22° ♐ 51'

22° ♏ 51'

U.S.S.R.—Herding Economy (National Chart)

beauty (Taurus on the 10th). They could control their prices because they created a monopoly around their product.

As long as there are no competitors, the system works. The guild is an early model for a factory or a cartel of any kind. A group of people get together to control the output and the price. Since the Arabs have always been a nomadic society which is the natural condition of the herding society, it is not surprising that they formed a cartel, OPEC, to guarantee that their product (10th) would command the value (Taurus on 10th) they determined it to be.

Communism

Communism is the modern form of the herding economy. Virgo (a changeable [mutable] sign) on the 2nd house of money, can mean a managed currency or an unstable currency. It can also mean that the needs of the workers dictate money policy. Virgo on the 2nd distributes the wealth to the workers. *Wages are determined by the number of workers, not by the amount of work produced.* The process of production is government controlled (Capricorn on the 6th), but the workers are the government. They gain control by not working. Saturn rules Capricorn and restraint.

Prices are fixed and inflexible (Taurus on the 10th), determined by the money available, not by market forces. Money is not as important as the distribution of wealth, because the workers already own everything. When surpluses and shortages appear, goods are exchanged by barter in order to establish a true market value. Like the feudal model, vast wealth centered in the government supports the arts (Taurus). The real market competition is in the area of health and fitness, Capricorn on the 6th, witness Russian domination in the Olympics. The major production is in durables (Taurus) or in things that will create peace, beauty, and safety. Consumables suffer. The Virgo economy need not worry about the post-industrial state, because it never really gets to the industrial.

We can see why there are persistent shortages in Russia in every area of the economy except the military, the athletic, and the artistic. State ownership is feudalism in modern dress. The Russian military machine is more defensive than aggressive. Ours evolves from a need to put our men and machines to work, coupled with a defensive posture that springs from our Cancerian preoccupation with security. If the United States had a more militant chart, we would try to take over the world.

Russia has a world of wealth in natural resources and in gold, but it is concentrated in the hands of a bureaucracy of workers (Virgo on the 2nd) that makes decisions about market needs in the absence of any market principles. In the American system any worker can be king (Virgo on the 10th). In the Russian system, the workers are just as much chattel as they were under the Tsars. This, alone, is why communism never took hold in this country. Marxist academics rhapsodize on the horrors of feudalism, when ironically feudalism is what they espouse.

Evolution of the Agricultural/Taurus Economy

Having created a primitive agriculture, our primordial family soon added livestock which could provide food, clothing, and fertilizer for their crops. Having created peace with their neighbors and relatives in the clan, they fenced off individual territory so that each family would be rewarded according to his work. They had discovered sharing tasks was seldom equal. When every man or every clan hunted for itself there was perpetual war. The logical solution was private property.

The agricultural economy is the first civilized economy for two reasons:

1. It need not engage in perpetual warfare to survive.

2. It need not put up perpetual defenses to survive.

It allows each individual to prosper from his special skills and effort according to his own initiative, taking the best of the hunting economy. It serves communal needs by guaranteeing protection, employment, and sustenance within the family's province. The success of the agricultural economy depends first on Mother Nature, second on the market for surplus, and third on the maintenance of peace.

Now let's see what happens when that evolves into a trading economy, an industrial economy, and finally into a money economy.

Taurus on the Second

The property, land, and raw materials are the 2nd house, Taurus, the natural sign of the 2nd house. The distinction between property and people is maintained. The distinction between property and authority is maintained.

Virgo on the Sixth

The 6th house and the sign Virgo both represent labor—in the form of animals, people and machines—the transformation process, the work put into the project. The work is not stable, as it changes from season to season, but the workers remain workers whether they are employed or not—they are not traded in the market place (the eternal job search in the Capricorn model)—they are not feudal commodities in whom is invested a source of wealth. One does not drop members of the "family" when the harvest is done. The work changes from season to season. A farmer is not a specialist. He always has another skill to fall back on.

Capricorn on the Tenth

As a trading economy develops, the agricultural model develops along mercantilist and colonialist lines, the government or the market controls the output. On a farm all activity is essentially family centered. Thus, nationalism is the inevitable result of the agricultural economy just as internationalism (wide open markets) is the need of a hunting economy. All production in a trading/agricultural economy is geared towards the market. Insofar as can be humanly calculated, only what there is a demand for will be manufactured or grown. When the demand dies the farmer/factory will shift to a new product.

The agricultural model is as surely demand side economics as supply side is that of hunters. The herding model is governed neither by supply or demand but by fiat. Guilds and international merchants form cartels to control production and set prices for the rest of the world, take it or leave it. The agricultural principle evaluates goods, land, and material on the basis of its intrinsic wealth, with an eye to owning the raw materials of its production. In trying to maintain a healthy cash balance to carry itself through downturns in the market, it will cut costs to increase profits. In boom times, it charges what the traffic will bear, and sets aside the overage in order to keep its production going and its workers employed in the down times.

Despite the horror stories of the industrial revolution, the factory system did, in fact, try in the early days to follow sound financial principles. The workers were housed in factory buildings. They bought from factory stores, and often the entire family worked for the company. Wages were kept as low as possible against the eventuality that costs could not be recovered in the

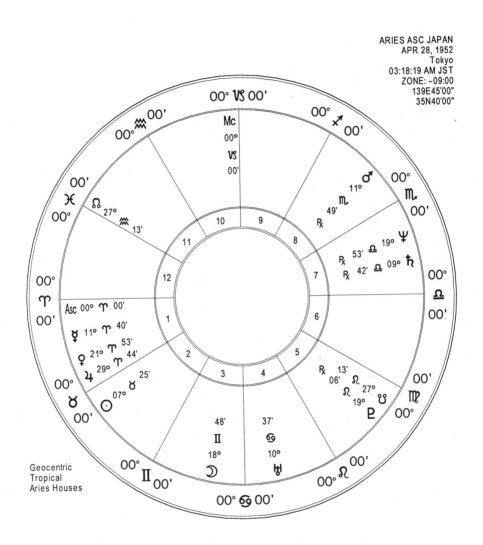

ARIES ASC JAPAN
APR 28, 1952
Tokyo
03:18:19 AM JST
ZONE: -09:00
139E45'00"
35N40'00"

Geocentric
Tropical
Aries Houses

Japan—Agricultural Economy (National Chart)

107

market place. The danger in an agricultural/industrial system is
that workers will be treated like farm animals. They will be
given enough only to keep them healthy enough to work. In the
best of all possible worlds the workers will be treated like family.

Another problem of the agricultural economy is keeping a
stable price. Since the market controls the price, it is above all
dominated by the law of supply and demand. Oversupply of raw
materials cuts the cost, oversupply of labor cuts the wage, oversupply of products cuts the price. Because a factory, unlike a
farm, does not guarantee sustenance, the work force has little
stability in an agricultural economy, unless the company adopts
family values, or unless, as in a farming economy, all workers
share in the bounty and all workers share in the profit.

The early years of the industrial form of the agricultural
economy were characterized by the search for cheap raw material and cheap labor. These were times of great exploration, and
colonization. The colonies supplied the raw materials. They purchased the finished goods. The colonies were paid cheap and
forced to buy dear, which is what the American Revolution was
really all about.

As the agricultural economy developed into a money economy, it chose a substance of intrinsic value as the basis of its
currency, the gold standard. Workers were paid wages, based on
productivity, that is, piece work. The final price depended on
cost as in any industrial economy, but production was limited to
what would sell. The agricultural model produces nowhere near
the variety of products a hunting model does. What can not be
sold internally (the surplus) is sold abroad.

Like any good farmer who wants the advantage all one
way, nations maneuver for a favorable balance of trade, buy raw
materials from abroad and sell back expensive manufactured
goods. We call this mercantilism. The down side of mercantilism
is that the favorable balance of trade bleeds the rest of the world
of resources with which to pay. The population is overrun with
wealth (Taurus on the 2nd), as are the banks. The economy is
either forced to save or whipped with skyrocketing prices. Eventually it buys abroad products its own economy ignores because
of low demand. Money flows out of the country, which fuels production elsewhere.

The down side of trade barriers and the insularity of an
agricultural economy, is the failure to satisfy consumer demand.
Capricorn on the 10th produces a necessity economy—not one of

abundance. Prices may put necessities out of reach of the workers and widen the gap between rich and the poor. When this happens or when the government takes control, the health and well-being of the work force declines, as do the quality of the goods and the lifestyle.

Japan is the model of a modern economy run on agricultural principles. Because they have so little land and so few natural resources they must operate on an international scale if they are to prosper at all. Because of its strong family tradition, they create a family-type corporation, where the workers give and get loyalty and protection. Not only their relatively small land mass, but the nature of their economic style is also one of respect for property and land, which is why they tried to buy up America.

Intrinsic value is the driving force of the agricultural economy. Land has intrinsic value, gold has intrinsic value, art has intrinsic value, all apart from what they can bring in the market place. Who tried to buy up all the platinum and art? Guess.

Destructive Tendencies

All economies contain the seeds of their destruction. Consumerism, waste, overproduction, and warfare are the destructive forces of the hunting economy. The United States was originally blessed with "free" land and resources, plenty of room to expand over the territory, expanding markets through unlimited immigration, and finally through the destroyed markets after the two great wars. It is feebly keeping overseas markets fueled by exporting its cardinal sin—debt.

If the United States is to avoid the welfare state and the decline of both its productivity and freedom, it must return to principles that are more in line with the natural economy, the agricultural model.

If the Soviet Union is to rescue itself from economic chaos it must relinquish its feudal/herding system, create a level playing field, and return to market pricing (which, incidentally, is not the U.S. model). It must allow workers to reap the benefits of their own initiative without losing the freedom from need they prize above all.

The United States hunting model is not appropriate for Russia's transformation from communism. The agricultural model is the safest for the transition as it contains elements of protection that hunting capitalism lacks and a demand focus that is of prime necessity in a time of breakdown. Supply-side production, as practiced in the United States, would create goods that no one would be able to purchase and compound the problem.

The agricultural economy must ease its insularity, under-production, aversion to risk, and tendencies to over accumulate. Money must be kept active in the best tradition of the enterprising innovative hunt.

We have watched England decline under the welfare state and the U.S.S.R. disintegrate under communism. The key may be a kinder and gentler agricultural model with open markets. We already have two examples: Tito-style communism[1] (where the workers, rather than government, ran businesses) and the Japanese family-style corporation. Translated into American terms: worker participation in the profits of the business, a narrowing of salaries between management and labor, and job security by everyone taking a cut if the business fails to make a profit.

Forecasts

United States

With Virgo on the 10th either the price will be determined by wages or wages will be determined by price. The latter is more conducive to the survival of the industry. Either the unions, the workers, or the government bureaucracy will control the economy. Neptune in Virgo confuses the unfortunate and the needy with workers. We can be ruled by the people who work (Virgo), or by the people who do not work—the institutionalized, the insane, the addicts, the impoverished, and the sick and retired (Neptune). If the latter, we will all become the "slaves" of government largesse.

Russia

Russia has no hunting competitive tradition. If it tries to adopt American capitalism, it will become a colony of multinational corporations at best. If it adopts basic agricultural values, it can over a long period of time maintain its collectivist herding impulses long enough to feed its people and transfer economic control to market driven rather than government driven cartels.

---

1. The break-down of international-style communism must not be confused with the current Eastern European ethnic/religious upheavals, which fueled the demise of Yugoslavian communism.

If it does so, it will be in the best position to meet the new challenges of the collectivist Aquarian Age and the collectivist Air Mutation, to be discussed in chapter six.

Japan

Because Japan functions on agricultural principles in a country without enough land for its population, it is as dependent on foreign markets as is the United States. Any collapse of either the world economy or of its chief market, the United States, will threaten and collapse its own. They will resurrect themselves more quickly than we because of their fundamentally sound practices, the reason for their great renaissance after being devastated in World War II. Germany and most northern European countries also practice fundamental agricultural economics. The European Economic Community will dominate world trade for the rest of the materialist tradition and most likely the New World Order, too.

Other Modes

Economies that have the appropriate mode—Cardinal, Fixed or Mutable—on their relative houses will fare better than those that do not. An Aquarian 2nd, Gemini 6th, and Libra 10th is the prosperous model of a human-centered value system, such as is likely in the coming Air Mutation and Aquarian Age. It is the true communist/guild/herding model: people and their needs determine production and price.

A Scorpio 2nd, Pisces 6th, and Cancer 10th is the ideal of the satellite economy or supplier of raw materials, including slaves, in a colonial system. The water economy is capable of servicing any of the other three, no matter what the dominant economic system.

With a Leo 2nd, Sagittarius 6th, and Aries 10th, the true hunting model, power determines product and profit, every man for himself.

The true service economy is an air or water model, incompatible with the earth impulses of the United States' product-earth economy. If we transform into a service economy, we will become (10th house) the servicers (Virgo) of the products of the world. That may not be a bad option for the coming air *zeitgeist*.

Sound economic respect for all elements of the economy: a mandated stable currency with a money expansion that services only a growing population; the health and prosperity of workers;

and a level playing field in the markets, will come as close to guaranteeing prosperity, comfort and protection for all as is possible in a shifting world. The government should only be a moderator and arbiter, a muzzle on the predators.

A government that controls the economy on a agricultural model is mercantilist and imperial. A government that controls the economy on a herding model is communist and elitist. A government that controls the economy on a hunting model is socialist or fascist.

The choice is ours.

Precautions, Patterns, and Profits

- Economies with *agricultural* values are the most stable and most able to satisfy the needs of their constituents over long periods of time. Wealth is distributed on the basis of productivity. Investment opportunities.

- *Herding* economies underproduce and distribute wealth on the basis of membership. They tend towards authoritarian management, subsistence and luxury production with little in between. Invest or trade the product, not the country.

- *Hunting* economies overproduce. Wealth is available to those who take the initiative and fight for it. They are innovative, wasteful, and need constant new markets to serve if they are to survive. Enterprise opportunities.

- Government controlled agricultural models are mercantilist and colonial. Good investment.

- Government controlled herding models are communist and collective. Bad investment opportunities.

- Government controlled hunting models are socialist or fascist. Bad investment.

- Russia and the Middle East are herding economies.

- Europe and Japan are agricultural models.

- The United States and many underdeveloped countries operate on the hunting model.

Part II

CYCLES

Chapter Six

THE LONG VIEW

Now that we understand the fundamental astrological definitions of money, productivity and wealth, and how they operate in our respective economies, we are ready to examine their historical and cyclic implications.

Astrology must be redefined for every age. Context always determines interpretation. Even the best astrologers fail if they do not understand the age in which they live and do not keep track of events. We cannot live in a theoretical vacuum, crunching numbers and symbols. Astrology is a tool of observation and analysis. The focus is facts. Astrology, as a very powerful tool of the intellect, prompts heroic projections based on little but the practitioner's skill, but the best and most accurate interpretations and forecasts are coached by an unbiased awareness of now and then.

We swim in the Piscean Age, our lights refracted by their watery context. We are beset by the passionate idea, ever searching for definition, never finding the edge, always sure that certainty is just around the bend. Mankind always functions in a 2,000 year frame. Twenty-five thousand years must lapse before a repetition, before mankind experiences every event in every context.

Though we cannot prove astrology has attained its 25,000-year-old majority, we can safely assume that the first act of cognizant man was to notice how the Moon changed its shape. The observation of the Moon gave birth to the calendar. History was its twin. Much has been written about the major cycles produced by the circuits of the outer planets and the cycles of recurrence, conjunctions of planets that repeat around the circle of the Zodiac and eventually return to their original place. Though these explain hundreds of years of changing attitudes and fashions in the history of man, only the Great Mutations specifically relate to the social and political amalgam of survival that we know as economics. The Great Mutation is a Jupiter-Saturn conjunction that begins a series of Jupiter-Saturn conjunctions that stay in the same element—Fire, Earth, Air, or Water.

The value of understanding the historical implications of the Great Mutations is an increased understanding of the fashions, fads, attitudes, and economic ramifications of heavy transits (Uranus, Neptune, and Pluto) through signs of a particular element. The Fire signs are Aries, Leo, and Sagittarius. The Earth signs are Taurus, Virgo, and Capricorn. The Air signs are Gemini, Libra, and Aquarius. The Water signs are Cancer, Scorpio, and Pisces. Transits of the outer planets through Fire signs bring attitudes similar to the Fire Mutation. Transits through the signs of other elements reflect events and attitudes of Mutations in that element.

The following helps you understand not only the repetitions of history but the trends in our economic and political life in the light of preserving your assets and those of future generations.

The Great Mutation Cycle

Jupiter and Saturn represent fundamental market psychology as well as shifting prices and market turns. The conjunction of Saturn and Jupiter is called a Mutation. At every Mutation the direction of society shifts, new leadership is born, and new attitudes towards wealth take hold. Saturn and Jupiter form a conjunction every 20 years. At the end of 60 years they have formed that conjunction in each of the three modalities, Cardinal, Mutable and Fixed. This 60-year modality cycle, which is discussed in chapter seven, is a sub-cycle of the Great Mutation cycle that runs its course for approximately 200 years. The particular Great Mutation cycle is defined by the element that dominates the successive Lesser Mutations.

The element of the Great Mutation determines the fundamental nature of the economic forces of the period. One element always dominates. It is the element of the first Jupiter-Saturn conjunction that represents a permanent change from the previous dominant element, even though anomalies may have occurred in the previous Mutation period.

Our present Mutation element is Earth, which tells of a materialist economy, focused on the ownership of property and the production of goods. The Fire Mutation created an ethos of power and force. The Water Mutation dispersed and explored. The Air Mutation was humanistic, international, and communal.

The Earth Mutation

1007-8 to 1226 (1186 Air)   1842 to 2040 (1981 Air)

The organization of economic forces towards mastery of the material world defined and defines an Earth Mutation. The first step is the distribution and control of property: land, raw materials, people and machinery to create products and structures we can see, touch, and turn to profit to maintain our lives and our sense of value and worth.

In our time we proceed scientifically to develop technology to master the material world. We create the machinery of production and vehicles of transportation and communication. Whatever we think of ourselves, we are preoccupied with what we can learn from a study of the material world, the visible and concrete, and the principles on which it is founded.

The Previous Earth Mutation

In the previous Earth Mutation, the material world was of equal concern. Having been through the rapacious Fire trigon, which always precedes that of Earth, the society freed itself from the terrors of rampaging nomads who recognized no boundaries. Towns that hovered in fear grew into communities that provided a market place for crops that could grow in peace. They created surpluses that could be traded for the produce of early manufacture and individual enterprise. Territories that once were claimed by force of arms developed into nations built on stable populations. Hunting economies developed into agricultural economies, which eventually prospered, and created markets and trading fairs.

At the end of the Millennium, instead of fighting off the Danes, the King of England, Ethelred "the Unready," paid a ransom. Gold, highly prized in the preceding Fire Age, became the standard of exchange, and a means of protection from potential devastation. The money economy created a process by which a commodity desired by all could form a standard against which all trade could be measured.

The technology of agriculture boomed during this period, which gave us the iron plow and crop rotation. The development of milling and woolen industries were primitive parallels to our much later industrial revolution.

Materialist phases always put a high value on land and property. The feudal system, which found its full expression in the subsequent Air Age, was in this period a very practical way to keep the land safe for agriculture. People attach themselves to the land in Earth Mutations, in our times by owning their own home, in feudal times by attaching themselves to the land directly. This strong sense of land identity gradually evolved into cities and nations that displayed their own colors and styles. The Norman conquest in 1066 at the end of the first 60-year subcycle, marked the beginning of the European nation state.

Stability and peace, fundamental to Earth values, enabled wealth to accumulate. Out of the surplus sprouted huge stone monuments, castles and cathedrals. Just as we build skyscrapers in our version of the Earth Mutation, our earth avatars equally matched our preoccupation with building structures of great size and power. A vast majority of the great cathedrals of Europe were either started, built, or completed during this period. The Mayans, another great breed of builders, revived about this time, though the great pyramids of the Mayans were built during even earlier Earth and Air Mutations.

The conquest of territory equalled the conquest of people's beliefs. The sword of the crusader challenged on behalf of Christianity, just as our atomic stockpiles were a battle between free enterprise and communism, one-party systems and two. The control of territory equated to the control of ideas. The Christians had infidels. The capitalists have communists.

With wealth, surplus, and material values, religion took on a singularly material aspect. Thousands travelled under great hardship to recapture the holy territories from the infidel. Our culture has equally attached its ideology to territory, be it democracy or communism, whether by political spheres of influence or fighting for one's cause—Korea, Vietnam, Cuba, Afghanistan. World War II was a fight for territory (*Lebensraum*), the people who blocked the territorial imperative were dispensable. An Earth Mutation has little regard for people— witness the concentration camps, the starvation of the Ukrainians and Albanians, and the pogroms. People are secondary to material goals.

In early times the battles revolved around distribution of land. Today they are about the distribution of material wealth.

To keep land you must defend it. The development of arms and weaponry has high priority in Earth Mutations. Body armor developed in the West. Explosives were used in battle for the first time by the Mongols under Ghengis Khan. Our age developed tanks and nuclear arms.

Because we are in the last subcycle of Earth and already invaded by Air, expect a continuing of the shift away from the arms buildup and more towards universal understanding and cooperation. Property and material goods will remain important, but your grandchildren will live in a very different world with values far different from our own.

Characteristics of Earth

- Nationalism. Loyalty determined by physical boundaries.
- High yield agricultural production.
- Surpluses that create markets.
- The shopping mall, a permanent version of a trade fair.
- Money economies, based on a universal standard of value.
- The substitution of economic influence for power and war.
- Skyscrapers, modern cathedrals and castles.
- Territorial expansion for ideological reasons.
- The development of weaponry.
- Fairness based on distribution of material wealth.

The great talents of the Earth Mutation, then and now, are in technology and in mastery of the material world. Imagination is subordinate to machination. Creativity is ruled by the numbers. Material wealth equals power. It is very important to note that in our culture we protest politically the inequitable distribution of wealth. We do not get upset about a person's inability to use his skills and talents to his or her best ability; we do not get upset about ancestry and the breakup of family ties; we do not protest unequal power, except purchasing power. We fundamentally believe that all these problems are solved by money. That is our bias and the bias of every Earth era.

The Air Mutation

1226 to 1365 (1186 first appearance)

The Air Mutation marks the age of humanism and common effort. It also begins the focus on what people can accomplish by working together and by expanding their boundaries beyond their nation states.

The foundations of modern democracy were fertilized in Air. The Magna Carta was signed June 15, 1215 (not long after the first preview of Air). In 1258 the Provisions of Oxford established a council of 15 barons who would advise the King. The first commoners became members of Parliament. Economically the age followed the herding model. Craftsmen joined together in guilds to control output, quality, and price. The building that continued in this period was accomplished by a highly organized group of skilled craftsmen who travelled about the land to do a specific job. Cathedral building was no longer a local effort but the result of a cosmopolitan group of cathedral builders. The work and the craft became more important than its materialization.

In Europe the universality of the Catholic Church undermined nationality and promoted internationality. In similar fashion a person's specialty or guild was more important than his place of birth. Capitalizing on the great increases in productivity and technology of the previous Earth Mutation, trade fairs multiplied as commerce and international trade grew more and more sophisticated. Marco Polo travelled to China in search of new markets and new sources of supply. The Hanseatic League, an early version of the European Economic Community, dominated the foreign trade of Denmark, Norway, and Sweden and almost that of London as well.

Air created a movement towards brotherhood and against materialism as embodied in the teachings of St. Francis of Assisi and the begging friars. The monastic movement reached its peak.

With prosperity came large increases in the population. With population increase came the problem of what to do with the numbers. Monasticism solved the problems of the many people who would not have survived under the old ways, people who would have been homeless. Land is limited. Division of the land eventually makes it worthless either as property or as a means of survival and subsistence. We see hints in our own culture in the trend towards landless condominiums, which are essentially communal, albeit private, living arrangements.

As to be expected, the Air Mutation saw the resurrection of ancient learning and intellectual development. Manuscript copying preserved the wisdom of past ages and kept Aristotle and Plato safe for us. At the apex of the learned community were the Scholastic philosophers who debated how many angels could be found on the head of a pin. Though modern science began as a close observation of the material world, it is becoming an instrument of mathematics. Instead of angels, scientists now debate the number of particles in an atom, and the trillions of stars they never touch.

Scientific thought began with the introduction of Arabic numbers in Europe. The Arabs created the sciences of astronomy and math. Learning thrived. Many great universities, begun in the Air Mutation, exist still, most notably Paris and Oxford. The flowering of the intellect seeded trials for heretics. The Inquisition cultivated panic and fear.

Although the printing press would not be invented until the Water Mutation, block printing began. Edward I in England standardized the yard and the acre. Spectacles were invented, a necessity if aging or youthful eyes were to read the dense letters of copied manuscripts.

Our present Earth Mutation is in decay. In 1981 we experienced our first Air Mutation. The Jupiter-Saturn conjunction in Libra presages the coming Great Mutation in Air. The European Common Market, now being born, will be a dominant western trading force over the next 200 years. Expect competitive organization and trade wars. As corporations lose their national significance, an employee is more likely to identify himself with his company rather than his place of birth.

The values of humanism and brotherhood are apparent as is the breakdown of the old values of patriotism and national heritage.

Our religion is science. The non-sciences, religion and astrology, are considered inferior and heretical. We could have a new inquisition for orthodoxy. Electronics could one day keep our minds and our behavior pure.

The new knowledge of the Air Mutation began with astronomy and math. Our forays into space bring back the same focus. Air pulls us into speculations of explorations of new space. It is a time where ideas and abstractions are more important than material fact. The ideological wars of the last 20 years are the seeds of what is to come. Brotherhood and community values will triumph. Individuality will decay.

An expanding population will force us to live communally. Those the economy cannot support may well retreat to "monasteries" directed by ideals as well as necessity. Homelessness is not a moral issue as much as it is an economic issue, provoked not by greedy capitalists or welfare con men, rather it is the logical outcome of the decline and limits of the economics of Earth.

We have heard the Age of Aquarius anticipated and lauded in tale and song. Aquarius, for all its seeming rebellion and independence, is also group-think. As the detriment of the Sun, it represents a denial of individuality and autonomy, as well as a denial of kingly authority. No dictator is more powerful than the one who rules in the name of democracy. No leader more powerful than when cheering crowds bow to his will.

Characteristics of Air

- Collectivization.

- Internationalism.

- Humanistic values.

- Preservation of learning.

- Abstract thought.

- Communal living.

- Guilds, cartels, and trade treaties.

- Standardization of behavior, thought, and production.

- Egalitarianism.

- A mandate of peace.

Just as the 1980s previewed the Air Mutation, the Air Mutation previews the Age of Aquarius. Today's Air impulses portend the transformation into the Age of Aquarius. Communism failed because it was premature. Communist countries failed to establish the Earth foundation on which an Air society rests. The evidence suggests that our materialistic individualistic system is gradually accumulating humanistic and communistic values. We will straddle both for at least another 30 years.

The Water Mutation

1425 to 1663 (1305 first appearance)

True to its element, the Water Mutation spilled all over itself, weaving back and forth into the Air that preceded it and the Fire that followed. Normally, there is one maverick Mutation that forecasts the future elemental change. In the case of Water there were many on either side. The old system broke down. The new system never really exerted itself. Water first appeared in 1305, but didn't establish itself until 1425, the start of the High Renaissance. The Water Mutation of 1583 was followed by two Fire Mutations before it popped back in 1643. Fire did not establish itself until 1663. Almost 100 years of flux coincided with some of the greatest artistic achievements of western civilization. In fact, Water was firmly in place for only 175 years. It seeped in or leaked out for 300.

Water is the universal solution, where all boundaries are lost, where man ventures where no man has ever dared. Water created an age of exploration and discovery: Vasco da Gama, Magellan, Cabot, Columbus. With the Renaissance came the intellectual flowering of man's struggle for survival in Fire, through his mastery of the material world in Earth, and the peace to develop his intellect in Air.

China saw the artistic greatness of the Ming dynasty. In Europe it was an age of great imagination, great intellect, and great art. Think of Michelangelo, and Rembrandt. Think of Galileo and DaVinci, telescopes, and plans for planes. Water created ideas and speculations that could not be realized until the inventiveness of Fire and the materializing ability of Earth could bring them to fruition.

International trade, still the driving economic force, was now controlled by the great banking houses, which were the great banking families of Italy. The three balls of the pawnbroker were part of the Medici coat of arms. The monied interests controlled the city-states and waged private wars among one another. Central authority declined. Banking and money lending facilitated both the burgeoning trade and the costly expeditions to lands unknown in search of new markets and new supplies.

Alchemy, once an intellectual pursuit, became a scam, and the Dutch tulip fiasco in 1637 presaged the wilder schemes that would appear in the Fire Mutation. The economy was anyone's game. Monopolies were licensed. Money begat money. The

Water element tells us that family wealth, debt, and money creation or inflation will dominate the economic agenda.

Because wealth could be made or destroyed by the fortunes of a single ship, the first marine insurance was issued, not unusual in a period that had no controlling principles. Life insurance followed. Bank checks and bank drafts appeared. Abstractions begin in Air. They become a necessity in Water. One cannot expand indefinitely without a great deal of slack. One might call the closing years the age of bankruptcies. Empires built on numbers died with numbers.

All authority either collapsed or was in such disarray that economic matters were left to the money creators and the money manipulators. The Great Schism in the Catholic Church further weakened the central authority—although the Inquisition itself lasted until the mid 1700s. Constantinople, once the bastion of the Eastern Church, fell to the Turks and became Istanbul. Rome vied with Avignon as the seat of the Pope. The Reformation and Luther fed on the rotting corpse.

Scholarship developed independent of the Church authority. With the introduction of movable type and Gutenberg's printing press came printing in the vernacular. Everybody could read for himself. The first newspapers appeared. The first postal systems developed. Ideas were accessible to everyone. Everyone was accessible to everyone else. Galileo may have had to recant, but soon Kepler would calculate the laws of planetary motion. The Ptolemaic universe was a thing of the past. Even the calendar changed. The Julian, long out of sync with reality, was replaced by Pope Gregory with the current model which bears his name.

Artists broke away from the strict crafts-oriented organization of the guilds and attached themselves to wealthy patrons and started to become individuals again.

Contagions, spread by the ever widening circles of contact in the Air Mutation, were rampant in Water. The Black Death in 1337 wiped out so many people it produced a labor shortage that doubled the average wage. Medicine was the preoccupation of the times. Hospitals, insane asylums, and orphanages were founded. For the first time doctors were regulated and researchers went to the source, not the ancients, for their medical knowledge. While explorers roamed the globe, medical explorers uncovered the mysteries of the human body. We need not ask how.

It was a visionary age, that strove for perfection and God with the right hand and dipped into the till with the left. As befit its place in the Piscean Age, it explored and studied for the sake of knowing. Where explorers went, missionaries followed. Souls the Church could not control at home were sought abroad. Nostradamus made his first predictions. The focus was other worlds and other realms in the material world and out.

Water closets were invented. Water power fueled the engines. The road to Cathay was paved with waves. The age was boundless in every detail. The Hundred Years War began in 1337 and didn't end till 1453. Civil wars raged in Japan. England fought the War of the Roses. The seas dominated the action and the thoughts. One willingly sacrificed himself for a belief or a dream. Money was an entry into immortality, not simply a means of trading goods for goods.

Characteristics of Water

- Decentralization.
- Decay of authority.
- Disruption and wars.
- Free thinking.
- Exploration and discovery.
- Idealism and perfectionism.
- Other worldly pursuits.
- Financial instruments.
- Insurance.
- Experimentation.

While none of us will live into the next Water Mutation, we can see possibilities of the credit card economy in full force, space exploration, and the transformation of everything we believe to be true today into a new intellectual model for the Aquarian Age.

The Fire Mutation

1663 to 1842

The Water Mutation was a perpetual romance with the unknown. The Fire Mutation was a love affair with power and force. Money was irrelevant. The world had opened up. Everything was there to be fought for and won. Everything was up for grabs.

The divine right of kings replaced the divine authority of the Church and God. France saw the reign of the Sun King. Gold was the sign of power, the means by which the have-nots could have. Ghana was an empire of gold. The wealth of the Caliph of Baghdad was immortalized in *1,001 Nights*. The quest for knowledge gave way to the quest for gold as the conquistadors ravaged the civilizations of the western hemisphere. The Aztecs and Incas were decimated by the age's overwhelming lust for gold.

Despotism spawned rebellion. The American Revolution and the French Revolution fought for democracy and individualism against divine right and privileges of birth. What you hated you fought. If you failed to fight you lost. The first slaves were brought to Virginia in 1619. Slavery accelerated where the subjugation of the weak to the strong was economically feasible. The Indo-American tribes were driven off their land to make way for colonists. It was a hunting economy all over again, survival of the fittest, to the victor went the spoils.

Free enterprise in England received state support in 1649. The first banknotes appeared alongside the last meeting of the Hanseatic League. National banks were formed. Statism revived. The first income taxes were levied. The first dollar notes were introduced in the U.S. The first pound notes and copper pennies appeared in England. With paper money came paper schemes, Mississippi bubbles and South Sea Balloons. The Paris Bourse opened as did the Vienna Stock Exchange. Free enterprise became a respectable gamble, how the strong could triumph regardless of class. Speculation was the civilized form of aggression.

The hunting corporations dominated the economy of the world. East India Companies—industrial armies—established colonies for raw materials and markets for finished goods. The English, French, and Dutch divided Asia among themselves with the authority and indifference of a conquistador. Power was strength. Risk made profits. Go for broke. Life was cheap.

Contagions took on the face of fever, as cholera and smallpox spread throughout the world. Famous fires dominated the news as the movement to the cities set up conditions for major disaster. Life in the cities meant every man for himself. No longer did people have land and families on which to depend. Workers became, in the more inflammatory rhetoric, wage slaves.

The urge to control vied with the urge to be free. Freedom of the press was championed along with civil liberties and international free trade. The writings of Locke and Rousseau, Quesnay and the physiocrats tried to find in nature the foundations of a social contract, where each would be a power unto himself. Yet, the urge to be superior and exclusive won out in the movements towards Freemasonry and brotherhoods.

An age of gambling and risk, horse racing and card games were very popular carryovers from the previous age.

Most of the great manufacturing machines were invented during this period, the spinning jenny and the cotton gin. These machines and steam power led to an industrial revolution in Britain that spread all over the world. The first balloon challenged the air. New surgical techniques took the emphasis off the chemistry of medicine. Canals tore into the land. Gas lit the night streets of London. Electricity, its future replacement, was discovered. Mining robbed the earth of its treasures. Ironworks rose into the sky and pounded out materials for railroads and the first iron bridge.

Technology and invention were the rule, not the exception. The first technical college opened in Paris. Academies of science furthered a new awareness of the mechanics of the world.

With this realization and with the power implicit in the owners of their tools of production came the trade union movement and restrictions on working conditions and hours at the job. In the beginning of Fire an emerging middle class overthrew the king. At its end, labor challenged their middle-class despots.

We can still hear echoes of the Fire ethic: rugged individualism, free enterprise, *laissez-faire* economy. A new order developed. A new order demanded power and force. The Fire Mutation gave us the Age of Reason, despotism, invention, and revolution. The face of the land was permanently changed by the purveyors of Fire. Whatever we may think of their methods, they established the new order. Without their sometime reckless daring, few of us would enjoy the comfort we do today.

Characteristics of Fire

- Might equals right.
- Gold.
- Conquest and colonization.
- Subjugation of the weak to the strong.
- Autocratic central governments.
- Rebellion.
- Invention.
- Self-interest.
- Competition.
- Schemes and scams.

In the past 20 years the United States, a hunting economy, largely reverted to Fire values because of the breakdown of the Earth Mutation and the long passages of Uranus and Neptune through Sagittarius. A decade of hostile takeovers, rapacious management practices, and an obsession with profit rather than production will merely hasten the demise of Earth and clear the way for Air.

Our dream of colonizing other planets must wait for the Fire Mutation. Only then will governments have the power to amass the necessary resources to undertake such expensive projects or the need because of the environmental and human demands of our shrinking world.

And so we come back to Earth. In Fire no boundaries existed save what could be established with superior force. In Earth the boundaries reappeared. Within a short period of time we settled boundary disputes with Canada via the Webster-Ashburton Treaty of 1842, the year of the Great Mutation. The war with Mexico, soon to follow, gave us our southern boundaries. We had nothing to stop us but the sea and our own ambitions.

Workers who once worked at home and raised their own vegetables and eggs now worked in factories in the cities, totally dependent on wages for their ability to keep body and soul alive. With this potential for oppression, unionism and communism thrived. Gradually the vote expanded. The power once held by the authority of Fire spread through the population. The new aristocracy would be the monied class and the bourgeoisie. Gradually the market, not the blade, became the *sine qua non* of power, as the agricultural economic model replaced the impulse to hunt.

Outer Planet Transits

History may seem irrelevant to investing or starting a business today, but it is quite useful to know where the future's popular excitement will be directed. The activities of these elemental eras give us a clear picture of how the elements express themselves in action. Heavy transits through the various elements express the same dominance: 20 years of Uranus and Neptune through Sagittarius gave us an adversarial press, an activist population, and a moral imperative of the freedom to do your own thing. Forty years of Neptune, Pluto, and Uranus through Libra gave us mass movements of troops, communal living, and a morality of universal brotherhood. Fifteen years of Uranus and Neptune through Capricorn is restoring a preoccupation with wealth and prosperity and a morality of materially visible accomplishment. Forty years of Neptune and Pluto through Scorpio reflect a breakdown of order, the glamorization of drugs and sex, artistic expression, and an anti-religious amorality and cynicism.

The impact is especially strong today because the outer planets are clustering in the same signs, or in signs that closely follow one another.

Uranus has a period of approximately seven years in a sign. Uranus represents public interest and taste, what excites people, fads.

Neptune has a period of approximately 14 years and represents what fascinates the public: glamour, fashion, film, music, the reigning ideologies.

Pluto, a longer and more irregular period, represents obsession and transformation. It represents the side effects and fallout of the previous mass movements, ideologies, and taste.

As investment plays, anticipate market building in the goods and markets of the element through which Uranus and Neptune are transiting. They are currently in Capricorn (Earth), an emphasis on traditional values, conservatism, discipline, material goods. In fashion and the popular arts: nostalgia, slim lines and skin, leather and furs, slenderness and bone structure. For recreation, outdoors and gardening, or very elegant status type pleasures and pastimes. All are very different from the baggy, ethnic, individualist, and chaotic fashions of the Sagittarius (Fire) transit. Expect mail order to decline, as well as purely conspicuous consumption. Capricorn likes its status symbols, but more as a sign of accomplishment than of power and wealth.

Because we are in an Earth Mutation, the Capricorn transits will accentuate our long term prospects, and somewhat counter the Air instincts of the most recent Lesser Mutation.

Pluto in Scorpio brings sexual diseases, the result of an earlier prolonged transit of Neptune through Scorpio, that glorified the seamy, the sexual and depraved. It also enhanced a tendency among people who were born in that generation to go into debt. Pluto in Scorpio brings bankruptcies.

The impact of these outer planet transits through signs of the various elements are also a demographic tool. To anticipate what certain age groups will be attracted to, or what they will need to repair, note the outer planet positions in their birth years. The people who were in college in the protest years have Neptune in Libra: ideologically they advocated love not war, in accumulating terms, they love beautiful things, especially personal adornment. Expect diamonds to replace love beads. They also have Pluto in Leo, an obsession with power and strength. The need to keep their energy level high forecasts an enduring market for exercise machines, vitamins, and medical miracles to prolong youth.

Outer planet transits can help you time investments and enterprises. As is true in most cases, invest early in the sign. Sell late. Although too complex to go into here, the passage of these planets through the constellations lags several years behind the zodiacal passage, with which we are all familiar. The effect of this is that the peak and flareout usually happens after the planets leave. The best move is still to buy or start the business early.

In the long perspective we can draw a number of conclusions not only about the nature of the elements and their economic import but of their impact on our current and future ways of doing business. All these Mutations operated and presently operate against the background of the Piscean Age. Their future expression will operate against impulses of the developing Aquarian Age.

The Piscean impulse is, of course, Water. Our Great Age is an age of dispersion, exploration, ideation, imagination, and unlimited expansion. It is no accident that scientists view the universe as expanding. Our systems would naturally lead us to develop instruments that would give us that data. The Aquarian Age, being Fixed, will lead to new discoveries that will see the universe as stabilizing or even contracting. As the knowledge of the Water Mutation totally contradicted the knowledge of the Air Mutation, we can expect all our systems of thought and even our ways of thinking to be drastically altered as the next Great Age begins. We are living in the seed time of the seed time. Though the Aquarian Age may not technically begin for another 200 years (depending on whose figures you prefer), our present Air Mutation within the Earth period and the coming Air Mutation will gradually turn our thinking from Piscean to Aquarian.

The dominant impulse of any great Age is balanced by the sign in opposition. Even as we directed our energies by principles mystical and religious, by an ideal of self-sacrifice and self-denial, by an attachment to dreams of faraway places and perfect worlds, we have been constantly and inevitably preoccupied with the material world, the Virgo lever that keeps us from flying off into the chaotic ether. Even as we build technology on technology and swell with the bounty of our discoveries, we deny and denigrate our material fortunes and hate ourselves for what we are. In Pisces we can never be satisfied. There is always something more or better to be done, to be discovered, to be known. In time we will lose that yearning.

In the Aquarian Age we will balance ourselves with Fire, the struggle to retain our individuality and power. In the Cancer Mutation the ingenuity of the Pisces Age dazzled with its brilliance. In the Capricorn Mutation, the balance asserted itself and materialized that ingenuity. We have been blessed. How wonderful to have lived the schizophrenia of an Earth Mutation in a Water Age.

Precautions, Patterns, and Profits

- Outer planet transits through signs duplicate the mass interests associated with their elements.

- Outer planet transits of Capricorn will briefly return us to materialistic Earth values.

- Long term trends are towards collectivist, humanist, international and secular values.

- International corporations and trading cartels will dominate the global economy.

- Science and technology will be the new orthodoxy.

Chapter Seven

EVERY SIXTY YEARS

The Sixty-Year Cycle, popularized by Ravi Batra in *The Depression of 1990*[1], is one of the oldest mundane cycles known to man. Apart from its astrological correlation, 60 years is the time it takes for experience to pass out of fashion. An adult who lived through a severe economic dislocation would be 80 years old or dead by the time the next dislocation was due. If he were in a position of power or actively involved in the dislocation, say age 40, the knowledge he gained from the mistakes he and his peers made would be lost in the marketplace within 30 years.

If John Smith sold his house and put all his money in the stock market in September of 1929, just as the market peaked, he not only lost his assets, he lost his home. He learned two valuable lessons:

1. *What goes up must come down.*

2. *Don't risk your home on a "sure thing."*

In a couple of more years, he would have learned several more new lessons: *don't trust banks, the only money you have is the money you have in your hand, always make provisions for the future, be as self-sufficient as you can be, what is bad can get worse.*

Assuming John eventually found a job or got his old job back when the economy revived, he and his entire generation of mature adults would be exceedingly cautious, even irrationally cautious about safe financial practices. A period of disaster always gives birth to a mass psychology of fiscal conservatism. As a result, the economy would crawl on and up, safe and sure.

1. Batra, Ravi, *The Great Depression of 1990,* Venus Publishing, N.Y., 1987

Thirty years after the original disaster, the 40-year-olds are totally out of decision making positions in the economy. Their children, who lived through the hard times, and those who were young adults have strong memories of the hardship or of the tales thrice told.

They also have strong memories of recovery. They expect the recovery to continue forever. It does not. The market merely stabilizes during the next 20 years and acts the way it should. It trades in a predictable range.

Eventually stability begins to look like stagnation. Those who were fiscally conservative and mildly experimental during the stable 20-year period are perceived as old fogies, who were unable to lead the rest into a new and glorious time of prosperity. A new breed of managers and entrepreneurs enter the financial markets and the banks. They were born and grew up in the prosperity of the recovery period. They never lived through or groaned through the stories of hardship except from the lips of their grandparents. They are raring to show the world a thing or two about making money. The middle generation, retiring or feeling like failures, are willing to let them have a go.

The result in the first half of the last cycle of 20 years is go-go banking, finance-driven corporate policies, mergers and takeovers, and everybody gambling on stocks. Making money, not production or work, becomes the goal. Of course the crash comes, because all the knowledge gained from the previous money hysteria and crash no longer fills the brains of the shakers and movers.

If you look at the graph of the Dow-Jones Industrials, you see repetitions of this cycle from day one. From 1880 to 1900 the Dow slowly and steadily rose. From 1900 to 1920, the Dow could never break 100. From 1920 to 1929, the Dow went wild. From 1930 to 1940 it could not recover from the crash. From 1940 to 1960 the Dow steadily rose. From 1960 to 1980 it couldn't break 1,000. From 1980 to 1990 it skyrocketed. We make the same mistakes because old experience dies within 60 years.

The Dow is not the only indicator of this cycle. Graphs of oil and silver shown earlier reveal the same pattern. Human beings forget history. Human beings repeat history.

We believe only our own history. We think it cannot happen to us. The major astrological components of the 60-Year Cycle are Saturn and Jupiter. Our old friends are back again, not only determining broad sweeps of economic, social and political activity, but the smaller dustings as well. They do not do it totally by themselves. Eclipses impose themselves as do movements in the Solar Field. But, if Jupiter and Saturn are not involved, the movements will be either insignificant to the economy as a whole or temporary. The stock market crashlet of 1987 was a market phenomenon, not an economic phenomenon. It was similar to the market crash in 1869. The market crash in 1929 was of economic import. Our economically important adjustment will dominate the 1990s.

Before we get into the celestial mechanics of the 60-Year Cycle, let us examine some other cycles that have been identified independently of astrology.

The Juglar Cycle

In 1860 Clement Juglar discovered an eight to ten year cycle that bears his name. Very clearly this refers to the Jupiter-Saturn oppositions and conjunctions that are classically associated with mundane affairs and with supply and demand. Independent of whatever else is going on in the skies, Jupiter and Saturn always operate during major market moves, although they do not necessarily indicate tops and bottoms. Extremes are the result of converging factors, not simply of major planetary events.

The 10-year cycle is also a function of eclipses. Eclipses in the same sign recur at 10 year intervals, though one will be a north node eclipse and the other a south node eclipse. Any event in a nine to ten year cycle will relate to nodes, eclipses, Jupiter-Saturn recurrences, and occasionally a Saturn contact of its position at an earlier date[2], since these occur at seven to nine year intervals, due to retrograde motion.

Cycles of recurrence also occur between the Moon and Mercury and the Moon and Venus every eight years, and between the Moon and Mars and Mars and Venus every 32 years (a multiple of eight), and between Mars and Mercury every 79 years (a near multiple of eight). The multiples of these cycles of recurrence and repetition indicate many possibilities for astrological identification of the Juglar cycle.

---

2. Any of these recurrences could be related to points and planets on individual charts to be discussed in chapter ten.

The Kitchin Cycle

The Kitchin Cycle was discovered by Crum and Kitchin in the 1920s. Its period is about 40 months, which astrologers have correlated to hard aspects of Jupiter and Uranus. Uranus turns any direction opposite to what is in effect. Since Jupiter is the planet of prosperity, Uranus would reasonably be expected to turn the direction of prosperity and growth.

There are a number of difficulties with the assignment of Jupiter and Uranus as a major cyclic pattern. Although they give the market a bounce, they do not time major events. The period from conjunction to conjunction is 14 years, half of a normal Saturn cycle, which indicates Saturn in opposition to its place 14 years before.

Jupiter and Uranus were not involved in the market run-up in 1929 nor the crash. Jupiter and Uranus were not involved the all time low of 1932. The combination was not involved in the crash of 1987 nor in the crash of 1869.

While the Jupiter-Uranus conjunction does have an effect on market prices, it is not an indicator of major tops and bottoms and is, therefore, of limited usefulness. Its conjunctions, squares and oppositions often occur when one or both are retrograding, adding more confusion as a forecasting tool and giving too much latitude in assigning it to specific phenomena. The contacts look good in hindsight. We do not have that luxury when we look ahead.

While the 40-month cycle could represent Jupiter-Uranus, it seems more likely that the Kitchin cycle is temporary, a matter of happenstance, or a correlation to an irregularly occurring 22-month contact of Mars and Venus.

The great argument for Jupiter-Uranus revolves on a reversal of the Kitchin cycle in 1940–1941, co-incident with a double contact of Jupiter and Uranus because of retrograde motion, but Mars and Venus had multiple contacts in 1940 also, which could have produced a similar effect.

Twenty-two months is the normal lapse time between successive conjunctions of Venus and Mars. However, the full cycle is not 44 months. It can have a lag of up to an entire year if Venus is retrograde when Mars makes his contact. If all things were equal we would see an approximately 22-month rising market, followed by a 22-month falling market. However, when

Venus retrogrades, Mars can make as many as four contacts over a period of a year, before the new up or down period starts.

In the early 1950s when the market doubled to reach new all time highs, most of the Mars-Venus conjunctions were multiplied because of retrograde Venus. By contrast, in the 1970s there was only one Mars-Venus spree, which corresponded to the high of a decade of normal trading ranges. Though the Dow never fell below the high of the mid 1950s, it was never able to break the firm top of 1,000, not permanently breached until 1982.

In all probability the actual movements of these cycles are a combination of Saturn's hard aspects to its own place at seven to nine year intervals, the Jupiter-Saturn conjunctions and oppositions, and the irregular cycle of Venus and Mars. All significant events show cumulative planetary buildups that mature at approximately the same time. Aberrant recurring cycles cannot be deduced from figures alone. They can only be spotted astrologically. Because of this, many market timing schemes work well for several years, then go haywire. Like Mars and Venus they do quite well by one another short term. Long term they have their fights.

The Kondratieff Wave

In 1926 Kondratieff wrote of a cycle of about 52 years that he observed in the economy of the United States. Depending on the author, the Kondratieff Wave is often stretched anywhere from 50 to 60 years, depending on the thesis and projections that are being supported. Richard G. Zambell in *Hyperinflation or Depression?*[3] outlined 10-year segments of Kondratieff thus:

Decade	Attitude	Effect
First	Conservative and protectionist	Recovery
Second	Maximize wealth, free trade	Growth, war
Third	Progressive, reform minded, free trade	Prosperity, war
Fourth	International, protectionist, scandals	Transition, stagnation
Fifth	Conservative with extreme protectionism	Depression

3. Zambell, Richard G., *Hyperinflation or Depression?*, Weiss Research, Inc., West Palm Beach, Florida, 1984, pp. 52–64

Apart from the fact that he covers 15 years in some "decades," we can safely say that the 50-year cycle (incidentally, one noted by the Mayans) is a timing of accumulated planetary patterns that occasionally hit at 50 years. It may also be a reflection of Mayan Venus cycles, not addressed in this work.

Recurring cycles like Jupiter-Uranus, Jupiter-Neptune, and Jupiter-Pluto happen at approximately 13 year intervals, which could account for a 50- to 52-year cycle. However, the 50-year cycle as described is more likely a function of the 60-year period. Kondratieff theorized a rise of about 20 years and a decline of about 30, with 10 years out of the decline a major depression or crisis. As we will see, the Mutation cycle is more descriptive of Kondratieff than he is of himself or his advocates are of him. The 60-Year Cycle is the most predictable and precise of all. In fact, it incorporates many of the elements of the shorter periods.

If we use Zambell's descriptions but call the 1930s the sixth decade we will see an apt description of the decades since:

FIRST: 1940s— recovery from the depression.

SECOND: 1950s—Strong growth. Because of the devastation of World War II, America becomes the producer of the world. Korean War.

THIRD: 1960s—Guns and butter philosophy of the Johnson administration, and great wealth within the country. Vietnam war.

FOURTH: 1970s—Stagnation. Oil crisis and a lackluster Dow.

Here's where Zambell's model breaks down. Both the 1920s and the 1980s reflect the real nature of the fifth decade, years of wild growth and scandals. They, not a period of stagnation, preceded the Depression.

FIFTH: Should be wild growth and speculation followed by

SIXTH: Depression.

Our history undeniably segments into six, not five, 10-year periods. The foundation of the 60-Year Cycle is our old friend, the Mutation cycle, plus certain cyclic recurrences that occur within it.

The Mutation Cycle

As stated in previous chapters, the Mutation cycle is the name given to the conjunctions of Jupiter and Saturn. It describes the complexity of supply and demand and the long term economic style.

Jupiter and Saturn represent fundamental market psychology as well as shifting prices and market turns. They are not simply buying and selling. Each can drive the market up for different reasons. When Saturn and Jupiter are in bad aspects to one another, growth is slowed or stopped. A lack of growth or abundance can drive prices up because of scarcity. Growth can lower prices because of abundance. Growth in the money supply raises prices because of an abundance of money. A shrinkage of the money supply drives prices down because of a shortage of money. To know which operates one must be familiar with market realities, with the phase of the Mutation cycle and the position of planets in signs.

Within the 60-year period, Saturn and Jupiter join three times, once in each mode, three 20-year segments. The movement is not from major disaster to major disaster, but from hard won experience to market wisdom. Each 20-year mode period is subdivided into a rising cycle of 10 years and a declining or adjusting cycle of 10 years. The 60-year period is also divided into a rising segment of 30 years, followed by a declining or stabilizing segment of 30 years. The major correction occurs when the 30-year turning point coincides with a 10-year turning point. This happens every 60 years, roughly 1870, 1930, 1990. This pattern holds true no matter what the Mutation element. The order of the modes, which represent the market psychology and trading practices, is backward: Cardinal, Mutable, then Fixed.

Cardinal Mutation Phase

During the Cardinal period, the market dominates. The economy stays in a trading range. Although it prospers overall and fluctuates (in the normal fall by half and double) nothing spectacular happens because the population does not fully understand the new conditions, especially the first 10 years. When the Cardinal phase began the Great Mutation cycle, as it did in 1842, the economy was in total chaos. The Cardinal phase is a time of *experience,* on-the-job training in how money really works.

Mutable Mutation Phase

After the opposition of Jupiter and Saturn which starts the next 10 years, the money controllers tinker. The tinkering leads to what we might call premature knowledge that brings us into the Mutable, experimental phase, the second 20-year period. The manipulations that worked a little bit in the late Cardinal phase are now given free play, with apparently wonderful results. The market soars. The activity is frenzied for the first 10 years of this period. Prices skyrocket. (1920 to 1930)

The mid-point of this segment is the 30-year-point disaster of the 60-year period that Kondratieff noticed. The 30-year buildup of the 60-year cycle is complete. Its downturn or stabilizing period is about to begin. The high point of the Mutable period has been reached. Its correcting or stabilizing period is about to begin. The second half of the Mutable period tends to be crash and burn, not only because it is a double downer, but because it was preceded by a double upper. From 1930 to 1940 the population got a real *education*.

Fixed Mutation Phase

During the Fixed 20-year period, the market strives to get back on its feet and establish a firm *foundation* (1940 to 1960). Wealth accumulates. Everybody knows what to avoid. Chastened by the excesses of the previous phase, the market makes its greatest gains. When the Cardinal phase returns (1960 to 1980) the stability begins to look like stagnation. Everyone is disappointed that the gains of the Fixed period are not being repeated. The tinkering begins anew. Whereupon we have another go at soar, crash, and burn, in the second half of the Mutable cycle (1980 to 1990).

Wave watchers expected the market to make a major correction in the 1950s. In fact, there was only a mild recession. The Fixed sign period is the least likely to have major upheavals on purely economic grounds. The devastation in Europe and Japan at this time was the result of war, not economics.

Mutation Cycle

Phase 1	Cardinal	Markets stay in a trading range.		
	20 years	1842–1861	1901–1921	1961–1981
Phase 2	Mutable	High speculation and growth.		
	10 years	1862–1872	1921–1931	1981–1991
Phase 3	Opposition	Severe correction and stagnation.		
	10 years	1872–1881	1931–1941	1991–2000
Phase 4	Fixed	Wealth building and steady growth		
	20 years	1881–1901	1941–1961	

Lesser Mutation Rounds

Each Great Mutation cycle contains at least three Lesser Mutation rounds of 60 years. In the first phase the world population learns to cope with the new social, political and economic order of the age. In the Great Earth Mutation, the problems were: structuring the industrial revolution, implementing the new technologies, and accommodating the flight to the factory from the farm. Round one ended in 1901.

From 1901 to 1961 the focus shifted from the problems of getting factories and workers organized to how to keep the playing field fair, how to avoid busts and booms. The Federal Reserve System, social security, workers' compensation, antitrust laws, were all part of what to do after the machines were producing. Despite 1929 and the 1930s, the stock market actually rose from a value of 40 to over 1,000 during this period. In the first period, it never got beyond its 20 to 40 range. Although much of that rise can be attributed to government induced inflation, there has nevertheless been a distribution of wealth among an incredibly large number of the population, more than the world has ever experienced before. Round two fine-tuned the results of round one.

The final phase, which began in 1960, is the decline. An Earth centered economy deteriorates into a sensation economy. Wealth produces a hypersensitivity to pain and puts an increasingly dull edge on pleasure. We think every problem can be solved with money. That was true when lack of money was a problem. Today the problem is too much. Round three deals with the problems of excess.

Second Round Mutation—Dow 1900 to 1938

Dow Jones Industrial Averages 1900–1938

Third Round Mutation—Dow 1960 to Present

Dow Jones Industrial Averages 1960 to present

4,000

3,000

2,000

1,000

0

1960   1965   1970   1975   1980   1985   1990   1994

Mutation Rounds

Round One   1842–1901   Structuring the materialist economy.

Round Two   1901–1961   Fine tuning and regulation.

Round Three   1961–2020   Excess and disintegration.

A word needs to be said about the 1950s in which the stock market shifted to a new multiple of 10 during what would normally have been a downward correction. The Taurus Lesser Mutation, in effect at the time, tends to hold value steady. It also tends to align money to its true value. The great bull market of the 1950s was not a growth in wealth, but an adjustment of the markets to the inflation in the system. The stock market and the currency were reset to their true value. A correction is a correction. Correction does not always mean down.

We also have an anomaly operating in the present Mutation subcycle. The last Lesser Mutation (1981) occurred in Air, which presages the Great Air Mutation in 2020. We skipped the Mutable Lesser Mutation this time around. In the past our presidents died during Lesser Earth Mutations because we have an Earth sign on the 10th house. Reagan survived the assassination attempt because this Mutation occurred in Air.

Sign Impact

The time pattern of the subcycles is complicated by the sign pattern. As Jupiter and Saturn move through the signs, significant adjustments or turns happen at 15° of a sign, especially the Mutables. The crash of 1869 occurred with Saturn close to 15° of Sagittarius, in 1929 Jupiter was at 15° of Gemini, in 1987 Saturn was just past 15° of Sagittarius. Because a crash does not occur at all 15° points we can only conclude that these indicate ripeness and a mid-sign peak, not an inevitability. A crisis needs more than a single point to materialize it.

War

War has an economic impact, but it is not a function of economic cycles. If it were, the whole world would be at war every few years. Zambell's model identifies certain economic decades with war. Although war can have an effect on the economy, especially for the loser, war itself does not turn an economy one way or the other. The war cycle is not an economic cycle. Technically speaking, the United States has been at "war" since 1942: World War II, The Cold War, Korea, Vietnam, the war on poverty, the

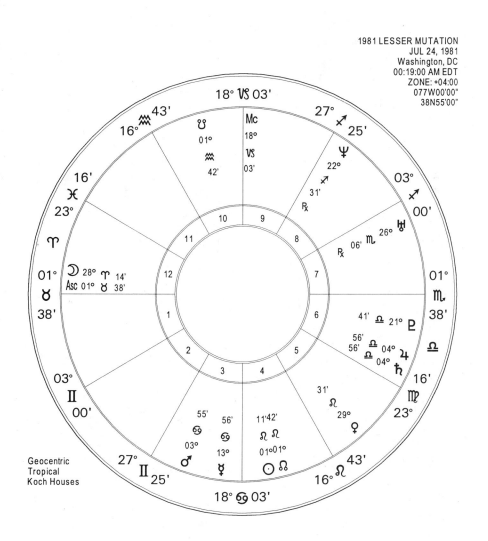

Lesser Mutation—July 24, 1981, Washington, D.C.

undeclared civil war of the 1960s, the oil war, the war against crime, the war against drugs, the war with Iraq. This is not unusual for a hunting economy. To put it a slightly different way, we have been spending and losing money all through these periods as if we were at war. The loss of property and lives as a result of violent crime and drugs has in all probability matched what an ordinary war would do to an ordinary country. Yet our economic flow still follows the arbitrary curves and the universal patterns of trade.

The impulse to go to war may well be the result of economic factors. Germany was almost destroyed economically in the aftermath of World War I. While it seems foolhardy they would start a war again, it is not so foolish if you understand their drive to get their enemies under control and restore their devastated economy. Although many economies had to start from sub-zero in the 1940s, the fact is that all economies flourished during this period. Japan and Germany, the losers, made the greatest gains of all. While the correction at the end of the Fixed era is often unpleasant, it is in fact, merely a signal that the stable period is over and the market period is about to begin. Occasionally the growth is stopped drastically until the market reaches its true level.

In 1842, the beginning of the Earth mutation, the United States was a developing country which entered the Earth mutation with no currency of its own and without a central bank through which to channel an orderly progress of trade. Not until 1849 did it begin to amass the necessary trading medium that would enable it to finance its growing production. The 1840s debacle was aggravated by the Mutation in Capricorn, which meant a prolonged transit of Saturn in its strongest signs through the U.S. 2nd house.

Ordinarily, Mutation conjunctions and oppositions time peaks and valleys. In the case of the United States, the peak crumbles and the valleys dip because of Saturn's simultaneous passage through Capricorn and Aquarius. The severity of any universal indicator is a factor of its impact on the national chart or on the chart of a particular institution: e.g., the stock market or a corporation. While the globe will experience the correlations of the Mutation cycles, not every place on Earth will experience it equally or in precisely the same way. Local and geographical impact will be discussed in chapter ten.

The conjunction of Jupiter and Saturn indicates a bottom and a building. The opposition indicates a top and a fall. The adjustment at the turn of the century was relatively mild. The 1840s were severe because they also indicated a major shift in financial, social, and political focus. The 1960 turn had greater political consequences than it did financial, although it marked the beginning of the guns and butter philosophy that eventually started an extended binge of government expenditures and federal deficits that are with us today.

Someone once divided the economy into four phases:

1. When you are poor and you know you are poor (decade six).
2. When you are getting rich and you think you are still poor (decades one and two).
3. When you are rich and you know you are rich (decade three).
4. When you are getting poor and you think you are still rich (decades four and five. Five is where the speculation and borrowing begin).

We can parallel these to the phases of the mutation cycle. Phase one is part two of the Mutable phase. The economy has just crashed. Everyone knows the meaning of poor. Phase two is the Fixed phase where everyone is painfully aware of poverty and does not trust one's ability to accumulate, despite evidence to the contrary. Phase three comes at the start of the Cardinal phase. One's whole attitude towards money takes on a facade of very high expectations. One feels in control. The markets and the government begin to make decisions on the basis of a perception of unbounded wealth. Phase four kicks in the second half of the Cardinal phase and culminates at the middle of the Mutable phase where the economy crashes. The borrowing always gets out of hand in phase four. If one thinks rich, any financial difficulty is merely a momentary embarrassment, therefore, borrowing until the luck returns is perfectly reasonable and acceptable. When a whole nation is standing on the dock waiting for its ship to come in, the dock sinks. Although we can find a correlation with this fourfold designation loosely within the Mutation cycle, the understanding of the movement from poverty to wealth and back to poverty is actually a description of the complex 60-Year Cycle and the progress of the planets that compose it.

The Sixty-Year Cycle

The 60-year cycle is somewhat elusive because it does not follow a mathematically precise astrological model nor a precise cycle of 60 years.

In addition to the Jupiter and Saturn recurring cycle, the 60-Year Cycle is two complete revolutions of Saturn, five revolutions of Jupiter, which means a return not only of Saturn to its beginning place but of Jupiter, as well, plus recurring positions of eclipses and nodes. Mercury and Saturn also have a recurring cycle of 59 years, which is also two progressed lunar cycles. Like everything in astrology the redundancy is monumental, nowhere more monumental than in this cycle of 60 years.

The redundancy is necessary so that the proper accumulation of astrological events can time the crises or turning points. At least one of these long term cycles must be operative at the same time as the short term when short term planetary data indicates corrections.

It will be demonstrated that Jupiter and Saturn alone can be used to time major economic events when used in tandem with the Solar Field for the medium to short term timing. One of the keys to astrological timing and forecasting is to know what to leave out. Unusual planetary configurations, particularly of the outer planets cannot and do not by themselves spell economic disaster as part of a financial cycle. Earthquakes cause economic disaster, but they are not economic in nature. Unusual configurations can have an economic impact, but only if they coincide with an actual financial cycle. They add import only to what is already in place. For instance, the San Francisco earthquake and North Carolina hurricane damage caused simultaneous damage in the insurance industry, but not right away. The worst of the insurance industry's problems followed the greater economic patterns. Their troubles emanated from their investment practices as well as client claims.

Saturn and Jupiter *always* have an economic impact, sometimes more important than other times. Eclipses often have an economic impact. Most of the time they are slight. Saturn and

Jupiter both drive the market up, though Saturn often constricts the flow of money and produces losses and falling prices. Falling prices can be good news or bad, depending on whether you are buying or selling. We seem to be obsessed with upward movements and view anything steady or down as bad. This leads to much unnecessary hysteria, the kind that kicks in the Saturnian fear.

Saturn and Jupiter are simply the planets that relate to man as a social and civilized creature. They relate to the economy in terms of confidence and fear. Jupiter is enthusiasm. Saturn is the price paid to satisfy the enthusiasm. Jupiter is conservation and expansion. Saturn is restriction and loss. Jupiter gets carried away on fashion. Saturn gets carried away with anxiety. Jupiter buys a beaded sombrero, never to be worn, as a memento of a trip to Mexico. Saturn buys the sombrero for fear of a sunburn or fear that the supply will be grabbed by other balding heads.

When Saturn went over the Ascendant of the U.S. chart, public confidence in the economy did not falter even though many of the doomsayers said that we were on the verge of collapse. The market went to dizzying heights in a short period of time because people were afraid they were going to lose out on this fabulous rise in the Dow. Jupiter in Pisces and Aries egged them on. Shortly after Saturn made its station at 14° of Sagittarius, the Dow reached a new all time high and started the decline that would end with the debacle of October 19th. From thence the population turned totally wary and pessimistic as befits both the Saturn in the 1st house and the cautious Jupiter in Taurus. To go back to the point about thinking rich when one is actually poor: until the banking system started to show severe strains, no one stopped borrowing—especially if he was not personally hurt by the crash or if he had any capacity to put his purchases on the tab.

After Saturn made its last opposition to Jupiter, the Dow continued to rise. Despite the experiences of the farmers in the midwest and the S&Ls, people still believe the banks are safe and the economy will muddle through. They are afraid, but they still think they have to get in there and take advantage before its too late. This is exactly the psychology of Saturn, struggling beside the hope and optimism of Jupiter. Buy now before it's too late. It is exactly the psychology of thinking oneself rich when one is actually poor.

Jupiter-Saturn Movements

How Saturn functions has to do both with its position relative to its own cycle and relative to its position to Jupiter.

Every seven to nine years, easily observed in an ephemeris, transiting Saturn makes a hard aspect—conjunction, square, or opposition—to the natal position of Saturn on the Mutation chart.

Every three years Jupiter does the same. The Jupiter return, its contact to its natal place, the Mutation, is the most powerful. This occurs every 12 years. Normally a very strong connection, it occurs in the sign of its weakness, Capricorn, the sign of Saturn's strength. The opposition, also a strong placement, is in Jupiter's sign of strength, Cancer, and occurs midway in its 12 year cycle. Every 60 years, Jupiter's bounty gets squashed by Saturn at their mutual conjunction. Every 30 years it peaks, then gets blocked by Saturn opposed.

In both the Earth and Air Mutation Saturn dominates. In Fire and Water Mutations Jupiter has the strength. In the previous chapter we saw great expansion during Fire and Water Mutations. Contraction is the norm of Earth and Air. Because Saturn dominates in this era, we will delineate Jupiter as a satellite to Saturn's normal contractions, his corrective contacts to himself.

The Saturn cycle begins with the Jupiter-Saturn conjunction in Capricorn. Saturn in Capricorn sees reality. Jupiter is limited and restricted by Saturn, lacking in confidence and hope. Phase one starts with a negative idea of one's position.

When Saturn reaches Aries, its first turn seven years later, Jupiter is in Virgo, its detriment. Things are still looking down.

At the Jupiter-Saturn opposition two years later, Saturn is in Taurus and Jupiter is in Scorpio. Still the pits. Nine years have now elapsed.

About 14 to 15 years later Saturn opposes the starting point in Cancer, but lo and behold Jupiter is now in Pisces. Things are looking up.

The next phase, roughly 20 years after the first conjunction, is another conjunction, this time in Virgo. Jupiter in Virgo is not very optimistic, but within a year, two at the most, Saturn in Libra squares its natal place. Jupiter will either be in Libra or Scorpio. Saturn is strong in Libra so the market is functioning well, but the fear of loss remains strong. Fear of loss multiplies other fears, which occasionally lead people to do foolish things and take foolish risks.

Jupiter in Scorpio thinks borrowing money is going to solve all the problems and that is exactly what happens in this phase. They go Jupiter-crazy through Sagittarius, breathe a bit in Capricorn, pick up in Aquarius, Pisces and Aries. This happened in the 1920s and it happened in the 1980s.

The next Jupiter-Saturn opposition generally occurs in Capricorn/Cancer. This is a double whammy, a Saturn return (Saturn conjunct its original place) that blocks the normal prosperity of Jupiter in Cancer. Just as things seemed to be permanently wonderful they turn bad. (This took place in 1930, 1989, 1990, and 1991.) The Jupiter in Cancer, Saturn in Capricorn opposition is a point of major adjustment because it represents a Saturn return plus a Saturn block of Jupiter. It is the end of 30 years of rising markets and expectations and the start of 30 years of stability or decline. This is the critical turn in the 60 Year Cycle. While the United States did not own up to recession till 1991, in Japan, the Nikkei started its drastic drop right on time in 1989.

Eight years later when Saturn enters Aries with Jupiter in Aquarius/Pisces, we have passed the worst. Within a couple of years the new Jupiter-Saturn conjunction takes place in Taurus. (1940–41) Jupiter in Taurus is promising for financial well being and stability, though the problems of Saturn will have to be overcome first.

In a few years (1945) Saturn in Cancer opposes its natal place with Jupiter in Virgo. Weak markets and little confidence. The bottom comes at the beginning of this cycle, the best place for it to be. The new Saturn-Jupiter opposition takes place either in Pisces/ Virgo, which is a correlation of the last Mutable stage or in Aries/Libra which is a function of the Saturn hard aspects to its beginning place. Either way, or a combination of both, they happen almost simultaneously, marking a major shift in the economy, difficult but manageable with the right moves. This occurred in 1951. The signs look good for this period, compared to what they have been. Saturn makes a second return to its natal place, Capricorn, this time with Jupiter firmly in tow. The cycle is complete and a new order begins, new opportunities for growth.

In the off years, if Jupiter is in a sign of strength and not
square to Saturn, there will be a spurt of optimism and growth,
otherwise, the markets will be lackluster, trading in a range.

The reasons we start with Capricorn are twofold. The first is
that Cardinal signs indicate starts. The second is that the Great
Mutation chart of 1842, the chart that dominates this Earth
trigon, is a conjunction in Capricorn. The coming Great Mutation
in Air will occur in Aquarius, a Fixed sign. Consolidation, not
enterprise, will direct this era. All passages are made more complex by the introduction of new Lesser Mutations along the way,
by the natural meanings of the progress of Saturn and Jupiter in
the signs (chapter two) and their progress through the chart of
the country or market involved (chapter ten). All of which means
one cannot make pinpoint projections, but must judge the degree
of buildup and its impact on specific charts.

The Lesser Mutation Charts

Although economic turns are forecast by the broad sweep of
Jupiter and Saturn to one another and Saturn with reference
back to itself, the actual peak or valley may be triggered by the
Lesser Mutation charts, the intermediate Jupiter-Saturn conjunctions after the first major one. Saturn squares and oppositions to its Lesser Mutation position can mark important turns.
The 1929 crash occurred when Saturn squared its position in
Virgo in the Lesser Mutation. This was also true in 1869. Saturn squared its 1981 position in September of 1989. The Nikkei,
a leading indicator in the world economy, began its long decline.

Where there are multiple conjunctions as there were at the
last Mutation, the last one appears to indicate a bottoming of
negative financial and economic indicators and the beginning of
an upward phase that culminates at the Jupiter-Saturn opposition. This was true in 1869. In 1989 when the Dow dropped 200
points, our economy was not visibly jolted by the Saturn square
to its 1981 Mutation, although conventional hindsight shows a
U.S. economic decline from that time. The last Jupiter-Saturn
opposition of this phase occurred Leo/Aquarius in May of 1991.
That put the final lid on this period of growth and marked the
start of the real economic downturn.

The great bull market of the 1950s represented, not a rise
in prices, but a successful price adjustment to the high levels of
money in the system. Whether the bull market of the 1980s will

follow suit is still to be seen, but the great drain of cash from the S&L failures and the precipitous decline of the Japanese and other stock markets will likely represent a shrinkage of assets and therefore of investment money in the 1990s. This is essentially the same scenario as the 1930s, when the stock market made an unsuccessful run at an inflation adjusted DJIA.

Major changes and upheavals usually take place in Mutable Mutations. Mutable Mutations have Cardinal Jupiter-Saturn oppositions. Mutable signs take us beyond the limits. Cardinal signs begin all over.

Crash Signatures

To make this even more clear, let's look at the last two crashes from top to bottom.

The crash of 1929 occurred in the Mutable phase of the Mutation triad. Saturn was in Sagittarius square the Mutable Lesser Mutation; Jupiter was in 15° of Gemini. The market actually peaked that year on September 3 with Sun in Virgo and did not hit its first bottom until late November with Sun in Sagittarius.

The all time low came in 1932 just before Jupiter entered Virgo. The worst point of the economy was in 1933 with Saturn in Aquarius and Jupiter in Virgo. This is precisely the pattern of 60 years earlier when in 1874 the banks failed and the economy hit its low: Saturn in Aquarius and Jupiter in Virgo. The combination is both hopeless and a sign that the bottom is reached and things are about to turn. This combination occurs approximately every 60 years.

The market high of 1987 occurred just as the Sun entered Virgo. Saturn was in Sagittarius. On crash day Saturn was still in Sagittarius. More important the market did not leave the bottom range until the Sun, Mercury, and Saturn were back in Sagittarius.

One of the most astounding observations that comes out of these researches is the position of the Moon. At the August high of 1987 the Moon was in Virgo as it was on the day of the crash. The all time low of 1932 occurred with Moon in Virgo. The Moon passed from Virgo to Libra on the day of the 1929 crash. The market could not have crashed that year with Moon in Virgo because Virgo was on the weekend. We can assume the psychology crashed that day. Even a casual observation of the monthly ups and downs of the Dow usually reveal a down day in Virgo. Virgo, the nothing-but-the-facts-ma'am sign, is most antagonistic to the speculative fervor of Pisces.

The key to drastic change is Mutables. The points of correction are conjunctions and oppositions. Expect contractions and bottoms when Saturn is in the signs of its strength, Capricorn, Aquarius, and Libra. The most severe pattern is the five year stretch of Capricorn and Aquarius. The constriction establishes itself in Capricorn and bottoms out in Aquarius. Expect constriction when Jupiter is in the signs of its weakness, Capricorn, Virgo, and Gemini. Expect growth when Jupiter is in the signs of its strength, Cancer, Sagittarius and Pisces, but the gains of the latter two are likely to be transitory—peak and crash. Expect sudden changes and major swings in all Mutable signs.

With Saturn you must know the markets. With Jupiter you can get away with interpretation. Saturn means you lack what people want to buy and lose out on a profit, or you have it and cannot give it away.

In trying to anticipate turning points do not get caught up in numbers. Saturn need not be precisely square Jupiter or precisely opposite. The buildup of energy is more important than movement from point to point. For instance, if Saturn or Jupiter is in a Mutable sign or a Mutable phase of the Mutation cycle, look for activity when the Sun is in a Mutable sign and the Moon is in Virgo. If other conditions, to be discussed later, are also operating you can estimate the critical point.

Do not forget that although Saturn and Jupiter are descriptive of the broader economic issues, the Sun, gold, the standard of value, is what controls everything around it. If that standard of value is going to be jolted in a major way, the Sun will be in a Mutable sign.

Sixty-Year Rules

- Sixty-year cycles are made up of three periods of 20 years each.
- The 20-year periods start with Jupiter-Saturn conjunctions.
- The Conjunctions occur once in each modality.
- The modality of the Great Mutation determines the starting point—in our Earth era, Capricorn.

Capricorn represents the start up Cardinal phase where human beings are confronted with a whole new set of circumstances they must master. By trial and error they attempt to manipulate and control their financial destinies or forget old knowledge and experiment with old failures in new conditions. In the Mutable phase, they learn the lessons of boom and bust. In the Fixed phase, they are cautious and wise. In Fixed phases they prosper.

Within the Mutation cycle is the phase of Saturn making squares to its own place. At the opposition points which occur roughly at 15 year intervals, the market makes a major shift, the severity will depend on the position of Jupiter at the time.

The first Saturn return has Jupiter in opposition, which is the disaster point of the 60-Year Cycle, and the point where the most severe dislocation occurs.

Saturn and Jupiter also respond according to the strength, weakness or neutrality in a given sign and point up areas of maximum constriction and maximum growth.

All major changes and shifts first show themselves in Mutable signs. Be particularly alert to the signs of Virgo and Sagittarius when looking for major tops and bottoms. The Sun and Moon are the chief timers of the Jupiter-Saturn movements, though eclipses and Mars provide a different kind of timer which will be discussed later.

Saturn is particularly dislocating when passing through Capricorn and Aquarius. When Jupiter in Virgo coincides, the absolute bottom has been or is about to be reached.

Observe the passages of Saturn and Jupiter through the houses of the national or market chart. Saturn in the first quadrant is very difficult. Saturn in the 2nd house is especially hard.

Eclipses

Eclipses are usually prominent when a market fails. Because we have two to five eclipses a year, an eclipse is hardly an indicator of a market collapse or economic crash. They are timers and triggers of other conditions.

Scorpio-Taurus eclipses are especially lethal as they indicate money and debt. Other eclipses are more relevant to individual charts. The United States has trouble with those in Aries-Libra and Virgo-Pisces. The keys to the eclipse appear to be its financial involvement with the entity chart and its south node connection to Mars. What an eclipse actually does will be discussed in chapter eight, the Solar Field.

Trends

Most of this discussion has centered around planetary interactions that are global in impact. We do live on a planet, Earth, and so we do and must partake of all general trends. As we become more and more a part of international markets these global indicators will have an even greater impact than in prior times, giving individual countries less leeway in solving their own financial difficulties.

The Saturn return with Jupiter in opposition took place in September of 1989. Even though the Dow rose higher, weaknesses in the economy began to display themselves. Corporate earnings declined. Real estate prices fell. Interest rates remained high. The boom of the 1980s came to a halt. We can expect a major correction locally and globally. Saturn passes Capricorn and Aquarius through 1993. However, Jupiter transited Virgo in 1992, a likely indicator of the major bottom globally.

Jupiter in Cancer for the United States means increasing taxes or increasing debt. Saturn in Capricorn means decreased purchasing power for the population and failing banks. From the perspective of the United States chart, Jupiter in Cancer means wealth for our enemies and allies. Since the major upheaval coincides with the onset of the European Common Market, it should initially have a negative impact on the global economy, either because of trade restrictions to counteract it or because of trade wars to achieve position and advantage.

This phase is also complicated by the Lesser Air Mutation, with which it began. Our decline will not look exactly like the last. We are turning to human and humane solutions for economic problems. If we are successful our prosperity will form around a slightly different social order. If we are not, we may jump prematurely into what Eastern Europe is trying to give up.

Precautions, Patterns, and Profits

- Expect a major market correction every 60 years.

- The correction occurs when Saturn opposes Jupiter in the mutable phase of the Mutation cycle.

- Any Jupiter-Saturn conjunction or opposition reflects a major disruption or correction in the economy.

- 1992 should be the bottom of the global downturn.

- Prosperity will be difficult before the year 2000.

- Jupiter-Saturn conjunctions are good buy signals.

- Sell just before the oppositions or sell short.

Chapter Eight

THE SOLAR FIELD

The Sun and its movement has always been the center of man's interest and man's observation, the heart of the calendar, the 24-hour day, the 365.25 day year. All planetary movement, by the nature of the Zodiac itself, is interpreted relative to the Sun. Although the ancients chose Earth as the center of the universe—it is, indeed, our center—they recognized the centrality of the Sun not only to all existence, but to all activity. Whether or not they could prove it as the physical center of our planetary system is moot. Philosophically, intellectually, and symbolically they placed it right where it is, at the core.

As we have seen in earlier chapters, we must have a financial base that creates stability, confidence, and predictability. So far, in the history of mankind, gold is the only commodity that has been able to fill that standard. The gold standard halted the banking crises of 1873 and 1933. In the latter part of the 19th century when the gold bugs battled the free silver advocates for domination of the currency the U.S. economy only sporadically got off the ground. Up until 1960, with the combination of massive gold inflow from a favorable balance of payments and a firm gold standard we prospered as we have never before in our history.

The Solar Field describes the fluctuations that occur in spite of a stable standard of value, and the fluctuations in the standard of value itself. No system grants stability. Markets are always flexible.

The Solar Field is defined by the Sun, the Earth, and the nodes of the Moon. The nodes of the Moon are intersections of the path of the Moon with the path of the Sun. In terms of planetary activity, they define the area where eclipses take place.

The Earth, of course, is where we are doing business. For the benefit of those who know little about astrology and for modern students who pay more attention to the mathematics of planetary motion than the actualities of planetary motion, the following explanation is in order.

The Earth is always in the sign of the Zodiac opposite the Sun. Whenever a planet or the Moon is aligned with the Earth (in conjunction), it is also opposite the Sun. The Earth and its satellite, the Moon, form a unit relative to the Sun. The Moon is a general indicator of value on the level of demand. When the Moon is on the dark side, from fourth quarter to New Moon to first quarter, the demand side is lighter. When the Moon is on the bright side, from first quarter to Full Moon to fourth quarter, demand runs high, often reaching a peak at the Full Moon, and dying out at the New Moon. Most observers in financial fields have noticed this loose, though like the inconstant Moon, not wholly reliable indicator of the monthly tides of human commerce.

In astrology we define the Earth activity primarily by the Moon. The measurable range of the Moon's travel along the ecliptic defines its area of operation. The nodes mark the edges of the Moon's travel along the ecliptic in the Solar Field. In the graph of the Solar Field they are the parallel lines that cross in the direction opposite to that of the Earth and Sun.

Throughout 1980 many astrologers warned against the dire economic consequences of the Uranus-Saturn conjunction. Each time it occurred, nothing outstanding happened in the market. At its most potent, it occurred outside the Solar Field. By the time it entered the field in December, it had already lost most of its punch. Do not confuse the economic playing field with the ability of severe planetary dislocations and aspects to reflect havoc on the earth. During that period of heavy outer planet conjunctions we were subject to a disaster a day—plane crashes, earthquakes, hurricanes. These have economic consequences to be sure, but not in the marketplace, which is what we are discussing here.

From this first rule of astrological reality, we can draw the conclusion: *all significant activity takes place in the Solar Field.*

The economic corollary is: *all economic activity occurs against a standard of value, regardless of the actions of governments and banks.*

Visual Patterns

Astrology began as an observation not a calculation. In order to understand what the planets do and what the true repetitive patterns are we have to understand what the heavens look like.

The planets fall into three classes. The newly discovered planets (Uranus, Neptune, and Pluto), which cannot be seen with the naked eye; the inner planets, Venus and Mercury, whose orbits lie between the Earth and the Sun; and the old "outer" planets (Mars, Jupiter, and Saturn), whose orbits lie outside our own.

For the purposes of this discussion we will cover only the classic planets. The planets beyond Saturn will be discussed at a later time. They are relatively unimportant to the design and function of the Solar Field.

Three bodies are capable of moving between us and the Sun; Moon, Venus, and Mercury. The others never cross between us and the Sun; Mars, Jupiter, and Saturn.

All planets beyond us, except Mars, cross the Solar Field once a year. Mars crosses the Solar Field about every two years. The Moon enters the Solar Field once a month, the two week period when the Moon and Sun are in the same area between the nodes simultaneously. Mercury and Venus are almost always in the Solar Field.

Venus and Mercury appear to us as satellites of the Sun just as our Moon would appear to others as our satellite. Satellites have phases. They also appear and disappear more erratically than planets that make a more stately and dignified progress across the celestial vault.

One month they are on one side of the Sun. We see them early in the morning before the Sun comes into view. Another month they are on the other side. We see them early in the evening shortly after the Sun sets. Sometimes they disappear like wayward children playing hide-and-seek. When either Mercury or Venus appear as morning stars, they forecast the rising of the Sun. They are messengers in the eastern sky that herald the light of day. As evening stars they set after the Sun in the west to warn us of the coming dark.

Mercury is the planet of trade. Venus is the planet of investment. Together they represent the two major types of financial transaction: short term buying and selling, and long term buying and holding.

When planets are in the Solar Field we cannot see them except shortly before sunrise and after sunset, because they are too close to the Sun. They are above us in the daytime sky. Planets that are directly above us, culminating, and those that are rising and setting are strong. Mercury and Venus are strongest when we cannot see them. Their position as morning or evening stars are the only things that give us a clue.

As we have indicated earlier, the Moon is the planet of consumerism, so though it has relevance to buying and selling particularly on the retail level, it has a very short cycle and often acts as a trigger of activity rather than a determinant.

Planets in opposition to the Sun have a similar importance though not as strong as the conjunction. They rise as the Sun sets and set as the Sun rises. They dominate the nighttime sky. Of these, Mars is the most prominent. At its opposition it is retrograde and at its closest point to the Earth. It hangs brightly and firmly in the nighttime sky.

The inner planets are called the personal planets because they are the ones we see the most, see the best, and give us the most information about ourselves in our daily lives. Venus is the prime determinant of bear markets and bulls. The Moon is the monthly variance. Mercury shows short term rises and falls, and Mars inexplicable market jumps.

While these planets are not determinants of precise rises and falls in the Dow-Jones Industrial Average, they do reflect general market psychology and inclination. This book's research is pegged to the Dow because: it has been around for 100 years and gives a much longer perspective on what has been happening in our economy; its multiples reflect the inflation in our economy in the appropriate *de facto* proportion; other market averages generally replicate its moves. Like the price of gold, it helps us put in perspective what money manipulation and statistics often confuse.

The Solar Field

On the 360° ephemeris, the graph of the Solar Field, we see the movements of Mercury and Venus as a spiral about the Sun, the caduceus, a symbol of healing, and the double helix, the fundamental structure of genetic information. As modern science comes closer and closer to truth, we discover that ancient symbols exactly describe the result. The Sun is the

Solar Field 1956—Ahead and Following

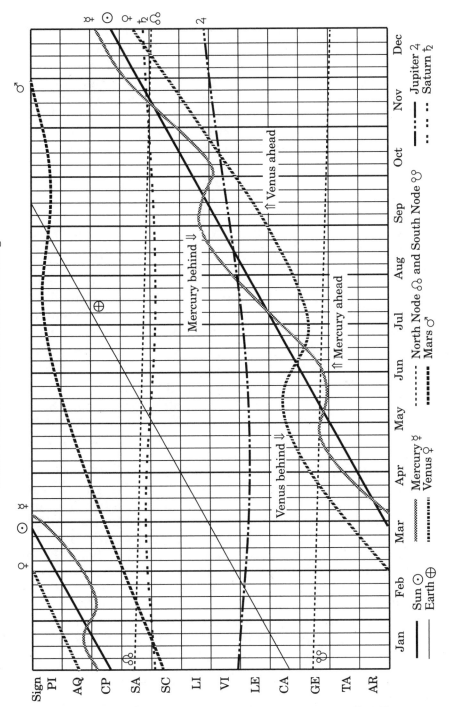

Sun ☉
Earth ⊕

Mercury ☿
Venus ♀

North Node ☊ and South Node ☋
Mars ♂

Jupiter ♃
Saturn ♄

⇓ Mercury behind

⇑ Venus ahead

⇑ Mercury ahead

⇓ Venus behind

planet of life energy. Mercury is the planet of information. Venus is the planet of balance and mating. In economics, the Sun is the standard of value, the vitality of the economy. Mercury is the process of trading, the intelligence that gives an accounting. Venus is the fair exchange. Mercury with its short cycle refers to traders and speculators, who move quickly in and out of the market for profit. Venus represents investors, who are looking for value, who are willing to wait a year or more to show a return.

Either planet heralding the day indicates calculation and confidence. All is done with the eyes wide open. Either planet heralding the night looks to past activity for profit, is nervous about the future, and seeks to get the best deal. Buyers and traders "sleep on it."

Although the following discussion may appear highly technical, it is quite simple if you refer to the illustration. The Sun is the bold line with the strong straight upward slant. Venus and Mercury curve around it. When either is above the Sun, it is an evening star, rising after the Sun. When below, it is a morning star, rising ahead of the the Sun.

Venus

Venus is a planet of modulation and balance. We have seen how the market tends to double and fall by half. From 1890 to 1920 the trading range was 40+ to 100. From 1933 to 1953 it was the same. The post 1960 market stayed in a trading range of 450 to 1,000 until the 1980s.

If a standard of value were maintained and no other factors intruded, the movement of Venus would correlate to a steady pattern of market advances and declines. Over a two-year term the market would circle the norm determined by the Sun and the Mutation planets. Of course, other factors intervene, some at predictable intervals, like the planet Mars. Others, though random to the mathematical eye, are predictable from mundane charts, those of countries and businesses.

The full Venus period of 588 days runs from the Venus Inferior Conjunction of the Sun to the next Inferior Conjunction. Because Venus revolves around the Sun between us and the Sun, she will align with the Sun (the conjunction) once when she is between us and the Sun, and once when she is on the Sun's far side.

Her Inferior Conjunction occurs when Venus is between the Earth and the Sun and in the same Zodiacal degree as the Sun.

This always happens during her retrograde period. Every eight years Venus makes the Inferior Conjunction within a degree or two of her original position, marking a full Venus round. On the graph the Venus line crosses the Sun line on a downward slant at the Inferior Conjunction.

Her alignment with the Sun on the far side is called a Superior Conjunction. On the graph the Venus line crosses the Sun line on an upward slant at the Superior Conjunction.

When Venus forms a conjunction, we lose sight of her. She disappears for about 14 days during an Inferior Conjunction—swallowed up by the light of the Sun. She disappears for as long as 84 days during the Superior Conjunction as her speed (from our viewpoint) is much slower.

When Venus is ahead of the Sun, moving from the Inferior to the Superior Conjunction, she acts like Taurus, buying everything in sight. When she follows the Sun, moving from the Superior to Inferior Conjunction, she acts like Libra, more inclined to sell or get her money's worth. When Venus disappears she acts like Pisces and either blows the bankroll or makes a fortune. Usually she does a bit of both, often a frenzy of activity up to the Conjunction, followed by a hangover after.

Mercury

The shorter term 115-day cycle of Mercury follows the same patterns of rising ahead and after the Sun. The Mercury line crosses the Sun line on a downward slant at Inferior Conjunction, when it is between us and the Sun, and on an upward slant at the Superior Conjunction, when it is on the Sun's far side. When it rises after the Sun (above) from Superior Conjunction to Inferior, Mercury acts like Virgo, profit taking, afraid to be left holding the bag. When it rises ahead of the Sun (below) from Inferior Conjunction to Superior, Mercury acts like Gemini, confident it has the market all figured out. When it rises ahead, the morning star, traders are cautious but acquisitive. They become buyers and investors. Mercury following the Sun indicates trader concern and selling, they go back to making tough deals.

Although Gemini Mercury never holds on to anything but paper profits, morning star Mercury is confident there will be plenty of Venus people to buy. Virgo Mercury is afraid the market will dry up.

The Inferior Conjunction of either planet signals the beginning of a buying phase. The Superior Conjunction signifies the start of a selling period. When Mercury goes behind the Sun for about 20 days on the Superior Conjunction and about 10 on the Inferior, we have a period of trader uncertainty as the currency and the market adjusts to more stable values. That leaves 40 days of buying or selling in between purely on the trading psychology and the manipulations of the Mercurial marketeers.

Constellations

The constellations tell us why we associate Venus and Mercury with bull and bear markets. Venus rules the sign of Taurus, which is the Bull, and a sign of accumulation. The constellation of the Bull lies in the Zodiacal sign of Gemini, which is ruled by Mercury. In a bull market both investors and traders are accumulating money and stocks. Venus acts like Taurus in a bull market.

The constellation of Ursa Major, the Great Bear, is adjacent to the constellation Leo (the Sun, gold), which is in the Zodiacal sign of Virgo, ruled by Mercury. Ursa Minor, the Little Bear, is directly north of the junction of the constellations of Virgo and Libra, and of the Zodiacal sign of Libra ruled by Venus. Libra is the sign of barter—when the Sun is "sick" in Virgo, Venus investors become Libra traders. Mercury traders turn Virgo and lose confidence. A bear market is in effect.

History shows us the great crashes in the American stock market occurred with the Sun in either Virgo or Libra.

The Bull Market

The fundamental bull market is marked by Venus rising ahead of the Sun, the period between her Inferior Conjunction to the Sun (retrograde) and her Superior Conjunction (direct). The bull market is very easy to see and predict with the Solar Field graph: the Venus line curves below the Sun, a sack ready to be filled. Investors are *in* the market and building assets. The psychological attitude is one of confidence.

A fundamental bull market began in October 1986 with a Dow around 1,900 and culminated in August 1987, when the Dow hit 2,700. The next bull market, as defined by Venus, started in June 1988 with the Dow around 1,900 and completed April 1989 with the Dow at 2,300.

Solar Field 1955—Bull and Bear

Venus Bear

Venus Bull

Sun ☉ —— Mercury ☿ ······· North Node ☊ and South Node ☋ ···-··- Jupiter ♃
Earth ⊕ Venus ♀ Mars ♂ ···· Saturn ♄

167

The Bear Market

The fundamental bear market is one in which investors either take profits or are reluctant to enter, have little confidence in the future, as represented by Venus rising after the Sun, from Superior Conjunction to Inferior. On the graph the Venus line curves above the Sun, dumping out her goods. The mass of buyers dry up. Investors become traders. The Dow stagnates, or stays in a trading range, as traders and investors try to take advantage of every rise as soon as it occurs. At worst, it sets the stage for disastrous drops when negative indicators add fear and panic. In essence this Libran Venus market tries to correct and stabilize.

The Venusian bear started August 1987 with the Dow at 2,700 and ended June 1988 with the Dow at 1,900, exactly where it began at the previous Venus bull. This is a textbook case of what would happen if there were no interference from other planets or outside economic forces.

The next bear began April 1989 with the Dow at 2,200 and ended in February 1990 at 2,500 having reached a top of 2,800. While that seems to go against the interpretation, two other factors intervened. Jupiter and Mars transits of the Solar Field should have driven the Dow to 3,000 or more, but the bear Venus did not have the confidence to hold on and wait. In the next bull market, the Dow nudged 3,000.

When Venus is ahead of the Sun, the ups will be higher than the downs overall. The disaster transits, which will be covered later, will not have as bad an effect as expected, or the market will quickly recover. When Venus rises after the Sun, the highs are usually lower than the previous highs as the market tries to correct down to previous lows. In the absence of disaster transits, the market will stay level. In the presence of disaster transits, the market will dive or crash.

Astrology indicates events by an accumulation of pressures rather than a point-to-point or specific pattern of planetary interaction. We can safely conclude that the market will not peak with Venus after the Sun, the Venus bear. It will rebound from a crash with Venus ahead of the Sun, the Venus bull, at least until Venus goes behind and everyone loses confidence.

In the disaster year of 1914, when the market closed for four months, it bottomed during the Venus bear. By the time it reopened and began a climb, Venus was in its bull phase. In 1974 the market peaked in July with Venus ahead of the Sun. It hit bottom in December with Venus behind the Sun. Although the market rose during this Venus bear, it never went beyond its 1974 high. It rose even higher once it entered the bull phase, which marked the start of a major extended rise. In 1929 the market crashed during the bull phase, which indicated that the fall had a long way to go. It hit absolute bottom during a Venus bear.

All things being equal, Venus ahead of the Sun will signify a bull market, and Venus following the Sun, a bear. If for other reasons, which will be delineated later, the market rises or falls: a rise in a Venus bear could be even better than it looks; higher highs are coming in the Venus bull phase; a fall in a Venus bull means you ain't seen anything yet. If, however, the rise in a Venus bear or fall in a Venus bull is due to Mutation factors, the interplay of Jupiter and Saturn, the above rule does not apply. Remember that we have two separate factors at play: the Solar Field and the Mutation cycle. They work independent of one another, though they produce a single result, market effects.

Venus is the great modulator. It keeps trying to maintain a consistent level. Venus tends to achieve the same price that it held during any similar stage in its relationship to the Sun. If two-thirds into its bull or bear phase the Dow was 1,200, it will, all other things being equal, be 1,200 the next similar phase.

Conjunctions

Conjunctions are alignments of any planets or points to other planets or points. The most important conjunction in the Solar Field is a conjunction with the Sun. On the graph it appears as a planetary or nodal line that crosses the Sun line. The traditional term for a planet forming a conjunction with the Sun from a 17° to 10° range is combust. The planetary energy is being swallowed up by the Sun. In practice, with respect to the actions of the market relative to the motions of Venus and Mercury, the orb appears to be 10°. When the planet forms an exact (also called partile) conjunction with the Sun, a situation called Cazimi, the Sun impresses its full power on the planet. One might call it a phoenix aspect. The body burns up, is regenerated, and eventually appears in a different form.

The Dow always rises when any planet makes a conjunction with the Sun. The rise may be large or small, depending on the planet, but there is always a rise that day.

Correlations to the DJIA show that a market shift (major or minor, up or down) when either Mercury or Venus is 10° from the Sun on either side. These are the points of disappearance and emergence. Mercury is the messenger of the Sun. Mercury-Sun conjunctions mark the times when Mercury returns to get the message. The message Mercury carries back into the market depends on the sign through which the Sun is passing.

Though the market gears for its bull or bear phase at the conjunctions, the phase does not begin in earnest until the planets show themselves. If the market is to remain stable, it will correct down during the disappearance so it can rise in a bull phase or correct up so it can fall in a bear phase. This happens in an orderly market, not one that is being shaken up by other factors, such as the frenzy stage of the Jupiter-Saturn Mutable Mutation.

Both Venus and Mercury appear to lose their influence when behind the Sun. Since Venus is the basic modulator, and Mercury is the planet of sharp trading, they subordinate themselves to the primary function of the Sun to stabilize the currency and level the playing field. During most of the recovery from November 1929 to April 1930, Venus was behind the Sun and not making a major impact. After she came back into view on the bear side, the market fell. When she reappeared after the Inferior Conjunction, the end of her retrograde period, on the side of the bull, the market showed an advance. It continued to advance until Venus went back into hiding prior to her bear phase, at which time it started its precipitous fall to the all time low just before she reappeared to signal the start of a new bull.

Ancient astrology was visual and observational. The appearance of Venus as a morning star was a bad omen. Correlations with the Dow and with any reappearance of Mercury or Venus suggests the reappearance marks a turning point, good or bad. They also confirm that the appearance of the planets relative to one another is more important than their mathematical relationships.

Solar Fluctuations and Gold

While Mercury and Venus weave in and out, the Sun is reflecting the money standards by its sign positions, which tell us of the relative value of our currency to gold and how it affects trade. The price of gold usually hits a high in Leo, an intermediate low in Libra, a turnaround in Sagittarius, a low in Aquarius and an intermediate high in Aries. Gold prices rise from the south node to the north node and fall from the north node to the south node. This means either the currency is getting stronger or the monetary base is contracting.

There is a general rise in prices from the Sun's passage from Capricorn to Cancer and a general fall in prices from Cancer to Capricorn. This represents the Sun's declination, most southerly at 0° Capricorn and most northerly at 0° Cancer. It crosses the equator at Aries and Libra, time periods when the market tries to correct.

If the Sun is in its bull phase from Cancer to Capricorn and Venus is in her bear, the market can stabilize or rise. The market also tends to rise when the Sun is going from south node to north node, which can counter Venus bear or bull indications.

The price of gold, however, rises from Cancer to Capricorn and falls from Capricorn to Cancer, counter to the market moves. It rises from the south node to the north node, the same way the market moves. The most difficult period of the Sun, where the greatest falls are likely to occur, is from Virgo through Scorpio.

The Sun in Leo puts a high price on gold and starts a contraction in the paper money supply. Gold supply and the trading medium contract through the signs of the Sun's weakness, Virgo through Libra. Prices fall because there is insufficient trading medium to cover this traditional time of harvest. As money is borrowed to bridge the gap, prices start to rise. The price of gold increases and peaks in Sagittarius as the commodity becomes plentiful, which, in turn, drives the price of gold down in Capricorn and puts more money back in circulation. Thus, the stock market tends to fall from the Sun's passage from Cancer to Capricorn and rise from Capricorn to Cancer. The price of gold does the reverse.

If this is hard to follow, an example may help. Suppose you want to buy a car. In August the price is $15,000 dollars for the car you wish to buy. You have $16,000 in your bank account, leaving you only $1,000 for other expenditures. Your car is a popular model, so people deplete the supply, the price either remains stable or rises. In December a new shipment rolls off the assembly line. In January car salesmen offer all sorts of deals to make buying attractive, the price falls to $14,000. If you waited, you not only have the car but $2,000 of discretionary income left over. The car squeeze, like the gold squeeze, drives the price up. The gold glut, like the car glut, drives the price down.

Lunar Fluctuations and Silver

The Moon, which represents silver prices, appears as a series of very steep lines on the Solar Field graph. (Not shown in the 1956 illustration.) Silver has always been a very volatile commodity, partially because it is so susceptible to overproduction. When the Lunar line crosses the Sun line, this is a New Moon. Silver hits the low for the month and starts to rise. When the Lunar line crosses the Earth line, this is a Full Moon, and indicates the monthly peak.

The highest prices for silver come at Full Moons in Taurus, Cancer, and to a lesser extent, Pisces. These occur when the Sun is in Scorpio, end of October through most of November; when the Sun is in Capricorn, end of December through most of January; and when the Sun is in Virgo, end of August through most of September. Except for these periods, silver prices usually follow the movements of gold.

The Interplay

As you can see from the graph, Mercury and Venus are sometimes on the same side of the Sun, at others they are on opposite sides. When they are on the same side in a Venus bull market, the Mercury traders are eager to buy and sell. When they are on opposite sides the traders find willing investors to sell to, though they are reluctant to buy themselves. When they are on the same side in a Venus bear market, both investors and traders are in a mood to take profits and unload. When they are on opposite sides, the traders buy on speculation, trying to guess the bottom.

Some Venus bulls start with Mercury selling, others start with Mercury buying. Some start in the middle of either. All ways will have slightly different impacts.

A balanced market is one that has buyers and sellers in it. Mercury and Venus on opposite sides of the Sun, regardless of their bullish or bearish positions, usually correlates with healthy trading, a rise on the Dow or a stable market. Buyers are available for those who want to sell. Sometimes the buyers are investors who find traders, ready to take a quick profit, confident the market will eventually go higher after the next correction, which they create for themselves. (Venus ahead of the Sun, Mercury following.) Sometimes they are traders willing to unload investors of their down stocks as they hold for future profit. (Mercury ahead, Venus following.)

Occasionally, the investors and the traders both sell, which create more serious downturns in the bear market. (Both Venus and Mercury following the Sun.) Occasionally they are both in a buying mood with nobody who wants to sell. (Venus and Mercury both ahead.) Though one would think that this would create a shortage and therefore rising prices, not necessarily. Sometimes there is simply no interest. The traders keep the market going. The investors sit back and hold on, wait and see. When the traders are holding, little happens. Early in the bull market, this condition usually correlates with a drop in the Dow. Late in the bull market, Mercury on the same side as Venus can forecast a feverish high, particularly if Mercury rises ahead of Venus. The sign of the Sun will indicate whether the mid-phase joining of Mercury and Venus either ahead or following, will equate to an up or a down.

Just as Venus is a natural planet of patience and caution, Mercury as the messenger of the Sun, is often a planet of speculation and confidence. Although Mercury usually appears between Venus and the Sun, it rises ahead of Venus towards the end of a mature bull, or appears rising ahead of the Sun alone when Venus disappears behind the great regulator. Look for market highs here, though they are a danger sign that the bull has run its course. This happened in August 1987.

As Venus emerges from behind the Sun, Mercury may set beyond her position. This happens at the beginning of the bear market. If the second condition follows quickly upon the first, a major correction is indicated. This was the situation between

August and October 1987. Anytime Mercury outstrips Venus, either leading her in rising or following her in setting, we have a condition where speculation outstrips common sense.

This is very easy to see on the graph, the Venus line gets very close to the Sun and the Mercury line is either above or below her. This situation occurs when Mercury and Venus make their Superior Conjunctions close in time to one another or Mercury makes an Inferior Conjunction while Venus is making her Superior Conjunction on the opposite side.

In either a Venus bear or bull market the direction of price movements generally follow the shifts of Mercury: rising during its direct motion, falling during its retrograde motion. In a Venus bull the rises are ever higher. In a Venus bear, they tend mainly to correct. The trading stays in a range.

Conjunctions, Oppositions, and Squares

Mercury and Venus form two kinds of conjunctions and four kinds of oppositions.

Conjunction I—Both Between Earth and Sun

When they make contact during their simultaneous retrograde motions, the market tends to go up as it did in June 1988. In forming conjunctions to one another, buyers and sellers pair up, as they are simultaneously being energized by the Sun. The time period is only 10–14 days, which indicates a short, sharp run-up in some commodity. In June 1988 it was sugar. In December 1989 it was oil. Speculation is rampant.

Conjunction II—Both on the Far Side of the Sun

When they join each other and the Sun in direct motion, the Superior Conjunction, we have a major turn in the market, such as the high of August 1987, which was followed by the crashlet of October. In this situation Mercury rises ahead of Venus when moving towards the Sun and rises after Venus when moving away. Both are danger signals that trading has overreached the amount of money available to finance it. Perception is more important than reality under these conditions. If the Sun's sign indicate an up market, Mercury and Venus will dive in with all the confidence in the world. If the Sun's sign is pessimistic, Venus and Mercury will pull it down after contact is made.

The Sun is an especially dominant force when Mercury and Venus are combust, that is, they are blotted out by the light of the Sun. In a discouraging sign or in its decline phase it brings the market down as it did after the Jupiter-Saturn opposition of July 1990. With Mars doing its buying frenzy in August 1990 in Leo it drove the market wildly up.

Opposition I

When Mercury is making an Inferior Conjunction while Venus is making a Superior Conjunction, they are on opposite sides of the Sun, and therefore, in a condition of heliocentric opposition from the point of view of the Earth. This indicates a strong turn to a bear market.

Opposition II

When Mercury is making a Superior Conjunction while Venus is making an Inferior Conjunction, this opposition indicates the beginning of the bull market. Oppositions always limit in some way.

Opposition III—The Square

When Mercury and Venus make a visually heliocentric opposition at the start of a Venus bull (one is a morning star and the other an evening star), there is usually a drop until Venus makes her station. At the start of a Venus bear, the market rises to the Mercury station, the point where the Mercury line changes direction, then drops.

Opposition IV—The Square

When Mercury and Venus are farthest apart from each other and from the Sun, there is usually a drop or turn in the market. This is not to be confused with a genuine heliocentric opposition, it is where they appear to be at extreme ends from the point of view of the Earth. The most severe is when they are in a sextile aspect (60° or two signs apart) to one another, relatively rare. The range is from 30° to 60° plus or minus and takes a bit of time to spot in either a standard or graphic ephemeris. It often happens a week or two from a heliocentric opposition. These represent a pause, much like a quarter moon.

Visual Patterns

The Bow

When one planet is direct and the other retrograde, you will see a definite crossover on the graph. If this happens simultaneous with a conjunction to the Sun, expect a major shift in market direction. This also correlates with a square aspect at the fullest parts of the Bow. When the Bow occurs on the ecliptic the market reacts to a square, an opposition, and another square in rather quick succession, producing a price fluctuation that resembles a heart attack.

This pattern was very strong in the 1929–1932 period when the market was in its greatest disruption. A spectacular Bow occurred in June–July 1932 just as the market hit its all time low.

The Sheaf

When Mercury and Venus form Superior Conjunctions with the Sun simultaneously, the market tends to top. August 1987 saw a spectacular convergence of Sun, Mercury, Venus, and Mars.

The Swirl

When Venus and Mercury form Inferior Conjunctions with the Sun simultaneously, a graceful S-curve forms on the graph. Because both planets are at their closest point to the Earth, there is usually a feverish up market somewhere. Highly speculative. The rise usually goes from the first retrograde to the last retrograde with a bump up in the middle. The intensity will depend on the sign of the Sun.

From 1981–1985 most passages of Mercury and Venus relative to one another did not sharply contact the Solar Field in any the above patterns. Approximations appeared, but they did not form sharp designs around the solar path. From late 1985 to 1987 individual cycles began to converge. Sharp correlations equate to major moves and major disruptions.

One other factor shows up in price levels relative to our two game players. Their phases are similar to the phases of the Moon. Prices tend to fall when either are at their greatest distances from the Sun. On the sell side they rise until they hit maximum elongation, then fall. On the buy side they fall to maximum elongation then rise.

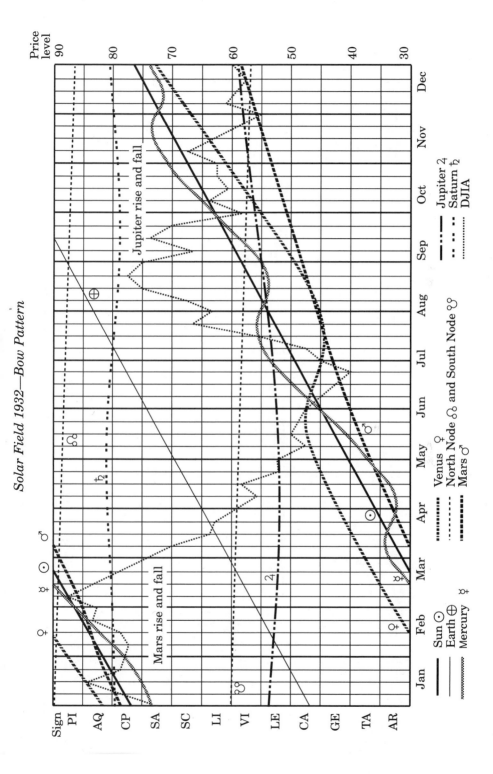

Solar Field 1932—Bow Pattern

Jupiter rise and fall

Mars rise and fall

Sun ⊙
Earth ⊕
Mercury ☿

Venus ♀
North Node ☊ and South Node ☋
Mars ♂

Jupiter ♃
Saturn ♄
DJIA

Price level: 90, 80, 70, 60, 50, 40, 30

Jan Feb Mar Apr May Jun Jul Aug Sep Oct Nov Dec

Sign: PI AQ CP SA SC LI VI LE CA GE TA AR

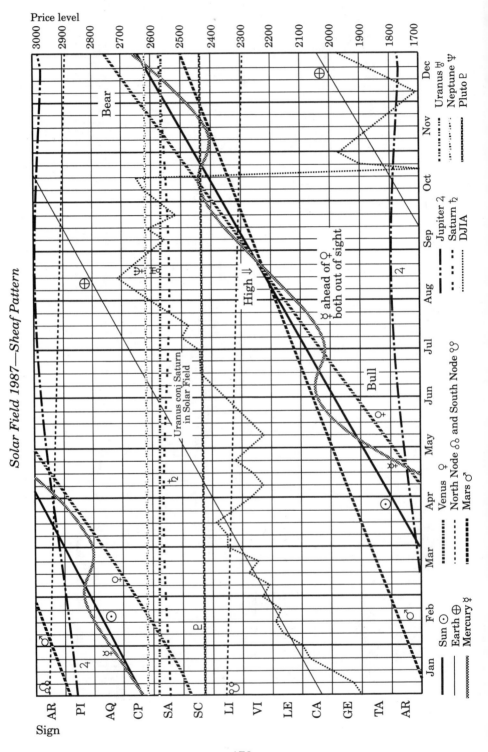

Solar Field 1987—Sheaf Pattern

Price level

3000 2900 2800 2700 2600 2500 2400 2300 2200 2100 2000 1900 1800 1700

Bear

Uranus conj Saturn
in Solar Field

High ⇓

♀ ahead of ♀
both out of sight

Bull

Sun ☉
Earth ⊕
Mercury ☿

Venus ♀
North Node ☊ and South Node ☋
Mars ♂

Jupiter ♃
Saturn ♄
DJIA

Uranus ♅
Neptune ♆
Pluto ♇

Jan Feb Mar Apr May Jun Jul Aug Sep Oct Nov Dec

Sign

AR PI AQ CP SA SC LI VI LE CA GE TA AR

178

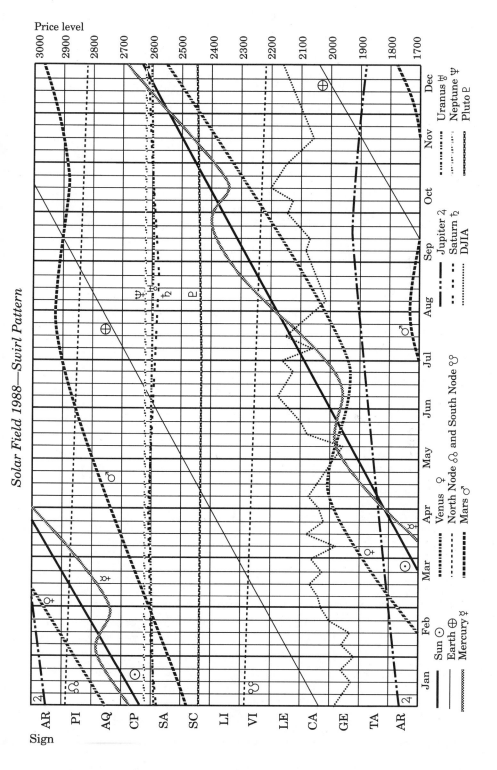

Solar Field 1988—Swirl Pattern

Price level

3000 2900 2800 2700 2600 2500 2400 2300 2200 2100 2000 1900 1800 1700

Sign

AR PI AQ CP SA SC LI VI LE CA GE TA AR

Jan Feb Mar Apr May Jun Jul Aug Sep Oct Nov Dec

Sun ☉   Jupiter ♃   Uranus ♅
Earth ⊕   Saturn ♄   Neptune ♆
Mercury ☿   DJIA   Pluto ♇
Venus ♀
North Node ☊ and South Node ☋
Mars ♂

179

Maximum elongation, the greatest distance from the Sun, occurs near the beginning and end of retrograde periods, when either appear as downward slants on the graph. The movements of Mercury in this respect are more noteworthy than those of Venus, because they happen more often. When either planet is at its farthest from the Sun, economic activity loses its economic moorings, its sound financial base. When Venus and Mercury are farthest from one another, buyers and sellers are far apart. If you are confused about what these planetary relationships mean, simply look at the picture of it. Far apart on the scale means far apart in life. The Venus curve on the bottom means the buyers are filling their sacks. The same curve on the top means assets are being given up or lost, the coffers are emptying. The same applies to Mercury.

Market Trends

When you try to analyze you will find that cycles offset each other. Do not be alarmed. That is perfectly normal. Major moves are going to be as striking with respect to planetary reinforcement as they are in life.

The Moon

The Moon is in the Solar Field about two weeks per month. On a graphic ephemeris the moon shows as a very steep line. When she crosses the node into the Sun's field, she will have a stronger impact than when she is outside. Her conjunctions to other planets have an effect when she is in the Solar Field. The effect is much less when she is outside.

The movement of the Moon from the south node to the north node generally signals an upward movement of prices, peaking out when she crosses the north node. The movement of the Moon from north node to south node indicates falling prices, the low occurring as she transits the south node.

The movement from New Moon to Full also creates upward pressure, while the movement from Full Moon to New creates downward pressure. Observations of this movement over a year in time show an increasing pattern of divergence of the two cycles then convergence at eclipses. Because these waves are not in sync most of the time, they require a special interpretation. The primary and strongest movement is the Moon from node to node. When the Moon is outside the Solar Field the New Moon-Full Moon pattern takes over. The market always changes direction when the Moon crosses the nodes, up from the south, down from the north. You always see a low and an upturn at the New Moon, a high and a downturn at the Full.

The market also experiences down blips at apogee, perigee, zero degree declination, and maximum declinations north and south. These do not appear to indicate trends, more likely daily aberrations. The Moon sign also appears to have some impact. We have noted market tops and bottoms in Virgo. Taurus is often a down sign, though Fixed signs generally maintain price levels. Mutable signs usually have an up day and a down day. Cardinal signs are indicators of new moves.

Eclipses

Eclipses reverse the Solar Field as the Sun and Moon cross the nodes. The price movement also reverses itself. Prices *fall* to a *north node* solar eclipse then rise. Prices *rise* to a *south node* solar eclipse then drop. A lunar eclipse with the Moon at the north node represents a drop followed by a rise and at the south node a rise followed by a fall. Often lunar and solar eclipses precede and follow one another rapidly, creating a major price swing and an immediate correction. When one occurs alone, the jolt is less severe. Often it indicates a long unbroken trend because there is no counterbalance. The reverse movement is only at the eclipse. The market immediately gets back to the normal price movement of up from south to north node and New Moon to Full.

In other words, a south node solar eclipse starts a falling market. A north node solar eclipse starts a rising market, especially if it stands alone or follows a lunar eclipse. Lunar eclipses appear to be more potent than solar eclipses, especially if they follow solar eclipses. A north node lunar eclipse signals a rise. A south node lunar eclipse signals a decline. Eclipses reverse market direction. Occasionally, they go contrary to themselves if other factors are strong enough.

If an eclipse also occurs on an important degree of a national or mundane chart, the adjustment will be more severe. On October 7, 1987, the lunar eclipse hit the United States Saturn, always a trouble spot for money.

Nodes

When the Sun crosses the node, planets that were in the playing field are suddenly out. Those that were out are suddenly in. These are the few times in a year when either Mercury or Venus or both are out of the playing field. Their upward or

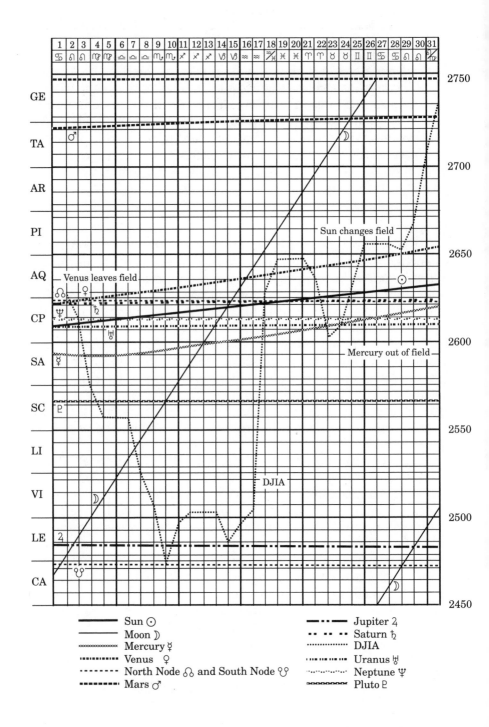

Solar Field January 1991—Solar Eclipse

182

downward pressure is removed temporarily. Eclipse conjunctions and oppositions have such a powerful effect because the usual modulators are knocked out of the field of activity. To see this on the graph, cover what has preceded the crossover point of any of these planets. On rare occasions, both Mercury and Venus will be either left in the old Field by the Sun or precede him into the new.

Mars

Mars, the planet of sex, death, and debt, visits the Solar Field every two years, fertilizes Venus, the planet of money and love, then goes his merry way, leaving the rest of us to pick up the pieces. As in all planetary visits to the Solar Field the contact of Mars and the Sun produce a rise in the market, often accompanied by feverish activity. August 1987 saw a rare convergence of Mars, Venus, Mercury and the Sun all at one time. After the Sun-Mars conjunction, there is a sharp drop. If Mars hits Venus after he hits the Sun the market will quickly recover. If he gets to Venus first, during her bear phase, there is no instantaneous reprieve.

The Mars line on the ephemeris stays the most distant from the Sun line and dips across the Earth line during its retrograde period (downward slant). When it enters the field it swoops down on the Sun and its companions. The market takes a sharp upward rise.

By itself Mars represents losses, cutting prices, and interest rates. As Mars enters the Solar Field and as it contacts the Sun interest rates fall. They tend to fall or stay low while in the Solar Field and when moving from north node to south node. They tend to peak at the Mars retrograde opposition to the Sun, when moving from south node to north node, and stay high or rise when out of the Solar Field.

As with all the planets beyond us, the Sun usually changes the Solar Field to bring them in. They rarely cross a node to enter it. The passage of Mars over a node is especially significant. Mars conjunct the south node heralds trouble. Mars crossed the south node on October 12, 1987. Mars over the north node often signals a peak though not necessarily a fall afterwards, much depends on whether it is moving into the Solar Field or out of it. If it is moving out the rise will be sustained. Mars moving in at either node is more likely to signal disruption.

Jupiter

Jupiter is the planet of bounty and confidence. As it moves into the Sun it pushes market prices up. It does the same with Mercury and Venus and everything it touches. A rising market will go even higher. A falling market will temporarily pull itself out of a slump. Once the contacts are made, prices fall, though not as drastically as they do with other planets.

Saturn

Saturn is the planet of reality and adjustment. Saturn is the great leveler. As it moves into the core of the Solar Field and interacts with Mercury, Venus and the Sun, the market rises and falls sharply after each contact. The rise is high if it contacts Venus and Mercury before it hits the Sun. The conjunction with the Sun produces an upturn then a sharp decline. Contact with Mercury and Venus after the conjunction with the Sun produce small rises and a more severe downturn.

Any contact with Saturn illustrates a market level, either a top, a bottom, or a trading range. When Saturn left the Sun and Mercury in December 1987 the market was about 2,000. It stayed pretty much in the 1,900 to 2,100 range until the start of the next Venus bull in June 1988.

Jupiter and Saturn

Because of their nature as timers of the larger economic cycle, these planets move to a rhythm of their own. The market always adjusts at their conjunction and opposition. The conjunction usually starts a rise out of economic difficulties. The opposition indicates the beginning of a fall. These were covered in an earlier chapter. *The Mutation has a cycle of its own and will drive markets up and down regardless of the conditions in the Solar Field.*

Uranus

Uranus is a planet of disturbances and reversal. It can indicate foreign money, a change in the rules, breaking the rules, or a sharp pullout of funds. The recovery after the December low in 1987 coincided with the passage of both Uranus and Neptune through the core of the Solar Field. Uranus, Neptune, and Pluto often break market barriers and price levels. They produce 100 point breakthroughs, up or down.

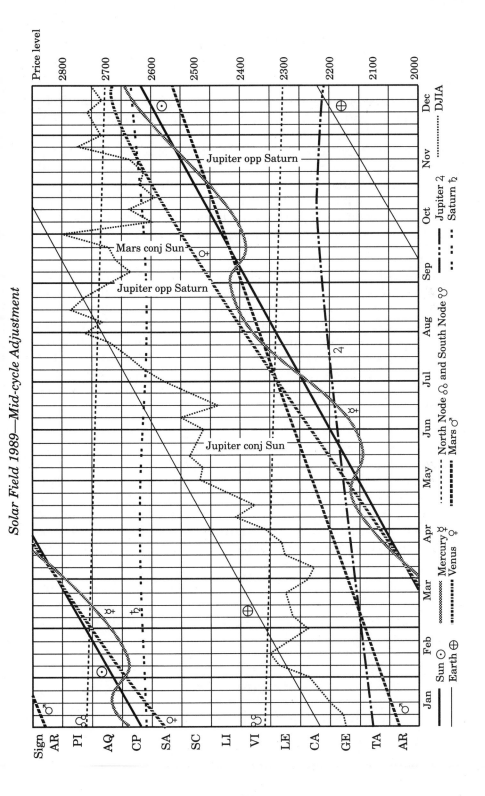

Solar Field 1989—Mid-cycle Adjustment

Neptune

Neptune is the planet of inflation and illusion, also an indicator of foreign funds and manipulation and deception. Its contact with the core of the Solar Field usually brings huge rises, often to new price levels, though the real gains may be illusory or temporary. Euphoria often accompanies Neptune in a bull phase, unease, uncertainty, and panic in a bear. Neptune takes on the coloration of planets with which it is in contact. If in contact with destructive planets during its passage, the mood is frightened. When you think of Neptune, think of excess.

Pluto

You like pain? Think of Pluto. Pluto is the wipeout planet. Pluto hit Mercury and entered the core of the Solar Field on October 6, 1987. It hit Venus on October 17, Mercury again on October 24, the Sun on November 2. As usual, the contact with the Sun brought the Dow back up, but Pluto hit Mercury again on November 19, and Mars on December 11, to bring the Dow almost back to the October low. Pluto is another debt/interest rate planet, that equates with massive money pullouts and bankruptcies.

Subcycles

Other subcycles exist relative to the Sun. The movement of any planet from conjunction to opposition, from when its line crosses the Sun to when it crosses the Earth, usually suggests rising costs/prices. The movement from opposition to conjunction, from its line crossing the Earth to its crossing the Sun, usually means falling. This is more useful in trying to judge market sectors and commodities than market averages.

Principles

To forecast markets, one must correlate a number of complex forces that often counteract one another, which is why in the long run in a non-inflating economy, there is little change in price.

Prices Rise

- From conjunction to opposition.
- From Sun in Capricorn to Cancer.
- With Venus rising ahead of the Sun.

- From the south node to the north node.
- From New Moon to Full.
- Any planet's conjunction with the Sun.
- High rises occur with Mars, Jupiter, Saturn, Uranus and Neptune passages through the Solar Field.
- When the inner planets form Swirls and Sheafs.

Some horary rules indicate that signs of short ascension mean low prices, just the reverse of the above rule. Others indicate that Capricorn to Cancer means you buy high and sell low. Cancer to Capricorn means you buy low and sell high. Observation of the Dow suggests the latter.

Solar conjunctions *always* indicate a price rise, no matter which planets are involved, though preceding contacts with Venus or Mercury may push prices down.

Prices Fall

- Prices fall from opposition to conjunction.
- From the Sun in Cancer to Capricorn.
- From the north node to the south node.
- From Full Moon to New.
- Immediately after conjunctions to the Sun, especially Saturn and Mars.
- At most Mercury retrogrades.
- Mercury 10° from the Sun.
- When Venus and Mercury move towards their greatest distances from one another, especially the sextile.
- With Venus rising after the Sun.
- Planets in Virgo.

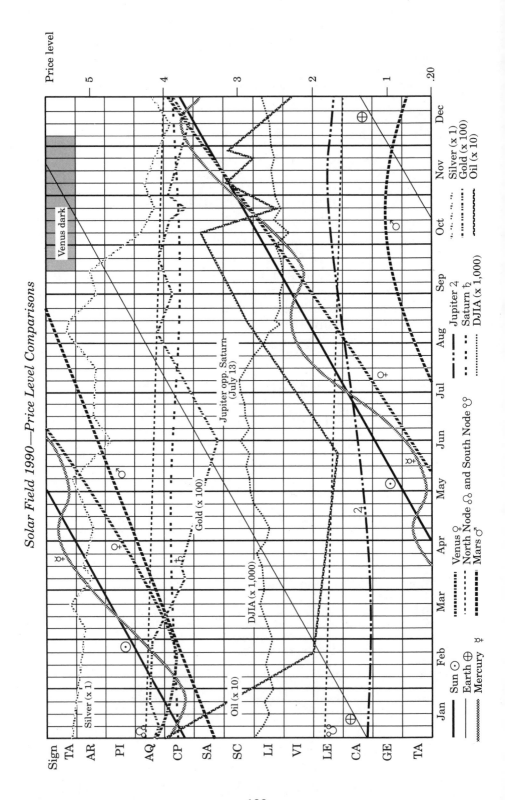

Solar Field 1990—Price Level Comparisons

Sign · Price level

Silver (x 1) · Gold (x 100) · Oil (x 10)

Jupiter ♃ · Saturn ♄ · DJIA (x 1,000)

North Node ☊ and South Node ☋

Sun ☉ · Venus ♀ · Mars ♂

Earth ⊕ · Mercury ☿

Venus dark

Jupiter opp. Saturn (July 13)

Gold (x 100)

DJIA (x 1,000)

Oil (x 10)

Silver (x 1)

188

Trend Breaks and Shifts

- Eclipses.

- Nodal passages, especially the Sun and Mars.

- Mercury outside the orb of Venus.

- Mercury and Venus invisible.

- Mutable sign passages, especially Virgo and Sagittarius.

- 15°, especially of mutables.

- Jupiter-Saturn conjunctions and oppositions.

- When the inner planets form Bows.

Mercury is a market maker, most stable when in the opposite phase of Venus: providing buyers for sellers and vice versa. Mercury has a reputation as a trickster. In the middle or late Venus cycle, he often pulls the market up when on the same side, according to the sign position of the Sun.

When the Sun, Moon, Mercury, or Venus cross the nodes, the inner planets and the Moon can be out of the Solar Field for as much as a month. Whichever one stays in will determine whether it is an accumulate or take profit time. Mercury and Venus lose power as regulators when they are 10° from the Sun. For Mercury this is 10 days before and after Superior Conjunction and five days before and after Inferior Conjunction. For Venus this can be as long as 42 days before and after Superior Conjunction and seven days before and after Inferior Conjunction. The biggest shifts in prices often occur in these "dark" times, up or down.

The periods of "hiding" for both Mercury and Venus equate to the economy's attempt to correct itself to find a true value. Venus went behind the Sun on September 22, 1990. After the Jupiter transit of the Solar Field drove the Dow almost to 3,000, the Jupiter-Saturn opposition drove it down. The north node lunar eclipse that followed the solar eclipse drove it down further. Retrograde Mercury tried to revive it, but right after its conjunction with the Sun, Venus went dark. If you look closely at the graph, you will see that when the Sun crossed the south node, Venus was bumped out of the Solar Field so her conjunction with Jupiter had no great effect. She got back in just as Mercury was about to turn retrograde and contact the Sun, but the effect was short-lived. In addition, the Sun was in the Cancer to Capricorn down period and Mars was about to turn retrograde, indicating that interest rates had just about peaked.

Price movements in commodities seem to be most affected at Mercury and Venus retrogrades. Pay particular attention to Venus and Mercury in the same sign as each other and the Sun.

With commodities the supply is opposite the price movement. Mercury usually correlates with some shipping difficulty or problems in moving the commodity from one place to another. Venus is the financial pressure itself and the demand. In the case of the 1989 oil run-up, the refining capacity was down, and the combination of extremely cold weather and disruptions in distribution aggravated the problem.

If we only had the Sun, Mercury, Venus, and Mars to deal with, we'd have a market that circles around a predictable level with an occasional jolt that drove it up on a fad or down on a disaster. But, we have governments and laws, Saturn and Jupiter, that give it an extra twist, to jump the high range and break the low. As we move into the global market, we add Neptune, Uranus, and Pluto. The numbers get bigger. The range expands. The dance remains the same.

Precautions, Patterns, and Profits

- All important activity occurs in the Solar Field.

- Buy from Venus stationary direct, to Venus conjunct the Sun. Sell from Venus' reappearance to her retrograde station.

- Buy from Mercury stationary direct, to Mercury conjunct the Sun. Sell from its reappearance to its retrograde station.

- Buy just as Mars enters the Solar Field. Sell at Mars conjunct Sun or sell short just before.

- Buy before Sun in Capricorn. Sell before Sun in Cancer.

- Buy after planets conjunct the south node. Sell as they conjunct the north.

- Sell at any Solar conjunction. Buy after.

- Buy gold in Aquarius and Libra. Sell in Aries and Leo.

- Buy silver at New Moons. Sell at Full, especially Taurus, Cancer and Pisces.

- Eclipses reverse the Solar Field and disrupt trends. Stay away till after the shakeout.

- Sell towards the Full Moon or the Moon conjunct the north node. Buy at the New Moon or conjunct the south node.

Part III

DESIGNS

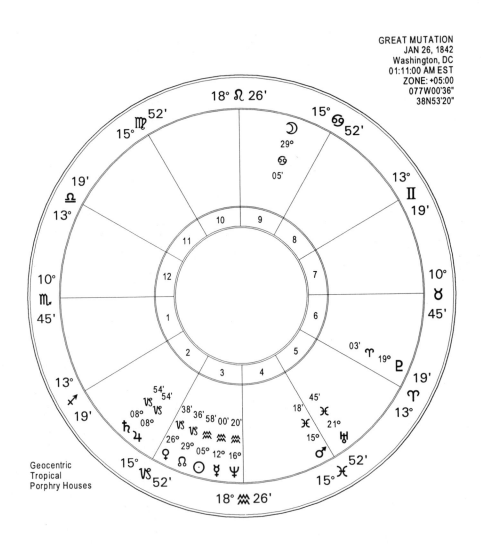

GREAT MUTATION
JAN 26, 1842
Washington, DC
01:11:00 AM EST
ZONE: +05:00
077W00'36"
38N53'20"

Great Mutation—Washington, D.C.

Chapter Nine

SPOT CHECKS

A lthough all economic activity takes place in a global context, every event does not affect every nation, every market, every person, or every tradable commodity with the same force. Each has its own rhythm of prosperity and decline. Certain celestial configurations impact markets and regions apart from any formal social or political organization. The global design is neutral. Only the targets experience good or bad. A blue sky is dandy for a picnic. Gray skies are best for staying in bed.

The focus of the world and its commodities and trade is the Great Mutation chart. The localized effect of the Great Mutation is the chart calculated for the longitude and latitude of the place. For a country it is its capital at the moment the Great Mutation occurred. Because of the revolution of the Earth, every location on earth has different critical points, the angles of the chart. The United States and Washington, D.C. have Scorpio rising, London has Capricorn rising, Baghdad has Pisces rising. Rising and culminating degrees (the Ascendant and Midheaven) can be calculated for any location on Earth for the Mutation's local and regional impact. The Great Mutation is not solely an economic indicator, but a social and political one, as well. Like national charts, it can help connect unusual social and political movements to their market effects.

Each planet on the Great Mutation chart represents a commodity or an activity of social, political, and economic interest. The degree in which it resides is critical to the variations in the price/supply of the commodity or economic sector it represents.

When Pluto transited 5° of Scorpio, the degree square the Mutation Sun, at 5° of Aquarius, the price of gold dropped over $100 an ounce. When Pluto transited square Neptune, the price of oil spiked during the extreme cold of December 1989. Pluto on the same degree in early fall of 1990 spiked oil prices because of Iraq's invasion of Kuwait. The first coincided with a dual retrogradation of Mercury and Venus, always a signal of high run-ups and speculative activity, the latter drove up the price apart from any cyclical or predictable market moves. These points, because they are on a chart that represents social, political, and economic realities, can spot moves in the market that do not come from the market alone.

Abstract and predictable cycles tell us the normal progress of financial and economic cycles. The Mutation chart gives us the convergence of these cycles, their locational impact, and more important, any non-cyclical changes in price and supply.

The following chart provides a quick reference for the impact of planets transiting the Mutation degrees. These are not part of any planetary cycle. They are simply degrees and their 15° shadows on the Great Mutation chart. This chart will remain in effect for the rest of the Earth Mutation. The Mutation chart of 2020 will shift this degree emphasis to their positions at the first permanent Mutation in Air.

To refresh your memory, the Cardinal signs are Aries, Cancer, Libra, and Capricorn; the Fixed signs are Taurus, Leo, Scorpio and Aquarius; the Mutable signs are Gemini, Virgo, Sagittarius, and Pisces. The planetary transits of degree areas are simple to pick out in a standard ephemeris. The impact of the planetary transits are in declining strength from the outer planets in: Pluto, the strongest, followed by Neptune, Uranus, Saturn, Jupiter, Mars, Sun, Venus, Mercury, and the Moon. Mars through Mercury have only a slight impact, mostly on a daily level, for the Moon only a couple of hours.

Mutation Degrees

For the United States, 10° Fixed and 25° Mutable act on the rising sign. The impact on the MC (Midheaven, 10th house cusp) is 18° Fixed and 3° Cardinal. The Ascendant represents the people and the social, political, and economic life of the country. The MC represents the president and the government.

Mutation Degrees			
Degree	**Point**	**Commodity or Condition**	**Major Impact**
5°/20°	Sun	Gold, heads of state, the standard of value, the money pool.	5° Fixed 20° Mutable
29°/14°	Moon	Silver, perishables, housing, the family, consumers, the public.	29° Cardinal 14° Fixed
12°/27°	Mercury	Mercury, transportation, machinery, exports, commerce, grains, and paper.	12° Fixed 27° Mutable
26°/11°	Venus	Copper, art, jewelry, treaties, land, sugar, cattle, money, and banks.	26° Cardinal 11° Fixed
15°/0°	Mars	Iron and steel, debt, interest rates, speculation, war, loss, and competition.	15° Mutable 0° Fixed
8°/23°	Jupiter	Tin, law, imports, abundance, growth, confidence, distribution systems, supply.	8° Cardinal 23° Fixed
8°/23°	Saturn	Lead, authority, production, scarcity, contraction, retail, and the market.	8° Cardinal 23° Fixed
21°/6°	Uranus	Electricity, electronics, technology, mutual funds, arbitrary acts, cartels, conglomerates, and revolutions.	21° Mutable 6° Fixed
16°/1°	Neptune	Oil, plastics, junk bonds, inflation, garbage, film, chemicals, alcohol, drugs, multinationals, and contagion.	16° Fixed 1° Cardinal
19°/4°	Pluto	Atomic power, toxic waste, violence, hostile takeovers, bankruptcies, venereal disease, addiction, commissions.	19° Cardinal 4° Fixed

The sensitive degree areas are: 0°, 1°, 5°, 8°, 12°, 15°, 16°, 19°, 20°, 21°, 23°, 25°, 26°, and 29° for everyone. For the U.S, the sensitive areas are 3°, 10°, 18°, and 25°.

Of these, the strongest are 8° and 23° (the degrees of the Mutation), and 5° and 20°, the degrees of the Sun.

Critical passages that produce multiple disruptions occur at 15°, 16°, 29°, 0°, and 1° degrees of the Moon, Mars, and Neptune confluences. One can understand the trading frenzy during the oil crisis of December 1989, particularly in the home heating sector, with Pluto at 16° of Scorpio.

The other highly critical areas are 5°, 8°, 19°, 20°, 21°, and 23°. Not only does this group together Sun, Pluto, Uranus, Jupiter and Saturn of the Mutation chart, but Mars, Neptune, and Uranus of the U.S. national chart and probably the Ascendant and Midheaven, too. Saturn made its station at 18°+ of Capricorn and was in this highly active area of the chart through most of 1990. The invasion of Kuwait precipitated the United States' gearing for war and gathering allies throughout the world. Both Pluto and Saturn were in these degrees at the end of the year and Uranus transited the Mutation degree. The late Capricorn eclipse on January 15, 1991 transited the U.S. Pluto, a planet of crisis and the ruler of its Mutation chart. War began the next day.

Much is made of aspects and their importance, and rightly so. However, any planet in the same numerical degree or 15° distant from it will have some impact, no matter what the aspect, no matter how slight.

The operative aspects are:

CONJUNCTION 0° separation

SEMI-SEXTILE 30° separation

SEMI-SQUARE 45° separation

SEXTILE 60° separation

SQUARE 90° separation

TRINE 120° separation

SESQUIQUADRATE 135° separation

QUINCUNX (or inconjunct) 150° separation

OPPOSITION 180° separation.

In order of importance: conjunction, opposition, and square.

A major difference between trines, sextiles, semi-sextiles and inconjuncts is the former has a slightly wider orb of influence under normal conditions. When marking degree areas the difference is irrelevant.

Actual semi-squares and sesquiquadrates are more important than the 15° addition that falls in modes that do not create the 45° and 135° aspect. However, they do operate. All 15° increments reflect the 24th harmonic, which operates in matters financial and economic.

While this may seem complicated, the key is to remember the numbers. If a planet or node is in the number that corresponds to a point or planet on the Mutation chart, or a factor of 15° distant from it, the commodity or trading will be affected.

How to Use the Degrees

While any transit, large or small, will have some effect while in the exact degree or its 15° shadow, if the Mutation degree is very early or late, (the Jupiter Saturn conjunction is 8°54' of Capricorn), there may be a slight lag over into the 9° area. More often than not, the effect lasts only through the actual minutes of the governing number. The question is not orb, but duration in the degree area as defined by the whole number, not the added minutes. Although not addressed in this work, the symbolic interpretation of the degree gives some clues as to the nature of the event or the people involved.

The two days of a Mars transit over 8°/23° usually coincide with a small drop in the Dow. A heavy transit over these points by Saturn, Uranus, Neptune or Pluto usually creates a major market disruption some time during their passage. Allow only 5' beyond the sign if the planet is in a very early or late minute of the actual degree.

One exception to precision in degree transits is the planetary Station. A planetary Station is the point at which the planet changes its motion from direct to retrograde or vice versa. This is marked in an ephemeris by D for Direct and R for Retrograde. On the graphic ephemeris the planetary line changes from an upward direction to a downward or vice versa. A planetary Station operates with a tolerance of a full degree on either side. Thus, a planet making a Station at 9° or 7° would effect the Mutation degree at eight.

The second exception is two planets straddling the degree. Uranus at 9° and Mars at 7° would affect Saturn-Jupiter at 8°.

Because these planets represent commodities on a world-wide scale, the Mutation chart represents overall world supply, demand, and price. Whether the price rises or falls depends on the nature of the transit and whether the investment is a commodity, a trade, or a speculation.

Interpretation

Commodities and trades usually operate inversely. A Pluto disruption of a *commodity* indicates a constriction or low supply in the commodity, therefore, the price rises. Pluto on the *market* degree, 8° of the Jupiter-Saturn conjunction, indicates a drop in price. The exception is gold. Pluto on gold, the standard of trade, drops the price of gold, which raises the value of paper money. Where gold is not the actual medium of exchange, the Pluto disruption of gold indicates a shrinkage in the money supply and therefore, a lowering of the gold price. Were gold traded as a commodity the reverse would be true. Today the gold degree is more an inverse scorekeeper of the value of our paper money than a commodity in its own right.

The major trigger for any social/political/economic activity is first, the Jupiter-Saturn conjunction itself; second, the particular entities a Mutation planet represents; and third, the impact on the particular country or geographical sector, as indicated by its rising and culminating degrees. All major world economic upheavals take place in the degree of the Jupiter-Saturn conjunction, 8° of Capricorn. Conjunctions, squares, and oppositions indicate major events. All planets in 8° of anything will have some effect. Twenty-three degrees of Fixed signs are next in strength but all 15° increments have some impact.

The second area of judgment is of the nature of the transiting planet. A transit of Venus does not have the effect of a transit of Neptune, or Mercury the impact of Saturn, but there is usually a blip in activity, particularly when no other movements are pulling in a different direction.

Uranus was in the 23° area of Sagittarius from July 1987 through November. The stock market rose, then crashed. Saturn was in 23° of Sagittarius in September 1929 when the market hit the all time high. Uranus was in 8° of Aries when the market crashed.

One may argue that these activities may not be entirely due to the harmonic of the Mutation Jupiter and Saturn. The United States has Neptune at 22° of Virgo, which may account for Mutable 22°/23° disasters. Uranus in the natal U.S. chart is just under 8° of Gemini. The combination of the Mutation numbers and the U.S. numbers account for the great activity in these numerical degrees, especially in the United States.

The markets as indicated by the DJIA rise or fall on transits to these places. The key issue is the duplication of energy on both the Mutation degrees and the degrees of the United States chart, which will be discussed in the next chapter. The combination is the reason for the localized effect.

Action of Transits to the Mutation Harmonic

- Sun—up

- Mercury—up

- Venus—up

- Mars and Pluto—down

- Jupiter and Neptune—up

- Saturn—up then down

- Uranus—instability

- Direct node—down

- Retrograde node—up

Uranus, Neptune, and Pluto in these degrees usually signal new market highs or lows, or breakthroughs of previous barriers. Occasionally these will be spectacular if other things support. Often, they indicate breaking a barrier or critical point: a 100 or 1,000 point barrier on the upside or the down or a change of 100 points.

Do not confuse the actions of these planets on the degrees with their fundamental or transit interpretations to individual charts. Uranus, especially, is inclined to some kind of disruption or break in the trend. It is rarely sustained. Think of Uranus as an explosion. Lots of fireworks followed by debris. The amount of debris is determined by other trends already in place.

The action of these planets on the degree of a commodity, relative to the behavior of that commodity, is slightly different. Mars and Pluto usually equate to feverish speculation. The supply of the commodity contracts, often through manipulation. The price rises. As mentioned earlier, the exception is gold. Pluto in the gold degree drops the price of gold, in contradistinction to Pluto in the Neptune degree, which raises the price of oil. While we should expect the planets of abundance to drop the price of commodities, this is not always the case. Inflation is the culprit. When Neptune and Jupiter transit a commodity degree, they indicate that the commodity price is absorbing its share of the inflated money base. In stable money times, this should be a drop in price. The caution in any commodity trading is to know the market and the climatic, social, and political events that could effect supply and distribution, to know whether Jupiter or Neptune is likely to be an oversupply or a flow of inflated currency into the product.

At the present writing, Jupiter is in the gold degree and is transiting the sign of Leo. Jupiter in Leo brings abundance of gold. The combination at this time indicates an oversupply of gold and a drop in price. If Saturn were transiting Leo, indicating shortages in gold, Jupiter on the degree could raise the price. When trading in precious metals reached the frenzy stage at the end of the 1970s and the turn of the decade, Jupiter in Leo gave an abundance of gold at the same time that Uranus and Neptune in a gold degree were indicating that gold was both absorbing inflation and creating a mania around itself. Any time the price rises drastically in a commodity, more of the commodity comes into circulation, especially if, like gold, it has been either dormant or hoarded. Such a condition eventually leads to a correction down.

Uranus

Uranus can go up or down. It usually does both. Mostly it is a danger signal that the trend is about to make a serious change. How serious depends on other indicators. Although Uranus can drive a market up, the price level will crash at some point.

Neptune

Neptune is usually unrealistically up. If other factors support, there will be frenzied buying. Neptune almost made it to 8° in 1987, but Uranus intercepted and crashed the market before it could go absolutely crazy. Interestingly enough in 1988 Neptune stayed in the 8° area as the market slowly and quietly pulled itself up. Though the market had risen by almost 400 points by mid-year (a rise that would have caused hysteria in earlier times) nobody noticed. Such is the fate of Neptune.

Though one might expect to see Neptune as a factor in a panicky slide, the degree involvement appears to be positive. After the disastrous bottom of the market in July 1932, Neptune entered 8° of Virgo. The market started back up. Neptune is hope despite all evidence to the contrary.

Pluto

Pluto is always down as a market factor, often disastrously down, but it can be either price or supply. Pluto was in 8° of Scorpio in October 1987. Pluto hits the bottom and lies there. Something else has to start the upward move. Uranus has more of a bounce.

Moon

The Moon is relatively insignificant since it stays in the degrees for under two hours. While it may have some effect on hourly movements within a day's trading, the Moon's action is hardly noticeable unless the planetary field is devoid of all other activity, a very rare occasion. Lunar eclipses have a great impact, of course: usually a reversal of the current trend.

One of the great problems in any astrological analysis of economic factors is the multiplicity of distorting factors. One seldom sees "pure plays" in a planetary sense. However, the research in this book covers over 120 years. Every now and then a "pure play" appears.

The Mutation Chart Interpretation

Sun

The Sun in the Mutation chart is at 5° of Aquarius. It is widely conjunct Mercury and Neptune. The Sun in its fall indicates that gold will not be highly valued during this period, even though it has classically been the standard of exchange, especially in materialist phases of history. The interim period between the first Earth Mutation and this establishing Mutation saw several experiments with paper money. The disastrous *assignats* of John Law and Louis XIV kept people very suspicious of paper before the 1840s. In the United States the Civil

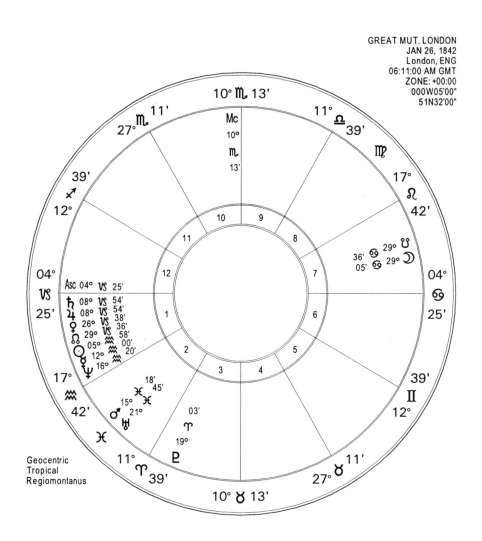

Geocentric
Tropical
Regiomontanus

Great Mutation—London

204

War occasioned new experimentation with paper. The Confederacy went bankrupt, as did the United States with "continentals" during the Revolution. Because the paper did fuel production throughout the 1860s, in the 1870s and beyond, there was a cry to restore the greenbacks that worked so well for so many during the Civil War.

One might say that the 20th Century has been the great experiment in learning how to replace gold with paper, an Air medium. The United States has been relatively successful—the 2nd house of the U.S. Mutation chart is ruled by the Jupiter of the Mutation conjunction. The United States represents one of the more successful efforts in this field.

London has the Sun in the 2nd. It is one of the major trading centers of gold. Berlin with Aquarius on the 2nd, its ruler, Saturn, conjunct Jupiter and the other, Uranus, conjunct Mars in Pisces has gone both ways. They had runaway inflation in the 1920s. They have shown great capacity to be prosperous and productive. Tokyo shows prosperity through other people's money. With gold in the 2nd, a great respect for the classic standard of value. In recent years the Japanese have been the major purchasers of platinum. Perhaps the Sun in Aquarius indicates that a new and rarer metal could supplant gold's position. Platinum would be a good candidate.

Sun in Aquarius also forecasts the spread of democracy and the fall of the monarchy. Today's despots fashion themselves as representatives of the good of the people, not would-be kings. The last great monarch in modern times was Queen Victoria. She was a woman, not a man.

Keep in mind the paper debacles between the establishment of Earth and its first appearance. Like Communism, the most likely social/political form of an Air Mutation, paper money collapsed during its first preview of the coming Mutation. Paper restored itself once the Earth Mutation established itself. Communism could, too.

Moon

The Moon, silver, is void-of-course in Cancer. Silver never seemed to go anywhere since the beginning of this Mutation. Before the Mutation the value of silver was $1.27 an ounce. It rarely ever made it close to that figure without government subsidies or highly unusual conditions, such as the Hunt silver maneuver of 1980–81. If silver had maintained its place relative to inflation, it should be selling at $12.70 an ounce. Historically, it has hovered around $.50 an ounce. Today it is below $5, an excellent signal to buy.

In 1963 silver was taken out of the currency, leaving us with no currency of any intrinsic value. Neptune hovered in the 14° area that year, the harmonic of the Mutation Moon. Pluto and Neptune stayed in that area through 1964. Even silver certificates were repudiated and discontinued. Silver and the Moon are inconstant commodities. Void-of-course in the Mutation chart, they were destined to go nowhere and to be insignificant in the economic practices of this Mutation period.

Despite great cries for free silver towards the end of the 19th century, silver was never able to maintain its value. Moon in Cancer makes silver plentiful. A plentiful commodity cannot be a standard of value.

Because Sun in Aquarius makes gold a non-plentiful commodity, gold could not be maintained as a standard of value during this Mutation either because there was insufficient specie to handle both growing productivity and growing populations, as well as the gap in time between the start of an enterprise and its profit at the marketplace. Gold simply is not fluid or plentiful enough for a production-driven Earth economy.

Mercury

Mercury in Aquarius indicates that trading will be highly organized, a group effort. It also points towards an ever increasing tendency towards an intellectual accounting rather than a material one, computer trading, the stock market, organized factory work, increasing depersonalization of trading. In short, instead of dickering, we have a price fixed by group consensus. The trading price fluctuates—Aquarius is not the most stable of signs. Many people determine trading transactions, not the old style one-on-one. Even in a world class bazaar like Hong Kong, though one dickers over every trade, it is often with reference to a price established elsewhere.

Aquarian trading took hold in the 20th century. The 1920s had their version of mutual funds as well as their mergers and acquisitions. Our stock market trading is almost totally dominated by the activities of huge pension funds, insurance funds, the billions invested in mutual funds. The debacle of October 1987 was precipitated by fund managers executing program trades all at once. If that does not represent Mercury conjunct Neptune in Aquarius, it is hard to imagine what does. When any planet hits 12°, the Mercury degree, unusual trading patterns occur. The nodes were in 12° of Scorpio/Taurus in the crash of 1929. Mercury made its station in 12°/13° of Scorpio in October 1987. Pluto made its station at 12° of Scorpio in July 1989: the S&L crisis that literally ripped billions of dollars out of circulation.

Venus

Venus is the planet of copper and of materials of intrinsic value, such as land. Venus in the late degrees of Capricorn forecasts the decline of copper, in value and in use. Several years ago, despite the fact that the copper in one cent pennies cost two cents, pennies continued to be minted. Copper prices fell to all time lows with Pluto in the late degrees of Libra. They are currently rising, but production lags. Venus in Capricorn indicates a burgeoning trade in manufactured goods and a market based economy. It also indicates government controlled economies. Venus conjunct the north node indicates that the money/manufacturing/government sector is a destiny driven factor in the era governed by this chart. With the south node conjunct the Moon, we can see the decline of agriculture and of home and family-based economic activity. People are no longer dependent on their families for survival but on their jobs.

Because the coming Mutation will be an Air and therefore, a collectivist era, we can see that this Earth Mutation has pulled us from the home and family into a group structured and group dependent economy that will naturally evolve into an impersonal and detached collective, where universal and international values will predominate over those of the clan and the nation, where brotherhood replaces motherhood.

Mars

Mars, the planet of iron and steel, interest rates and crashes, is destabilized and erratic because of its conjunction with Uranus in Pisces. We see how our industry was badly diminished by excessively high prices for iron and steel. We see how our system plays with interest rates to control the effects of inflation. Mars, as one of the ruling planets of the U.S. version of the Mutation, shows very clearly our own boom and bust pattern based on borrowed money, speculation (5th house), and risky group enterprises. Fifteen degrees is often involved in sharp market turns, both because it represents a movement half way into a sign and because it represents a hard contact with the Mutation Mars. Jupiter was in 15° of Gemini in the crash of 1929. Saturn was in 15° of Sagittarius in the crash of 1987.

Uranus

Uranus is the planet of unexpected turns and modern technology, particularly those connected with electricity—electronics, computers, and all transportation and communication systems, both global and extraterrestrial. Although the immediate effects were not economic in 1961, the first men orbited the Earth with Uranus making a station that year in 21° of Leo, quincunx the Mutation Uranus. Neptune passed over the U.S. Mutation Ascendant and Pluto trined the conjunction itself. In 1966, first Neptune, then Uranus hit the 21st degrees of their respective signs as unmanned vehicles landed on the Moon. On June 21, 1969, the first man stepped on the Moon. Pluto had made its station at 22°/21° of Virgo the month before, less than a degree from the opposition to Uranus, and was still in the 22nd degree. We did indeed slip the "surly bonds of earth." Note that Uranus rules the 4th house of the U.S. Mutation chart, and Neptune at 22° of Virgo in the U.S. natal chart also rules the 4th house. A rather fortuitous combination for a U.S. citizen's breaking his ties to home base.

Neptune

Neptune rules the chemical industry in general, and oil and oil-based products in particular. Neptune refers to all highly toxic, highly concentrated, and refined substances, anything that has undergone a process that removes it from its natural state. Neptune rules poison, drugs, alcohol, places of retreat and retirement, including hospitals, and all and any forms of self-destruction. It is glamour and hype, the film industry, all modern variations on old artistic processes and products. Jupiter in Pisces is a painting, Neptune in Pisces is a photograph.

The great oil debacle of the late 1970s occurred with major transits in the 16° area, the degree of the Mutation Neptune. Through 1977, 1978, and 1979, Saturn, Neptune, Pluto, or Uranus was always in a Mutation Neptune degree. The eclipses of 1980 and 1981 straddled the degree and oil prices topped. OPEC never reached the same level of power again.

Pluto

Pluto is nuclear power. It is debt of global proportions, which is why it has been so costly to produce the means to nuclear power. The underworld rises with Pluto, as do all forms of destruction. On the positive side Pluto kills to heal. It takes the deadwood and the hype out of the system, as it takes the diseased organ out of the body. Heroic measures to save lives as well as heroic measures to destroy life come under the realm of Pluto. The Mutation Pluto was not involved in the crashes of 1929 and 1987. Neither of them leveled the markets. Pluto came later at the bottoms.

The Mutation Pluto was opposed by the transiting Pluto in the oil, gold, and silver ploys of 1979 and 1980, where the prices were driven way beyond reason by the OPEC cartel and the Hunts' determination to corner the world market on silver. All the efforts collapsed as Pluto moved on. Pluto works in the dark and crashes in public, bringing hatred and disgrace.

Pluto is also the planet of hostile takeovers and the selling off of assets to reap huge profits that leave the corporation with nothing but streamlined debt.

Pluto always takes away the unhealthy and the ill-gotten gains. Unfortunately, many innocents are hurt in the process. Pluto is ultimately a planet of killing. Uranus is a planet of transmissible diseases. Neptune is a planet of epidemics. Pluto diseases always end in death.

It becomes very clear that the more planets of the Mutation chart are involved in any event, the greater the possibility for upheaval.

The United States Mutation Chart

The United States became a global economic leader because the Jupiter-Saturn conjunction occurred in the 2nd house of the U.S. natal chart and is heavily involved in the 2nd house (money and goods), and the 3rd house (trade and exports) of the U.S. version of the Mutation. It is an ideal combination for a production-driven, hunting economy, such as the U.S. economy.

With the passages of Saturn and Neptune over the Conjunction, our balance of trade became more and more precarious. We will not complete the dislocations until Uranus finishes its transit of the Mutation in 1991. After that, the United States will have a better chance of establishing more stable patterns of international trade.

Interpretation Recap

Look for important and heavy transits to the degree area of the planets on the Mutation chart. In most cases, the planet will have to be in the exact numerical degree to have an effect. However, in the case of Stations and eclipses, add a degree on either side. The orb is also extended if two planets straddle the degree. Conjunctions have the greatest impact, followed by oppositions, then squares and half-square configurations. Trines and sextiles follow next in that order. Their effect is of the nature of the planet. Trines and sextiles offer no resistance to bad things, they do not force good or bad. Semi-sextiles and inconjuncts are similar. Every movement in the same numerical degree has an impact. Planetary stations in the degree will be extremely strong no matter how light the aspect.

If the world is going to fundamentally change the way it does business, the Jupiter-Saturn conjunction will be affected. If it is going to have a major crisis in a particular area or with respect to a particular commodity or group of commodities, the planets will be affected. There were two eclipses in the 8° area, one in Taurus in 1976 and one in Libra in 1978—the oil crisis not only changed our way of doing business, but it redesigned our cars, and shifted a high degree of power to the Middle East oil producers. OPEC did not take over economic dominance of the world, but it became an important factor.

The Jupiter-Saturn conjunctions in 1981 at 9° and 5° of Libra mark a very serious shift in the balance of economic power on a global scale. Japan superseded the United States in many of its markets, the United States experienced severe economic problems with respect to its internal and external debts, and politically we saw an increasing trend towards conservatism.

The entry point of major global movements into a particular country will be primarily through the degree of its Mutation Ascendant. The ruling planet of the chart is important, as well. As in all astrological analysis, a buildup of factors will take precedence over any simple transit. If a buildup of factors occurs in both the national chart and the Mutation chart, a relatively light transit of either Ascendant could trigger the event.

The market crash of 1987 saw Venus, Mercury, and Pluto straddling and collecting light on the Mutation Ascendant degree. The August, September, and October time period has always been critical for the United States in terms of market highs and lows. In an earlier chapter we saw how the Sun in

Virgo through Scorpio reflected this lag time between major orders and their deliveries and therefore, between delivery and payment. The banking system is always strapped for cash during this period.

Astrologically, the Sun passes from the top of the Mutation chart in Leo (the 10th) and the critical point of entry of Scorpio (the 1st). If the United States is going to get caught in a global movement or activity over which it has little or no control it will happen in this last quarter of the year. It will be triggered by a transit in Scorpio. In the crash of 1929 the Mutation Ascendant was at the mid-point of the Sun at 5° of Scorpio and Mars at 15°. The south node was at 12°, the rising degree of New York. Because this event had global implications Uranus was at 8° of Aries, opposite the place where Mercury had made a Station at 8° of Libra the week before.

If we are looking for a causal factor in the world economic upheaval we can easily point to Uranus square the Mutation degree. In 1923, the year Germany experienced runaway inflation, Pluto was opposite the Mutation degree. Somebody's economic system was going to be destroyed. Neptune transited 17° to 19° of Leo that year, the rising number of the Berlin Mutation and its 8th, equal house. Saturn made a station at 19° of Libra square the Ascendant. Uranus made a station at 17° of Pisces. September saw an eclipse at 16° of Virgo. The 17° area is not important on the U.S. Mutation, nor is it important on the U.S. natal chart. In fact, the United States had Jupiter transiting the Mutation Ascendant. We did quite well.

Again we see a buildup of degrees and the importance of the rising degree in timing important national economic events. The rising degree represents the country itself and its people. Though economic events may be triggered by government activities, they often have little impact on the government, itself. The people always take the hit.

Scorpio Rising

Although we may not like to admit it, with Scorpio rising, our country thrives on the difficulties of others. Scorpio creates destruction or profits from it. As other nations become more prosperous we find our own prosperity in decay. We are at a serious turning point in the world economy. The coming transits to our Mutation chart suggest a worsening of our trade balances as

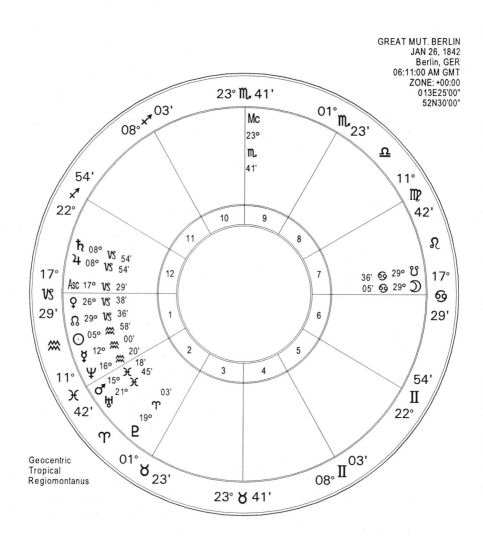

GREAT MUT. BERLIN
JAN 26, 1842
Berlin, GER
06:11:00 AM GMT
ZONE: +00:00
013E25'00"
52N30'00"

Great Mutation—Berlin

212

Saturn, Uranus, and Neptune transit the 3rd house of exports in the next few years. Exports determine our prosperity on this chart. The decline in exports on the Mutation chart corresponds with severe economic dislocation on the U. S. natal chart. This is exactly what happened in the 1930s.

Transits

- Uranus, Neptune, and Pluto as transits over these degrees, indicate unusual conditions, bubbles and crashes.

- Saturn and Jupiter represent normal rises and falls, which often have Mars as a timer.

- Mars does no great damage in and of itself, but will trigger many disasters.

- The Sun and the passage of any of these planets through the Solar Field also have a major impact when combined with any of the Mutation degrees.

- All major upheavals, either positive or negative, will be guided by the Jupiter-Saturn transits and major outer planet passages of critical Mutation degrees.

Bankruptcy

The outer planets indicate bankruptcy or incipient bankruptcy. Uranus does not pay its bills. Uranian money difficulties are usually handled by going into Chapter 11—interestingly enough, the number of its associated house. Neptune is too confused to realize the severity of the difficulty, is overly optimistic, and too muddled to reorganize. Matters drag out for years. Pluto is a willful bankruptcy, a tool to escape payment. Pluto steals. Neptune steals with excuses and good intentions. Uranus steals with group or government approval.

Uranus, Neptune, and Pluto materials are usually toxic and dangerous. When involved in economic activity, they are equally hostile to one's health, even when they seem to be creating prosperity. An arms manufacturer may achieve great wealth. His product still kills.

Houses

In interpreting mundane charts as to economic events and potential economic events in a given area, the nature of the planet and the house it rules are more important than its sign position alone. The planetary sign positions are, after all, the same for everyone. The signs on the Ascendant and MC are the most important, the others mainly as they impact their houses.

In individual, market, and national charts the signs are a clue to an understanding of how the entity will cope with circumstance on an impulsive basis. The Mutation as the global economic field is much more limited in its capacity to be effected by the will or the actions of its individual human or government components.

If we ever achieve a global government, maybe this will change. Should this occur, we can assume that the timing would be either the world capital or where the conjunction occurs either on the Ascendant or MC. The Jupiter-Saturn conjunction of the present Mutation occurs on the Mutation Ascendant of London. Great Britain did see the greatest days of her empire in this era and despite her ills, still continues to be a world power. England, in fact, led the Industrial Revolution and put in place business practices that would become universal. The Mutation is also conjunct the Sun and MC of the British national chart. Britannia indeed ruled the waves at the height of the Earth Mutation.

The progress of the transits over a Mutation angle moves from west to east. Thus, California is hit before New York, Los Angeles and San Francisco before Washington D.C. The crime connected to the drug culture, now reaching brutal proportions on the east coast, are the end result of the lawlessness of the drug culture that developed in the 1960s when Pluto was transiting the California Libra Ascendant. As Pluto swept east so did drug crime.

Consider California Mutation charts as an early warning system for the rest of the country—good or bad. Their heavy involvement with Pacific Rim economies and the passage of Neptune and Uranus through their 4th house will give us some clue to real estate and allocations of natural resources in the coming years. Pollution controls, the softening real estate market, and the shortage of water are likely to foreshadow increasing government power over the daily lives of American citizens.

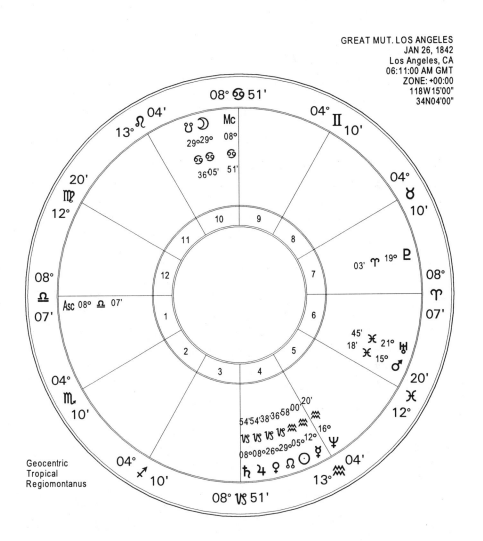

Geocentric
Tropical
Regiomontanus

Great Mutation—Los Angeles

215

While it has appeared that California has thrived in spite of deteriorating conditions in the rest of the country, it is only that outer transits can take several decades to show up in the East. California, with the Mutation in its 4th Mutation house, foreshadows the ultimate breakdown of property values. With the Air Mutation on its Ascendant, Californians will be the first to install the new consensus model of equity and trade.

The Mutation chart is what Mother Nature deals us. The national and individual chart, to be discussed in the next chapter, is what we do about what she does.

Precautions, Patterns, and Profits

- Degree areas of the Great Mutation chart represent general and specific areas of commodities and trade.

- Transits of Mutation chart degrees reflect non-cyclic moves in the market or the commodity they represent.

- Outer planets in the Mutation degree and its shadow, 8° and 23°, indicate market breakthroughs and advances or declines of 100 or more points.

- New point indicators will take over at the next Great Mutation in Air in 2020.

Chapter Ten

UNITED STATES CHARTS

Three charts forecast the impact of universal economic activity:

1. The natal chart of the country, company, or individual.
2. The Great Mutation, calculated for the capital or the geographical location, discussed in previous chapters.
3. In the United States, the chart of the New York Stock Exchange, as the primary trade mechanism of our capitalist system.

In this chapter we deal with astrological correlations to the relevant charts of the United States. The same rules apply to other countries, organizations of people, and individuals.

The inception or natal chart of a company, market, or nation helps us understand its attitudes towards the assets it controls, what it is likely to do in crisis or under stress, and its potential for making and losing money, how and when. The chart of the United States[1] shows it to be an economy run on debt. Because debt, in the long run, is inimical to the creation of lasting wealth, the United States experiences periods of boom and bust. The long period of prosperity the United States has enjoyed since the Great Depression was, as will be demonstrated, due to special conditions that created wealth for the country, not its normal pattern of buildup and decline.

---

1. The United States national chart appears on page 97.

Natal Chart

To understand a nation as a political entity, how its people organize themselves around their assets, production, and ideologies, we look to its natal or inception chart, the map of the heavens at the time of its birth, incorporation or charter. The persistent difficulty with the U.S. chart from an astrological point of view is the lack of consensus on the date, rising sign, and degree.

The chart used here is July 4, 1776 with 5° of Sagittarius rising. This chart is chosen because the July 4th chart is most widely used and is the date on which the birthday is celebrated. The choice of time is explained in Appendix III. This chart is used because it is descriptive not only of the conditions under which the United States moved to become independent, but because it works accurately in matters financial and economic.

Before you can make money and protect your assets in any particular country, native or not, you must understand how things are done and their likely results. The following descriptions correlate external appearance and circumstance to the houses of the U.S. inception chart.

The Houses

First house: Sagittarius rising, the country in general, and its population in particular. We are a rather tall, plump, friendly people, caught up in our own belief systems which we preach to the world. We are extremely prosperous. We love to travel. We are confident and optimistic, convinced we are the best. We are generous to a fault, even if we have to borrow to do it, ruler Jupiter in the 8th. We are spenders, not savers, who value assertiveness and initiative, typical of a hunting economy.

In a personal or company chart, the 1st house is the entity or self, and how that self is perceived by the world.

Second house: Capricorn on the cusp. We are perpetually in need of money and often preoccupied with achieving wealth. With Pluto in the 2nd and its ruler in the 11th of government money, we can see that the government, despite our protests to the contrary then and now, always seems to get or try to get control of our cash. The 2nd house rules banks. The banks are federally regulated and are the means by which the government raises cash. Through a system of borrowing and taxing, the government exerts great control over our assets, both personal and corporate.

In a personal or company chart, the 2nd house represents one's assets, how they are accumulated and spent.

Third house: Aquarius on the cusp of trade and exports. We have always had a very vigorous international trade. We export our debt, ruler of the 8th in the 3rd. Borrowed money on all levels fuels our trade. Our domestic trade is driven by consumerism, Moon in the 3rd. Since the Moon rules homes, we also see why the building cycle is one of the great indicators of our economic health.

In a personal or company chart the 3rd house represents the ability to communicate, trade, and move goods in and out of one's storehouse of value.

Fourth house: Pisces on the cusp of the land and its wealth. No one can deny that we are famous for our agriculture and our natural resources, ruler of the 4th in the 10th. The co-ruler, Jupiter in Cancer, the sign of its exaltation, indicates great bounty. We always put our resources into the hands of both our friends and our enemies, ruler of 4th in 8th.

In a personal or company chart, the 4th house represents one's base of operations, the home, the headquarters, the manufacturing plant. It represents land and property as a nontradable asset, the produce of the land, its wealth, and tradable raw materials, supply.

Fifth house: Aries on the cusp of gambling, investment, speculation, and the House of Representatives. Although we like to call our stock market a place to invest, it is actually a place of speculation. Aries is a sign of risk taking, which enhances the gambling fervor of Sagittarius rising.

Investment is where the fundamental value of the purchase stays constant and profit is made on interest, dividends, or rent. Speculation is where the fundamental trading value changes: return on investment is not as important as profit taking on a future trade. The expectation of attack, ruler Mars in the 7th of enemies and allies fuels much of our speculative fervor. We do not invest, we speculate. During the war with Iraq the stock market made a big bounce—up.

The House of Representatives is disruptive, egalitarian, and often functions in its own self-interest and against the people by whom it is elected. In practice it engages in short sighted populist policies that encourages venture capital to flee abroad and disrupt domestic markets, particularly through tax policies, co-ruled by Mars. The Smoot-Hawley Tariff, passed by Congress in the early 1930s, exacerbated our economic difficulties by killing our export/import trade, both of which are fundamental to our economic health.

In a personal or company chart the 5th house represents the same, as well as its creative offspring: children and risk taking ventures, plus the energy consumption and quality of manufacturing processes and products.

Sixth house: Taurus on the cusp of physical labor, health care, employees, the police and the military. The transit of Uranus through the 6th house during the 1930s equated with massive unemployment and the flight from the Dust Bowl.

Our workers are among the highest paid in the world, ruler 6th conjunct Jupiter and the Sun. Our agricultural production is unparalleled, yet we subsidize farmers and have a work force that is perpetually on strike. Neptune rules the 4th of farmers and is in the natural sign of the 6th of laborers. The 2nd of the 6th (labor's income) has striking Mars and Uranus. Our hunting economy with Virgo on the 10th makes the workers the real controllers of our productivity and success. Neptune makes them see themselves as martyrs. The government goes along for the vote. The 6th also governs the utility workers of the state: police, firemen, and the military.

In a personal or company chart, the 6th house rules health, working habits, employees, co-workers, and the tools of production.

Seventh house: Gemini on the cusp of partners and enemies. Mars and Uranus confirm that most of our wars have been fought on foreign territory; our perception that our allies need our help and that our enemies attack first. Our domestic trade is targeted for or controlled by foreign markets, ruler of the 3rd in the 7th. Our productivity and military buildup results from the constant focus on the military force of our enemies. Our country began in war, it maintains a warring posture, even though our Sun and ruling planet, Jupiter in Cancer indicate a non-warring defensive posture.

In a personal or company chart, the 7th house correlates to competitors and consultants, our ability to engage other people on our side or fight people who are not.

Eighth house: Cancer on the cusp of debt and taxes. Except for a short period in the 1820s the United States has always carried heavy debt. Our joint stock company system is really a different form of debt, a debt that need never be paid as long as a willing shareholder can be found. In this case the lender/owner does not sell the debt back to the company but to someone else who is willing to buy. Our whole taxing and spending structure is no different. Our ruling planet, Jupiter, Venus, Sun, and Mercury are all connected to the 8th, indicating the peculiar phenomenon of great wealth through debt.

The only time we have severe financial dislocations is when we start to pay off our debts. The greatest prosperity in the history of this country parallels the greatest increase in our federal debt. If this does not argue for the Sagittarius rising chart, nothing does.

In a company or personal chart the 8th house is the place of crisis, death, and debt. It is the partner's assets, shared money on which the entity can rely for support.

Ninth house: Leo on the cusp of imports and the judiciary. Leo on the 9th bespeaks our fascination with foreign goods. The Sun conjunct Jupiter and Venus in the 8th of other people's assets, reflects our massive purchases of foreign goods. These planets in the 8th house also mean imports aggravate our debt structure. Hence, the trade deficit. We are a nation of law and democracy, Sun, ruler of the 9th, conjunct ruling planet, Jupiter, natural ruler of 9th and significator of the U.S. population.

For a company or individual, the 9th house indicates foreign travel, the distribution system, advertising, contacts with the law or regulatory agencies, and religious and moral value systems, ethics.

Tenth house: Virgo on the cusp of the government in general, the President and the Executive Department in particular. Normally our president is weak. However, the power of the President and of the Executive grows on hardship and compassion. Because the ruler of the 4th is in the 10th, it would not be impossible for the government to confiscate the lands and resources of the country at some point. We could well be headed for a welfare state ruled by an inept and swollen bureaucracy, Neptune in Virgo in the 10th.

In a company or individual chart, the 10th house represents the reputation and social standing, ability to gain publicity and become prominent or successful, the Executive Board, CEO, and the salable product in retail outlets.

Eleventh house: Libra on the cusp of Congress in general and the Senate in particular. Saturn, ruler of the 2nd, in the 11th is another indicator that our government has the astrological capability of confiscating the property of its people. It has already happened. In the 1930s owning gold was declared illegal. The people who turned in their gold were given a piece of paper that was equal in trading value (set by the government, not by popular consent or by the market). In terms of intrinsic value the trade was considerably less than equitable. Paper has no intrinsic value, only a value based on trust.

By law the government cannot have money of its own. Saturn in the 11th, which is the 2nd of the 10th, verifies this and also its tendency to pass what it takes from the 2nd of private wealth into the 8th, the Treasury. The government pulls in less than it needs legitimately, so it resorts to debt to make up for the loss, or sends the money to enemies and allies both.

For companies and individuals the 11th house refers to organizations or groups of people who associate voluntarily, but who are not bound by contracts beforehand. Thus, it is the customer and his money that fills corporate tills, profits from the retail product, (2nd from the 10th), or friends with whom one socializes for business or personal reasons. Because there are no contractual obligations with the 11th house, it rules matters not under one's control, the unexpected, the faddish, the unanticipated and unforeseen.

Twelfth house: Scorpio on the cusp of the bureaucracy. Although the bureaucracy, as the natural 12th house, is by nature the secret enemy of any nation, Scorpio on the U.S. 12th is especially deadly. Largely the bureaucracy has grown through "crisis", military involvement, and increases in poverty and crime. The ruler of the 12th, Pluto in the 2nd, demands taxes to pay for the crises, and with co-ruler Mars in the 7th, is a natural enemy of the country. The tax demands of the bureaucracy enable us to get into international entanglements and war.

For companies and individuals, the 12th represents research, secret activity, customer relations, and self-undoing, the tendency to take action or be caught in situations that are not in one's ongoing and immediate self-interest, thus, charity, retirement, and incarceration.

Before the outer planets gained power and control, the U.S. chart functioned fairly productively. Since the discoveries of

Pluto and Neptune, we have become more and more rapacious as to tax and income distribution. The founding fathers created a very prosperous chart that guaranteed the citizenry and the law would dominate. The original chart is a chart of capitalism, the use of shared money to create wealth. The addition of the outer planets has distorted a relatively safe debt instrument based on group ownership, stocks (Uranus), into less safe bonds, promises to pay in the far future (Neptune), and on into highly unsafe leverage (Pluto) junk bonds.

The government, to counteract private sector excesses, has moved towards socialism and fascism, without removing or compensating for the evils of the debt structure, itself. These outer planets, that represent mass movements and ideologies, can make us a kinder, gentler nation or create government chaos. Pluto can bring us debt and death, or restructuring and transformation.

The following charts break down the house meanings for countries, companies and individuals. While the complexities of chart delineation are beyond the scope of this book, transits

---

Mundane Houses

1st	The population, its attitudes, and identity.
2nd	Wealth, banks, and assets of the population.
3rd	Exports, internal trade, transportation and communication, primary education.
4th	The geography, bounty of the land. Opposing party.
5th	House of Representatives, speculation, games.
6th	Labor force, police, and military.
7th	Enemies and allies. Internal opposition.
8th	Debt, taxes, stocks, and waste. The Treasury.
9th	The Judiciary, imports, foreign relations, colleges and universities.
10th	Government in general, President in particular.
11th	Congress in general, Senate in particular, corporations, the stock exchange and buying public.
12th	The bureaucracy, charitable, health, and research institutions.

Corporate Houses	
1st	Identity, middle management, how it does business.
2nd	Assets, how it transforms money into the means of production
3rd	Shipping and receiving. Internal communications.
4th	Location, suppliers. Manufacturing plant.
5th	Energy costs and quality control.
6th	Mechanics of production.
7th	Wholesalers, competitors, consultants.
8th	Debt and waste management. Joint ownership.
9th	Advertising, distribution systems, government regulation.
10th	Top management, retailers, the product and reputation.
11th	Available capital, profits, customers.
12th	Research and development, customer service, allocation.

through these houses and to the individual planets on the chart will show stress areas and timings for the specific country or market. Planetary positions are available in inexpensive annual ephemerides or in many of the popular monthly magazines.

Market Houses	
1st	The non-professional trading public.
2nd	The pool of money available to trade, bankers.
3rd	Specialists and accounting systems.
4th	The trading floor and commodities.
5th	Speculation and margin buying.
6th	Trading methods, mechanisms, and facilitators.
7th	Trading professionals.
8th	Bonds and debt instruments.
9th	Foreign markets and trade. The SEC.
10th	Directors, brokers, internal regulation, price averages.
11th	Equities and stocks.
12th	Institutional investors.

Transits through the Mundane houses of a corporation are an indication of internal capabilities, the ability to turn a profit, and where to anticipate problems or luck that comes from outside.

Individual Houses	
1st	The self, how you cope with conditions generally.
2nd	How you deal with money, your potential for wealth.
3rd	Ability to communicate, learn, trade, and keep accounts.
4th	Your home and real estate.
5th	Children, speculating urge, family wealth.
6th	Your work habits, how you deal with co-workers and employees.
7th	Clients, competitors, consultants, partners, and spouse.
8th	Debt, inheritance, alimony, your partner's wealth.
9th	Legal matters, travel, advertising, higher education.
10th	Reputation, achievement, publicity, success.
11th	Casual associates, customers, profit from business, groups.
12th	Retirement, plans, schemes, and dreams.

In 1929 and 1987 the passage of Saturn in Sagittarius, the sign on the cusp of the speculation 5th of the stock market chart, indicated a shrinkage of money available for margin buying. In both instances the market made precipitous drops.

Because of the importance of the angles, the 7th house can be both customers and clients. The distinction is mainly between who comes to you for service, 7th, and who pays for what they buy, 11th. The ruler of the 8th in the 11th brings people who pay.

Planets in Houses

Planets transiting houses have slightly different meanings than planets contacting one another either in the sky or on the chart. Planets in houses take three forms:

1. A planet in the house on the inception or natal chart indicates a permanent attitude, impulse, or set of conditions.

2. A planet contacting a planet or ruler of a house is an event.

3. A planet transiting a house is a set of conditions that either drag or build to an event. They indicate background practices, conditions, and attitudes that create or destroy wealth.

Pluto *in* the 2nd house of the United States chart indicates a population that is always in debt, that sees debt as a way to increase assets. Debt succeeds in the United States in creating assets and wealth. Since debt is not a normal way to increase wealth, the economy is subject to periodic trauma: the other side of Pluto. When we export our economic techniques to other countries in the form of loans, they inevitably fail, because our prosperity is unusual and unique.

Transits *through* the houses of a chart, planets that stay in the particular sector over a period of time, indicate the changing conditions and attitudes against which the more permanent placements operate. The transits of Jupiter through the 2nd house of the U.S. chart indicate a period of wealth creation or expansive spending, which does not have to be borrowed to finance. However, with Pluto in the 2nd house, this wealth tends to be used as the foundation or collateral to create more money to stimulate borrowing even more. In an ordinary economy, it would indicate simple asset growth and prosperity for the country and its citizens.

Transits *to* planets indicate events that are of the nature of the planets involved either ongoing in the sky or to a planet on a mundane or personal chart. The house in which the contacted planet is situated and the house the planet rules are both affected. Saturn rules the 2nd house of the United States chart, the wealth of its citizens and banks, and is situated in the 11th, corporations, stock ownership, and market wealth/retail profits. When the radix (natal) Saturn is activated by a transit, such as the lunar eclipse just before the crash of 1987, expect some disruption in money matters in the United States. In 1987, the people who invested in the stock market either through direct investment, mutual funds, or pension funds, lost assets. The corporate structure and trading groups, 11th house, also lost money and were forced to make difficult decisions as their profits and their ability to raise money through stocks seriously and precipitously declined.

The continuous squares to radix U.S. Saturn from transiting Uranus and Neptune through 1991 and 1992 indicate serious problems in the banking system, corporate profits and stocks, and banking disruptions and failures that will produce a *de facto* loss of assets by the public as a whole.

In January 1991 the Bank of New England failed when Neptune squared the U.S. natal Saturn and an eclipse occurred on the U.S. natal Pluto, the planet of bankruptcies.

As handy rules of thumb the planetary passages indicate: Sun, health and focus; Moon, daily timing; Mercury, discussion and trading; Venus, financial return; Mars, trouble and loss; Saturn, shortage or constriction; Jupiter, growth; Uranus, upsets; Neptune, distortion; and Pluto, restructuring and loss.

Transits Over a Chart

SUN Triggers action. Calls attention to the house or planet involved. Increases wealth. The month.

SOLAR ECLIPSE Reversal of existing conditions and attitudes. Major change can be good or bad.

MOON Appropriate focus on the houses or planets involved in larger activities. Destabilization. The day.

LUNAR ECLIPSE A revelation or implementation of plans. The effects of earlier eclipses to the same place end.

MERCURY Messages, given or received, discussions, adjustments.

VENUS Money or support for matters touched. Stability.

MARS Triggers activity. Disputes, accidents, war, and loss.

JUPITER Luck, promotion, publicity, or legal matters. Growth. Confidence and optimism stimulated. Foreign travel.

SATURN Tough decisions. Restrictions. Confrontations with reality. Obligations. Loss. Adjustment. Limits to one's ability and actions are clear. Paying dues.

URANUS Accidents, excitement, invention. Cartels. Chaos, rebellion, erratic and irresponsible behavior. Collectivism.

NEPTUNE Confusion, self-destruction, mass hysteria, escapism. Lies and propaganda. Retirement and contagion.

PLUTO Destruction, crime, murder, violence, coercion, and death. Research, revitalization, and restorations. Taxes and confiscation. Surgery and venereal disease.

History

When Saturn transited the 2nd house of the U.S. chart in 1873, the banking system failed. When Saturn transited the 2nd house of the U.S. chart in 1932, the banking system failed. Saturn started its transit of the 2nd house towards the end of 1989. We see the same massive bank failures that preceded the previous collapses. We have no good reason to believe that things will be different this time around.

Uranus and Neptune transited the 2nd house of the U.S. chart in the 1820s, just as they are doing today. The 1820s were a very prosperous period in our history with massive reductions in the federal debt. The first Bank of the United States, an arm of government, controlled the money and facilitated trade. During this dual transit the United States experienced a great influx of foreign money, since it had no stable currency of its own.

Today we see a great influx of foreign money. The Japanese and Europeans are spending and investing the money we spent on their goods, to buy and build corporations and real estate over here, invest in our stock market and buy government bonds. The dollar is unstable and on a floating exchange rate.

With Uranus, the planet of democratic nationalization, transiting the 2nd it is not inconceivable that a new government bank will replace the system that is now in place. We already see a variation on this with the Resolution Trust Corporation, the agency set up to sell off the assets of failed thrifts. Total government control of the financial assets are a small but seemingly inevitable step towards increasing, maybe even total, government control of the economy.

Neptune transits the 2nd house simultaneously with Uranus in the early 1990s. Since this is the first appearance in this sector since Neptune's discovery, we do not have incontrovertible historical evidence of its operation. We do know Neptune steals. The overthrow of the Manchu dynasty by Sun Yat Sen and the communists coincided with the passage of Neptune through the Beijing Mutation chart. We know they confiscated the wealth of the Manchus. We can presume they took control of all wealth as is normal for a collectivist society. In the 1930s, Neptune transited the 2nd house of the U.S.S.R. The crops of the Ukrainians were confiscated to feed the Russians. Millions of Ukrainians died of starvation. Neptune as the ruler of inflation steals the value of one's assets even as they multiply by the numbers. The least we can expect is increasingly confiscatory inflation and taxation.

Progressions

Progressions, an astrological technique beyond the scope of this book, indicate very long periods over which attitudes and conditions may change relative to the inception or natal chart. Unlike transits, where the planets from the Sun through Mars are relatively unimportant except as month and day triggers, these same planets take on a dominant and dominating thrust. The progressed Sun transit through the U.S. 2nd house produced a massive influx of gold into the country and averted the normal correction of the Jupiter-Saturn opposition of the Taurus Mutation. The progressed Venus in Pisces also indicates the creation and distribution of great wealth, along with increasingly high though productive inflation. The movement of progressed Venus into Aries, the sign of its detriment, in 1992 indicates the start of a prolonged period of economic and financial difficulty, which could result in a devaluation of the currency or even a total loss in its value.

We have recently seen Saturn transiting the U.S. 2nd—a decrease in the wealth of the country, especially the purchasing power of the inhabitants and a severe strain and great losses in the banking industry. We continue to have Uranus in the 2nd: severe disruptions and reversals in the wealth of the country and in the banking system in particular, possibility of a nationalization of assets. Neptune in the 2nd: great inflationary pressures on the wealth of the country and the income of the inhabitants, collapse or confiscation of the banking system, influx of foreign currency.

Two other factors appear in the secondary progressions of the U.S. chart. Progressed Venus, mentioned earlier, is negative for the stability of our currency and trade. Progressed Sun in Aquarius, the sign of its detriment, is another indicator of declining currency value. When the progressed Sun entered Aquarius, the gold standard was totally denied. Citizens were allowed to own gold again. The government sold off gold reserves to underscore their "lack of value." Since that time we have amassed a trillion dollar debt and a currency that has rapidly lost value against other currencies. Venus in Pisces, its exaltation, protected us from financial disaster. Venus in Aries, plus Neptune and Uranus in the 2nd could presage runaway inflation or a totally revalued and devalued currency.

The Mutation Chart

The Mutation chart calculated for a specific location reveals the impact of broader global movements. While it will tell much about what happens and who does what to whom, it is best used in conjunction with the national chart to understand not only what happens, but what the individual or nation does both to cause and cure it.

A closer look at the 1960s phenomena will help us understand the lag time between the universal and impersonal causes of any situation and the actions that are taken in response to it. As Pluto transited the western ascendants, creating sex, violence, and disrespect for law (Libra), Neptune began its transit over the U.S. Ascendant. Large segments of the population, especially Sagittarian/college students, became involved in drugs. The combination of the two, drugs in the East and in the country as a whole and lawlessness in the West presaged the lawlessness today. The generation most closely associated with the drug movement were born with Neptune in Libra. They were drawn to California as it appeared to be the expression of their birth Neptunes. As they wore flowers in their hair, smoked pot in the streets of San Francisco, and protested the war in Vietnam, Pluto was simultaneously breaking down law and order and spreading venereal disease. Lest this discussion be unnecessarily negative, great spiritual, occult, and transformational movements flowered as well. Had the United States been a one religion or fundamentalist nation, we might have experienced religious oppression instead of anti-religious license.

Since a national chart represents, in most cases, a willful act of humanity with respect to social, political, and economic organization, governments do not become involved or do not have sufficient power to become involved until the transits hit the more willful chart, that is, the birth chart of the country, particularly if the Mutation chart shows no government intervention. China's Mutation chart showed government intervention at Tiannenmen Square. The U.S. chart showed no federal intervention in these international populist movements. Local police and national guard engaged in various stages of protest and demonstration, but the Federal government, though the target, was little involved.

The United States government was not strongly involved in the Mutation chart during most of the 1960s. The masses succumb to the world *zeitgeist* in proportion to their government's ability to exert power and authority, with the will of the people or without. Although the 10th house of the United States Mutation is ruled by Leo, its ruler is in Aquarius as befits a democracy. Beijing has the Pisces Mars-Uranus conjunction in the 10th. Revolution and upheaval has been the condition of China for this Mutation, its governments violent and arbitrary.

In the case of the United States it seems clear that because the government on the Mutation chart is the will of the people it can and does take a whole sign passage for the U.S. to respond to problems that involve the people. The lag time is exacerbated by Neptune in the U.S. natal 10th, indicating a government that is better at propaganda than at hard-nosed response. Furthermore, a Neptune addicted government is unlikely to counterbalance a Neptune/California Ascendant generation and a Neptune addicted or escapist population. By the time Neptune reached the Ascendant of the U.S. chart in the early 1970s, drugs, though prohibited, were widely accepted.

To spot trends for the population, start in the West, particularly California, with Libra transits by outer planets for early signs of changing attitudes and taste. Note the consequences, good and bad as the same planet moves through Scorpio, the Mutation chart, and expect the full effect and social and political action to be taken when the planet reaches Sagittarius, the U.S. birth Ascendant.

For new trends in homes, real estate, land and resource management, we can look to California for trends, as the outer planets transit Capricorn, its 4th house sign. These trends will culminate in the U.S. natal chart when they reach Pisces. By that time the nation could be awash in its own toxic waste.

Pluto on the Ascendant of the U.S. Mutation chart brought us massive defaults in the S&L industry, tumbled the economies of the Northeast, created the AIDS epidemic, and made Washington, D.C. the murder capital of the world. Earlier, as Pluto swept across the United States and its moving Mutation Ascendant, farmers went bankrupt and Texas collapsed. The problem was not considered "national" until Pluto hit the eastern Mutation Ascendant degrees. Then the government started to see it as a crisis.

The United States as a people or a government are unlikely to deal with this Pluto passage or fully feel its effects until Pluto transits the Sagittarian Ascendant of the national chart in the late 1990s. That is when the corrective legislation will be enacted. By that time the population is likely to be living in fear of violence and disease. The people could vote for government repression and suppression. Expect drugs to be totally outlawed when Pluto squares natal U.S. Neptune and the MC. We may move towards a police state, such as Germany did when Pluto transited its Mutation 7th house in the 1930s and achieved when Pluto transited their national Uranus, ruler of their 10th.

Although we are proud that we have mostly avoided wars on our own land, the Pluto passage over the U.S. Sagittarian Ascendant does correlate to a period when war was fought on this territory—the French and Indian War. Whether or not there is combat, people are likely to continue to die as if there were unless something is done to counteract the deadly Pluto transit.

Obviously, investment forecasts for the decade of the 1990s will mass around repair, rejuvenation, security, crisis, military, research and debt instruments. Nuclear energy will come back into fashion. The ecology movement and waste management will dominate.

The Mutation chart used in conjunction with national and individual charts is useful in timing market moves, economic trends, and for reinforcing and confirming interpretations. If something appears on all three charts, consider it of major importance. As a handy rule of thumb, look at the Mutation chart as the time when problems are created and the national chart as the time when they are addressed.

The Stock Market

The stock market chart reinforced the financial difficulties of the Mutation and national charts in 1987. Pluto was square its Ascendant when the market dropped 500 points. Look at your own chart to see if your financial fortunes duplicate the fortunes of the United States or go against them. If you had it bad in the "roaring eighties," you may do well in the "groaning nineties."

Although the New York Stock Exchange chart has Sun, Mercury, and Venus in Taurus, a sign of its connection to asset building and banks, Mars in the 2nd house, Moon in Aries, and an angular Pluto mark it as a vehicle of speculation and debt. Margin buying was one of the factors in the 1929 crash. Expect serious disruptions in trading or severe declines in assets when Pluto passes through the late degrees of Scorpio in 1994 and 1995.

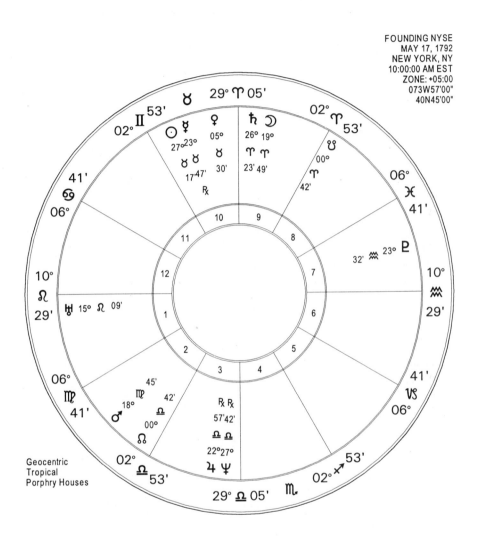

FOUNDING NYSE
MAY 17, 1792
NEW YORK, NY
10:00:00 AM EST
ZONE: +05:00
073W57'00"
40N45'00"

29° ♈ 05'

02° ♊ 53'

02° ♈ 53'

☉ ☿ ♀
27°23° 05°
♉ ♉ ♉
17'47' 30' 23' 49'
℞

♄ ☽
26° 19°
♈ ♈

02° ♈ 53'

☋
00°
♈
42'

41'
♋
06°

06°
♓
41'

10°
♌
29'

♅ 15° ♌ 09'

32' ♒ 23° ♇

10°
♒
29'

06°
♍
41'

♂ 18°
♍ 45'
♎ 42'
00°
☊

℞ ℞
57'42'
♎ ♎
22°27°
♃ ♆

41'
♑
06°

02°
♎ 53'

29° ♎ 05'

♏

02° ♐ 53'

Geocentric
Tropical
Porphry Houses

10 9 8
11 7
12 6
1 5
2 3 4

New York Stock Exchange

233

Note also that the stock market chart reflects a herding economic style. As stated earlier, the market is driven and controlled by small groups of men. It is no place for the little guy, unless he is aligned with one of the major players. With the ruler of the 10th in the 2nd, the banks control its wealth. If banks fail, so does the system.

The stock market is neither a leading nor lagging indicator of our overall economic health. The charts of the NYSE and markets are affected in major ways only by economic downturns that coincide with their charts. Their planetary activity is only significant economically when that activity is duplicated on national and Mutation charts. The first Jupiter-Saturn opposition of 1989, which started the present economic downturn, resulted in a 200-point drop in the Dow which fairly quickly recovered and went on to new highs. Given the concurrent transit of Uranus and Neptune through the U.S. 2nd house, we can conclude that an expanding money supply plus foreign and group (pension and mutual fund) trades keep the averages up.

Unless you are buying futures on the Dow, Dow-watching will not make you a millionaire. However, general market trends are useful in buying and selling real estate and for investing in mutual funds which tend to perform similar to the broader averages. The key to success in all markets is vigilance. Conditions always change. You must be willing to move your money around and operate with a clear and open mind.

Local and Personal Impact

Mundane transits (as current planetary configurations with respect to one another are called) and the condition of the Solar Field and Mutation planets indicate universal and global patterns. The degree of importance and impact on a specific country, company, market, or person is corroborated by the individual chart and the Mutation angles, drawn for any given geographical location. A further factor in specific charts is the ruler of the chart. The chart's ruler is the planet that rules the sign on the Ascendant. Mutual aspects involving the ruler of the chart and any other transiting planet often time events. In May 1991, Jupiter (the ruler of the U.S. chart) was opposed by Saturn. Throughout the period of Saturn-Jupiter oppositions the United States was forced to make serious decisions concerning: money and banks (Saturn rules the 2nd), the war with Iraq, natural

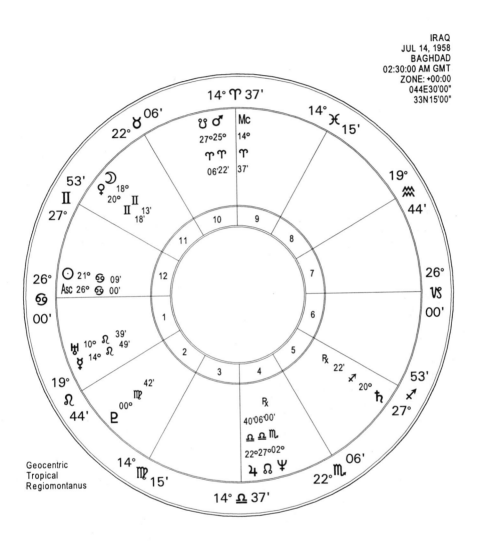

IRAQ
JUL 14, 1958
BAGHDAD
02:30:00 AM GMT
ZONE: +00:00
044E30'00"
33N15'00"

14° ♈ 37'

22° ♉ 06'

14° ♓ 15'

� ♂
27°25°
♈ ♈
06'22'

Mc
14°
♈
37'

19°
♒
44'

53'
♀ ☽ 18'
20° Ⅱ
♊
27° Ⅱ 13'
18'

10

9

8

11

26°
00'
☉ 21° ♋ 09'
Asc 26° ♋ 00'
♋

12

7

6

26°
♑
00'

♅ 10° ♌ 39'
☿ 14° ♌ 49'

1

2

3

5

4

℞ 22'
♐ 20°
♄

53'
♐
27°

19°
♌
44'
♇ ♍ 42'
00°

℞
40'06'00"
♎ ♎ ♏
22°27°02°
♃ ☊ ♆

22° ♏ 06'

14° ♍ 15'

14° ♎ 37'

Geocentric
Tropical
Regiomontanus

National Chart—Baghdad, Iraq

235

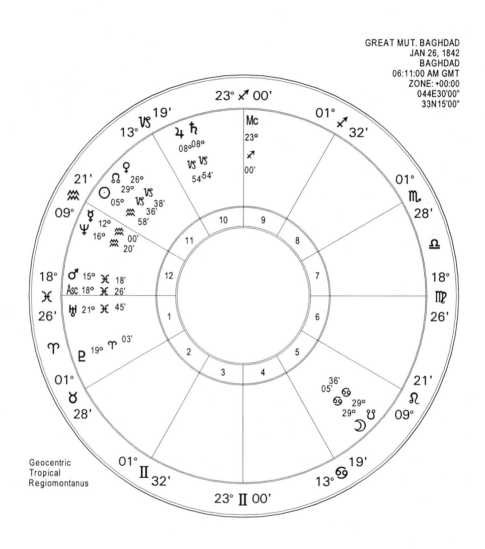

Great Mutation—Baghdad, Iraq

236

resource issues that could have an economic impact (Jupiter rules the 4th), and most recently, President Bush's heart problem, which caused concern and worry in the population relative to his "mate," the vice president, 4th.

Locating Significant Activity

- What is the nature of the problem?

- What does the Mutation planet signify?

- On whose charts does that planet have prominence, either in an angle or ruler of the ASC or MC?

- Examine national charts to confirm the activity and pinpoint the location.

Pluto on the Mutation Neptune signifies a high handed and illegal activity concerning oil. Neptune rules the rising signs of most Mutation charts in the Middle East. Kuwait's Saturn falls on Iraq's 7th house of allies and enemies. When the Jupiter-Saturn opposition fell across this connection, Saddam Hussein decided to rid Iraq of its obligations to Kuwait. The earlier Pluto on Neptune, December 1989, did not have a strong impact on the charts of the Middle East. There and then it was the usual wrangle over OPEC nations' honoring the provisions of their cartel. In the United States, Saturn concurrently opposed Venus, Sun, and Jupiter on our natal chart, indicating the oil problem would impact our wealth.

Conditions under which a country must operate reflect the Mutation chart, people as geographical masses of humanity. What the country does about it reflects the national chart, people as politically organized entities. If an activity occurs only on a national chart or the nation's Mutation angles, the impact is most likely national in scope. If it occurs on both simultaneously, it could have global impact.

Conflicting indicators describe a market in balance. Note unusual configurations that tilt the market up or down. Remember two fundamental truths: Markets rise slow and fall fast. Markets always seek a balance.

Economic Forecasting

- Always move from the broad indicators to the specific.

- What is the element of the Mutation?

- What is the progress of Jupiter and Saturn? What phase?

- What Mutation degrees are affected? What is the commodity?

- Are the Mutation angles of the country affected?

- What is the economic outlook on the national chart?

- What response to Mutation conditions does the national chart forecast?

- What is the condition of the Solar Field, bull or bear?

- Is the Sun, Saturn, or Jupiter in mutables?

- Is Saturn or Jupiter at 15°, conjunct or opposing a Greater or Lesser Mutation degree?

- Examine the Solar Field for planetary passages and eclipses. Note which planets are in and which are out.

Precautions, Patterns, and Profits

- When outer planets transit a chart's 2nd house, assets deteriorate through debt, inflation, or confiscation—keep a portion of your wealth in vehicles of intrinsic value.

- Transits to national and specific angles and planetary rulers of those angles, indicate localized effects of global or national activity. Watch the trends from their start in California and their movement West to East.

- Because of continuing outer planet activity in the U.S. charts through the 1990s, prepare worst case strategies for your investments and acquisitions.

- Be on the alert for signs of runaway inflation and bank failures.

- Watch Jupiter through the houses for areas of safety and growth.

Chapter Eleven

ASSET GROWTH

A strology gives us the tools to anticipate economic ups and downs, to create models of what is to come. Whether the models materialize depends on the astrologer's skill and on the decisions of those whose activity and power direct the course of events as they materialize. Every astrological symbol contains myriad possibilities. Uranus can mean ignoring reality as much as it can mean an action that goes against the norm. It can be uplifting or arbitrary and confiscatory. Neptune can mean being deceived by the economy or being oblivious to what is going on. It can precipitate altruistic activity or fraud. Pluto can take out a loan or fail to pay it.

To know which, you must be alert and aware of the local and global context, the tendencies of governments and leaders, and be free of as much political and social bias as is humanly possible.

Life does not happen in a vacuum. Neither should astrological interpretation and forecasting.

Market Timing

The number of factors that move market averages and affect individual potentials for asset growth are many and complex. While this makes pinpoint predicting of ups and downs, tops and bottoms, difficult, it does not in any way inhibit an individual's ability to use astrological information to enhance his own wealth creation strategies.

Two things must always enter any calculation of future movements: close observation of present conditions and an astrological monitoring of future planetary events. It has been said that life is one-third fate, one-third circumstance, and one-third will. The fate and circumstance as depicted on astrological charts give us an almost 70% chance of being correct in market predictions. If we have the will to discipline ourselves through our adversities and uncertainties, to restrain ourselves from our own enthusiasms when they counteract observation and common sense, we can certainly up the percentage in our favor.

Market Forecasting

- Clear your mind of the current wisdom and all personal, political, social, or moral bias.

- Study the current wisdom and judge it against the astrology. If in conflict, choose the astrology.

- Study context. Always check your conclusions against what you can observe, not against the theory.

- Know your subject. Know how the company, country, or individual has behaved in the past and what it is doing now.

- If your interpretations coincide with what you would logically expect, you are probably correct.

- If your interpretations do not coincide, check your interpretations for what you may have overlooked.

- If they still contradict, go with the astrology. It is the only tool that can anticipate the unpredictable.

You cannot mix political points of view with market forecasting. You cannot judge future events solely by patterns of present and past.

In trying to anticipate oil prices for 1990, the indicators showed a potential for a sharp rise in oil prices in late summer and early fall. Since this was an unseasonable jump, it was dismissed as having no major impact. Although transits showed some potential for war, disputes, and disruption of supply lines on the U.S. national and mutation charts, it did not seem all that likely or important. One can be too smart. Iraq invaded Kuwait and the rest is history.

Situations like this point up two serious problems for the forecaster, professional or amateur:

1. Having the *sang-froid* to choose the unthinkable or the unwanted.
2. Knowing which country will provoke the action.

In the case of corporate raiders, you would also need a handy reference of who might be vulnerable to attack, often indicated by Pluto transits to the corporate chart. These procedures were outlined in chapter ten.

Asset Multiplication

Wealth can be accumulated in good times and bad. Much depends on your understanding of the dynamics of your own chart and of the conditions that operate in broader economic fields. In times of rapid growth and inflation, even sloppy practices create assets. In difficult times, the fundamentals always prevail.

Good planets in your money houses are no guarantee of wealth. Jupiter in the 2nd can indicate a spendthrift. Saturn in the 2nd is often a person who amasses great wealth, because he never feels he has enough.

The natural order of material success is Taurus on the 2nd, Virgo on the 6th, and Capricorn on the 10th: the changing of one's assets into a marketable commodity that return wealth to the owner and transformer.

Ruler of the 2nd in the 6th; Ruler of the 6th in the 10th, Ruler of the 10th in the 2nd is the signature of a person who engages in a career or in activities that return him wealth. It is the mark of a country or an economy that produces wealth for its inhabitants as shown in the chapter on economic styles.

If these planets move otherwise, your attitudes and practices reduce your potential for wealth. If the ruler of your 2nd is in the 10th, you spend money for recognition. Recognition and reputation is more important than making money: ambitious, true, but not terribly profitable.

No matter what the prospects on the chart, good money practices always produce wealth, just as in bad times everything does not turn bad. Some companies thrive, some go under. In picking a company or a mutual fund in which to invest examine their prospects from a chart of their incorporation date. This information is usually found in the prospectus or in *Moody's* handbooks and *Donahue's Mutual Fund Almanacs*. Because you rarely have access to the time of day, keep track of its financial history to uncover down years that have no obvious planetary correlation, except that Saturn or Pluto must have been in the 2nd house or on an angle. Graphs of stock price movements provide the necessary background history. Otherwise, use a chart calculated for noon to get some idea of how the company is managed.

When making the actual purchase pick a day where the Moon is well-aspected. The Moon and Jupiter both rule growth. Pick times when there are favorable transits to your own angles and pending favorable transits to the benefic planets (Jupiter and Venus) and the angles of the company in which you wish to invest.

When you are under severe transits from Saturn and Pluto, avoid taking on debt or assets. Debt will grow. Assets will shrink. Take a breather or buy a broken-down house and fix it up. You cannot function totally independent of your transits. Buy as good ones come into play. Sell before the bad take hold. If you wish to make a great deal of money, you must be willing to trade. If you prefer safety, buy the best and hold, but remember that wealth multiplication is Libran and Piscean, the Taurean approach only guarantees little or no loss.

If you are under Neptunian transits, things that look good will turn out to be bad, things that look bad usually turn out to be good. Everything turns out different. If you want to be safe don't believe anybody, put your money in a vault and throw away the key. If you have money to burn, take a gamble, but know it is a gamble and be willing to be wrong.

Before You Buy

A good deal is not a good deal unless you can afford it and unless it has potential for future growth. Assess your financial reality according to the cornerstones of wealth addressed in an earlier chapter.

1. Taurus/2nd house of your cash. Do you have enough money to buy what you want? Is the product of sufficient value to get equal value from the trade? Examine intrinsic and transaction value. Make sure your barter value remains constant. Examine transits to all 2nd houses and natal Venuses involved.

2. Leo/5th house of speculation and the cost of commodities and consumables. Will your purchase maintain its price? Will your sale enable you to purchase another product of equal or greater value? Because Leo is associated with gold, check the inflation rate and its 10 times multiple to see if the price has outstripped inflation. Understand relative value. Make sure the product has lasting value, whether that is accounted in pleasure or cash. Be proud of any product you buy or sell. Examine 5th houses and Suns of the charts involved for the degree of speculative risk.

3. Scorpio/8th house of debt and shared resources; how the trading partner or seller values his goods and for stocks and bonds. What will it cost you to maintain your purchase? If you buy a dog, his cost is also his upkeep. If you buy gold, you may have to pay storage and assay costs. Understand upkeep and repair. Make sure it will not cost you more to own it than to buy it. Examine 8th houses, Mars, and Plutos of charts involved.

4. Aquarius/11th house, what the market will bear. How many other people value the product—is it in fashion? Is the pool of money sufficient to support the price? Understand the premiums that popularity demand. Make sure you sell in fashion and buy out. Examine the 11th houses, Saturns, and Uranuses involved.

Although outside the scope of this work, the election and inception charts of the purchase or trade, especially in real estate and long term holdings should be examined according to the above rules.

Financial Analysis

The following analysis sheet can help you to sort out the mass of data available for forecasting. It will help you pinpoint what is strong and important, and whether it will have global, national, corporate, market, or personal impact. It will help you identify trends and turning points. If you see an accumulation of up or down indicators, you can expect a major market move. If most indicators balance off each other, you can expect the market to stagnate or trade in relatively small ranges.

Use the graphic ephemeris to spot patterns, and pending configurations, contacts, and inner planet cycles. Use the

Financial Analysis		
Context	Sign, Planet, Degree, Dates	Up/Down
Great Mutation		
Mutation Subcycle		
Sign of Saturn		
Sign of Jupiter		
Venus—Bear or Bull		
Mercury—Buy or Sell		
Sun—Up or Down		
Patterns		
Venus Condition		
Mercury Condition		
Eclipses		
Conjunctions		
Mutation Degree 8°/23°		
Lunar Phase		
Node Transit		
Moon Sign		
U.S. Mutation Chart		
National Chart		
Market Chart		
Individual Chart		

standard ephemeris to spot the mutual configurations, Jupiter-Saturn contacts, planetary sign and degree positions, to pinpoint the days, weeks, or months in which major moves are likely. There are also astrology software programs available which will provide all the information of standard ephemerides, and some that will produce the necessary graphic ephemerides as well.

We will examine financial analysis sheets for August 1987, the Dow peak and for October 1987, the Dow crash.

August 1987 Financial Analysis

The market hit at the time an astounding 2,700 on the Dow. Most of the indicators are strongly *up* into the middle of the month. Saturn and Jupiter retrograde indicate a market turn. The Sheaf pattern and the Sun's entry into Virgo all presage a very highly stimulated market about to reach a peak. The limit was reached, not at actual stations and transits, but when the Moon and Sun entered Virgo, the sign of corrections to reality.

October 1987 Financial Analysis

The Dow dropped 500 points on October 19th. The slide started at Mercury retrograde on the 16th. Apart from the cycle indicators which were mostly down, there were two danger signals: the lunar eclipse on U.S. Saturn and the Mars transit of the south node. The other danger signals were Uranus and Pluto in the Mutation degrees.

You can see a considerable difference between this chart and the August chart. They share two qualities, the Neptune and Uranus activity and the Moon in Virgo on peak and fall day. Two contacts localized the activity on the national and market charts. Saturn squares Mars in the 2nd of the stock market chart, bringing much grief to traders and accounts for much of the pessimism that followed. The eclipse across the Saturn of the U.S. chart meant a great loss of assets in the country. Many foreign funds retreated from our markets during this period, so the recovery was stalled for lack of sufficient money available for investment. The north node lunar eclipse ordinarily would have signalled a fall followed by a rise, which would have mitigated some of the other negative indicators. But, this eclipse was not simply a mundane and universal occurrence, it hit the U.S. Saturn, a strong and deep loss.

August 1987	**Financial Analysis**	Dow Peak
Context	Sign, Planet, Degree, Dates	Up/Down
Great Mutation	Earth—Libra preview	unstable
Mutation Subcycle	phase 5, speculative to 1989-91	up
Sign of Saturn	15° Sagittarius station 19th	critical
Sign of Jupiter	Aries station retro 20th	up
Venus—Bear or Bull	Bull to 22nd conj. Sun	up
Mercury—Buy or Sell	Buy to August 19 Conj. Sun	up
Sun—Up or Down	Leo to August 23rd up then	down
Patterns	Sheaf	up
Venus Condition	invisible, no regulation	
Mercury Condition	invisible, Sun sign Leo to 24th	up
Eclipses	none	
Conjunctions	Mars to Sun August 24th	up
Mutation Degree 8°/23°	23° Sun, Venus, Mercury 16th to 18th	up
Lunar Phase	New Moon, August 24th in Virgo	down
Node Transit	Moon conjunct south node 27th	bottom
Moon Sign	Virgo on the 24th	turn
U.S. Mutation Chart	transiting Saturn sqr. Mars 18th	turn
National Chart	Uranus square Neptune, Neptune on 2nd	crazy
Market Chart	Jupiter conjunct MC public high	up
Individual Chart		

October 1987	**Financial Analysis**	Dow Crash
Context	Sign, Planet, Degree, Dates	Up/Down
Great Mutation	Earth—Libra preview	unstable
Mutation Subcycle	phase 5, speculative to 1989-91	up
Sign of Saturn	17° Sagittarius	unstable
Sign of Jupiter	23° Aries 24th	up
Venus—Bear or Bull	Bear visible September 29th	down
Mercury—Buy or Sell	Sell Retro 16th	down
Sun—Up or Down	Libra Scorpio	down
Patterns	Irregular Bow	down
Venus Condition	visible adjusting	down
Mercury Condition	invisible, Sun sign down	down
Eclipses	lunar 7th north node 13° Aries	fall/rise
Conjunctions	Mercury to Sun 28th	up
Mutation Degree 8°/23°	23° Uranus 8° Pluto to 10th	danger
Lunar Phase	New Moon 22nd in Libra	down
Node Transit	Moon conj. south node 20th Mars,11th	bottom
Moon Sign	Virgo on the 19th	turn
U.S. Mutation Chart	Uranus in 23°	danger
National Chart	eclipse across natal Saturn Uranus square Neptune Neptune on 2nd	danger crazy
Market Chart	t Saturn sqr. Mars on 26th	loss
Individual Chart		

While there is a mass of data to be sorted in any financial analysis, using these or similar analysis sheets can help you spot and focus on what is major and important. If there are no outstanding indicators in any given month, the markets will trade in a range. When there are no big jolts the movements of Sun, Mercury, Venus, and the Moon will have a stronger effect.

If you are active in trading the markets, apply these transits to your own chart, particularly your 2nd house, Venus, Jupiter, Saturn, Ascendant, and ruling planet. If your planets coincide with up or down indicators of major moves, you will be caught in the momentum. With astrology you can figure it out ahead of time and take the appropriate action. You can do the same for companies and businesses with which you are involved as investors or employees.

Investing Precepts

In the absence of any great expertise in astrology or in financial forecasting, keep in mind the principles delineated in previous chapters:

- Get in early when planets change signs. At those points, enthusiasm peaks for things that are about to fail or total aversion develops for things about to get hot. For investments: buy Jupiter early, buy Saturn late. For commodities: buy Saturn early, buy Jupiter late.

- Buy at the bottom. Sell at the top. While obvious and almost impossible without experience and help, it is less difficult astrologically. Jupiter-Saturn conjunctions are long term bottoms. Jupiter-Saturn oppositions are long term tops. Planets moving to a conjunction to the Sun indicate a peak and a fall. After the fall, there is a slow rise to the planet conjunct the Earth (opposition to the Sun) followed by a slow decline or stabilization until the next Sun conjunction.

- Sun conjunctions and oppositions are selling times. Buy before and after. Buy when Venus appears to signal the start of a bull market, rising ahead of the Sun.

Sell when Venus conjuncts the Sun. Do the same for Mercury. Buy when Mercury is on the same side as Venus. Sell when on opposite sides, before they start to turn back towards one another. These are contrarian moves.

■ Buy at the south node; sell at the north except at eclipses, when the trend reverses. You reverse, too. Buy at the New Moon; sell towards the Full, especially for personal purchases.

■ Sell products to the public according to outer planet fashions. Go contrary to the public when investing: Sell to Uranus and Neptune, buy to Pluto transits of the Solar Field.

■ Avoid retrograde periods of Venus and Mercury. Generally Mercury retrograde is a down market, except when Venus is simultaneously retrograde, but not always. Venus retrograde can go either way. These are correction periods which enable the ensuing prices to rise or fall in accordance with attempts to stabilize and equalize prices and markets.

■ Avoid eclipses unless you are very familiar with the current trend. Eclipses reverse trends.

■ Follow good money practices. Save enough to have money to trade and to spend in way that will increase your assets. Simply holding on to assets takes money out of circulation and reduces your ability to multiply your wealth. Keep debt short term and asset backed for maximum safe leverage. Buy goods in line with market value and personal value. Sell to market scarcities and fads.

■ Watch the Mutation degrees for unusual price movements in the markets and in commodities. These happen unexpectedly and change equally fast so you must be well prepared in advance.

The problem of personal timing can be handled by following the above rules. Problems of universal event timing can be handled by preparing a list of Mutation chart ascending and culminating degrees around the world. The Middle East has

Pisces rising and Sagittarius on the MC generally. All their
activity has relevance both to general price levels, ruler Jupiter
is intrinsic to the Mutation itself, and co-ruler Neptune, is the
planet of oil. To locate the specific country, examine the various
national charts.

Look to the rising degree when an event impacts the population or is driven by the will of the people. Look to the 10th
house where the government dominates. Looks to the rulers of
the Ascendant, for the actions of the leaders of the people,
whether in power or not.

If we look back at history we can see that countries ruled
by Jupiter or Saturn on their Mutation charts are most likely to
precipitate events that have a world impact. The United States
has a Jupiter in Cancer ruled national chart, which is why we
always respond to events rather than start them. Our Jupiter,
Sun, and Venus are very close to an opposition to the Mutation
degree, 8° Capricorn, therefore, we always feel we have an interest in whatever happens.

Do not fail to examine international charts when trading in
commodities not under the control of the United States. While no
astrological assessment is without complexity and difficulty,
astrology provides all the information you need to understand
and profit from what you can read about and see.

Precautions, Patterns, and Profits

- Buy and sell when you have good aspects. Jupiter transits to the lights, angles, and to the ruler of the commodity, property, product, or company. Also look for favorable mutual aspects between your ruling planet and Jupiter and Venus.

- Avoid both good and bad aspects to the above from Saturn, Mars and the outer planets.

- Invest in companies and people who have good Jupiter and Venus aspects to your chart.

- Before obtaining a mortgage or loan look at future Pluto transits. A debt taken out at the start of a series of Pluto transits to critical points means difficulty paying off.

- Avoid serious purchases when you are under the domination of Neptune and Uranus. Neptune makes the good seem bad and the bad seem good. Uranus gets carried away with excitement. Keep someone with a clear head beside you at all times.

- When buying real estate make sure the Moon and Venus are well-aspected. The election or inception chart should have the Moon in a money house for endurance and in a sign of her strength to maintain value in down times and promote growth in good.

Chapter Twelve

TOMORROW

We stand at the Millennium, the turn to a new century and a new eon of 1,000 years. The Millennium always brings upheaval and fear of annihilation, the end of the world prophesied in the Bible, a growing sense that "the center cannot hold." Astrologically we are in the breakdown stage of the Earth Mutation and on the threshold of the Aquarian Age. Our greatest concern and our greatest fear is of what is to come. We can anticipate both the Aquarian Age and the Air Mutation by examining the Jupiter-Saturn conjunction of 2020, the time in which our children and grandchildren will live, if not ourselves.

The New World Order

The chart of the Air Mutation in 2020 is the chart of the New World Order. For the United States, Taurus rising with Venus in Sagittarius in the 8th continues a debt-oriented economy. Uranus in the 1st suggests an attempt to mesh cutting-edge technology and shared ownership as the fundamental standard of material value. Its strong connection to the Aquarian 11th of groups and corporations suggests a primary identification with one's company and/or the corporate dominance (ruler Saturn in the 10th) of the national economy. We may try to cling to our land and our capitalism, but our identity will be with our group.

Gemini on the 2nd of money gives us an accounting system in place of material assets. Its conjunction with the Sun in the 9th portends fiat money, a credit card economy, regulated by law, not assets. The Sun, ruler of gold, is conjunct Mercury (ruler of the 2nd and 3rd houses) in a Earth sign. Gold may increase in value, but in the 9th, it could be controlled by law.

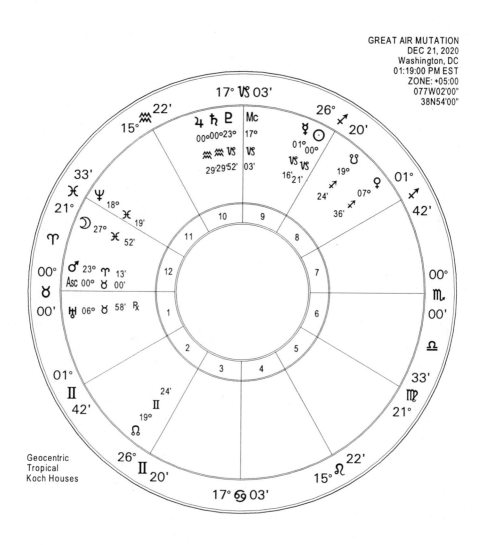

17° ♑ 03'

15° ♒ 22'

♃ ♄ ♇ Mc
00° 00° 23° 17°
♒ ♒ ♑ ♑
29'29'52' 03'

26° ♐ 20'

☿ ☉
01° 00°
♑ ♑
16' 21'

☊
19°
♐
24'

♀
07°
♐
36'

01° ♐ 42'

33'
♓
21°

Ψ
18°
♓ 19'

☽ 27°
♓ 52'

10   9

11   8

12   7

1   6

2   5

3   4

♂ 23° ♈ 13'
Asc 00° ♉ 00'

⛢ 06° ♉ 58' ℞

00° ♉ 00'

00° ♏ 00'

♎

01° ♊ 42'

24'
♊
19°

☋

26° ♊ 20'

33'
♍
21°

15° ♌ 22'

17° ♋ 03'

Geocentric
Tropical
Koch Houses

Great Mutation in Air—New World Order

254

Jupiter, Saturn and Pluto in the 10th suggest Plutocratic authority and despotic government or one beholden to allies and enemies (Pluto rules 7th) because of debt. The Mutation in the 10th gives the government control of the economy and corporations, or, the global economy takes the place of government. With Saturn square Uranus, democracy is compromised. The square from Mars to Pluto and from Uranus to the Mutation, with the lingering Earth values of Taurus and Capricorn, suggest a rebellious struggle between the individuality that a free-booting material economy afforded, and the autocracy that democratic despotism usually bestows. At its best, the United States could be a model of the transition from a materialist economy to an economy of travel and trade. At its worst it could be totalitarian.

The United States will amass great wealth through international trade (Mercury-Sun conjunction in the 9th) and may become the nexus of global import/export trade.

The Moon in Pisces indicates increasing homelessness or an increasing collectivist style of living, the disintegration and obfuscation of family ties, and the demise of the one-family home and property ownership. The bureaucracy (12th house) will swell, along with institutions: hospitals, prisons, retreats, a repeat of the religious withdrawal from the community that the previous Air Mutation witnessed.

The combination of Moon in Pisces and Uranus in Taurus, rising, both indicators of the population, suggests increasing isolation of the population from one another. Mercury, ruler of the 6th of work, in the 9th house, means work far away. Workers, Mercury trine Uranus, connected to their jobs electronically, need never go to the office. They can live at their places of work just as guild members did centuries ago. Women may lose much of the independence they won in a money economy. Mother martyrs come back in style.

The home may well be the only place of retreat and of privacy in an electronic age. We may all become couch potatoes, wrapped in our electronic cocoons.

It seems unlikely that the new world order will ever achieve one world government. The Catholic Church almost achieved a universal rule in the previous Air Mutation, intellectually, spiritually, socially, and politically. Broad masses of people who identified with each other by race and culture developed a centralized moral government through religion: Catholicism,

Islam, Buddhism, Confucianism, as befits a Piscean, other-worldly focus. In the Aquarian Age it will be humanistic and secular. Because of the breakdown of the nation state and the petty rivalries of medieval monarchies, governments were unable to counter or control the universal and global trading impulses that created a world economy and a market domi-nance. Rulers, unlike the church and its quasi-universal clien-tele, simply did not have the money and the power to achieve great global power and control. Global power developed in the Fire Mutation.

Although internationalism will be the dominant economic force, racial, ethnic, religious, and corporate structures will define individual loyalty and alignment.

To profit from the New World Order, think global, think people, think groups and cartels, think communal living (con-dos, retirement communities, apartments and hotels), think electronics and nuclear power. Go with the multinationals, not nations. Expect credit cards to replace cash. Anticipate data banks that will contain all the information needed to know anything remotely "public" about anyone any time. Privacy will be a precious commodity. It could be a good investment for the transition.

The Service Economy

The service economy is a harbinger of the New World Order. As we have seen in earlier chapters, all wealth comes from the ground. An industrial economy creates wealth because it is predicated on materials that are mined or produced from the bounty of the land. A service economy does not create wealth, it merely shifts it around.

The first sign of the post-industrial service economy is the shift from durable goods to consumer items. Consumer items are the perfect vehicle for a hunting economy because they are used up and must be replaced. But, as the work force (including both labor and management) prices itself out of world markets, consumer items fueled by high wages and inflation begin to fall prey to foreign competitors. Since our system is a "free enter-prise" system, we are loath to raise trade barriers. We cannot afford the backlash. Up to now we have been able to replace human labor with machines and shift our labor force to main-tainors, designers and purchasers of those machines. We have been able to keep ourselves going with the fat of our own wages through consumer items. The next step may well make us all salesmen for foreign products, and servants to those who have or control great wealth. Salesmen and servants are paid less than skilled workers on any level.

A service economy pays lower wages. Lower wages cannot buy the amount of products needed to keep the factories running. Having lost our manufacturing base, the product is no longer a thing, but a service. (Virgo is the sign of service.) A service person buys mostly necessities.

Starting an industry requires either an accumulation of wealth or a high risk entrepreneurial courage. The service person with a little extra wealth starts small businesses. Capricorn on the 2nd is the individual entrepreneur with little but his own skills to carry him. His businesses start with little capital investment: tax accountant, dating service, typing service, travel service, etc. Since foreign goods flow into the economy and foreign tourists as our dollar falls in the world economy, we will essentially service the enterprise of foreigners. It becomes apparent that a service economy is not a viable form for a fundamentally materialist and product oriented system.

If we lose our manufacturing base, we could ultimately move from capitalism to socialism. Because of escalating prices in the economy due to inflation, the increasingly lower wage earners will not be able to afford health care, our first step towards the welfare state. Virgo, the sign of the worker, is also the sign of health. In a Virgo dominated economy the health of the worker, the farm animal, the machinery is paramount.

The 10th house is also the sector of government control. Historically the government has legislated in favor of labor and the unions, a quick and easy way to buy votes. In an economy where the worker tends to price himself out of a job provision must be made for unemployment created by government policy, especially the minimum wage: unemployment compensation; Social Security; universal health care.

Our shift towards a welfare state has already begun:

1. Lower wages because of the shift to the service economy.

2. Minimum wages that price us out of world markets.

3. An emphasis on freedom and individualism that breaks down traditional family values and company loyalty,

coupled with an adversary relationship between labor and management.

4. An increasing dependency on the state to manage the economy—the means of production, the profit and loss, the cost of doing business, both through taxation and regulation.

5. A need for the state to provide crisis care for a work force that must keep spending in order to keep the machinery going at all.

If you want to have a look at America in the 1990s take a look at Great Britain from the 1960s on.

The end result could be state control of all goods and resources: Capricorn, the sign of government on the 2nd. It could be the national wealth tied up in service industries and in the health care system (the 6th house) whose goal is to serve the needy and the unemployed, Neptune in Virgo in the 10th.

Neptune in the 10th house of control and outcome, indicates foreigners could control or flood our markets, and the needy could determine our politics and the distribution of our wealth. Confiscatory taxes to pay for it all (Pluto in the 2nd of money) could stunt any hope of resurrecting our industrial machinery. We will have an elite of doctors and bureaucrats, a declining standard of living, and "security" from cradle to grave.

No, we will never be communist—communism spurts from an entirely different spring—but there will be little difference. The alternative is even less palatable—fascism. Contrary to popular belief, fascism is not a bunch of Nazis marching down Main Street, it is government control of private ownership. We see its seeds in regulated utilities and rent control.

It would appear that the only way we can maintain our industrial base and be competitive in the world is to eliminate the adversary relationship between labor and management, redistribute the wealth within the company, and allow labor to share the profits as an incentive to cooperate. Hunters tend to resist any authority but their own. It won't happen without a fight.

Collaborating and sharing impulses are replacing the Earth values of territory and ownership. Although these changes are happening in an Earth context, we can see a positive erosion of Earth values in the breakup of the Soviet Union, the formation of the European Common Market, a growing global financial interdependence that makes us all sink or swim together.

We also see the shift from the product economy to the service economy. Earth oriented countries will have a difficult time adjusting to this shift in economic value. Air countries and herding economies will come into their own.

To put it a bit more clearly, the concern of corporations will not be profit, *per se*, but a level of productivity that will not only perpetuate their own existence but guarantee jobs. Aquarius is a sign of consolidation, not growth. The capitalist system will give way to communal ownership. Businesses will be owned by employees, not investors, speculators, or stockholders. They will be directed by "unions," not CEOs.

Humanism, cooperation, and internationalism are the waves of the future. We get to sample some the next 20 years. Put your money on the people who deal best with people. A new wave can lift or drown us. The new wave is Air.

The Nineties and Beyond

The mid-range Jupiter-Saturn opposition in May 1991 marked the end of the Mutation bull market and the beginning of the great correction. Not only are we in the final phase of the Earth Mutation, a period of breakdown, but we are in the breakdown period of the third subcycle.

Transits and progressions of the U. S. chart indicate a rapidly falling value of our currency and of the value and wealth of its population. Pluto in Scorpio on the U.S. Mutation chart, a precursor of events on the national chart, created economic havoc in our banking system and in the general economies of the eastern part of the country. Pluto on the national Ascendant could mean great deprivation among the population, not to mention increasing violence and epidemics.

On the positive side it means a total change of attitude of the population, a transformation in the way we conduct our affairs. Let us hope that bankruptcy does not force the change.

This stage of the 60-Year Cycle historically equates to mass mania and plutocratic control. Germany gave us the storm troopers and the gas ovens. Salem gave us witch hunts. The post Civil War period gave us the KKK.

Countries and global economic forces are not individuals. Some of the greatest fortunes were amassed during the Great Depression. Only one rule applies: Stay out of debt. Hold on to your money to take advantage of the bargains a downturn brings.

Remember, too, in a contraction lower prices do not mean loss of value, just lower numbers on the price tag. Likewise, escalating inflation does not mean an increase in value, only higher numbers on the receipt.

If you invest in instruments of quality, quality does not deteriorate with price. Quality is constant, no matter what you pay. A good company will still be a good company, no matter what the price of its stock. A good piece of real estate remains good regardless of economic conditions. Value is not a function of numbers.

The general economic indicators bottomed in the fall of 1992. If you do not have the stomach to play a down market, invest in fundamentals, in companies soundly managed, those unlikely to fail. The world economies should gradually improve. The United States economy will not. To guard against a collapse in the dollar, put a portion of your money in silver and gold. Gold under $400 an ounce is a good buy. Silver below $4.00 is a deal.

Assume a worst case scenario for the 1990s. Our government is rife with the idea that we can spend ourselves out of a recession. With a debt at a 10 times multiple we should be able to. With a debt at a 100 times multiple, we were not even able to raise the Dow to the multiple of 10. Although we had a surge in the Dow beginning in late 1991, it occurred after the last Saturn- Jupiter opposition and is unlikely to be sustained without hyper-inflation. So far the Dow has failed to go beyond the high reached in May 1992 when the industrial average was 10 times the price of gold. The Nikkei likewise failed to advance beyond a similar convergence, when it began its long slide downward.

Should the Dow and the broader averages begin to rise wildly, jump in and out quickly. This is a signal of possible hyper-inflation. Convert your profits equally fast into tangible assets and property.

Expect tariffs and trade barriers when Saturn enters the 3rd house. Expect consumer inflation when Saturn leaves the 2nd. The best investment is debt-free real estate that can be rented when it cannot be sold. The best investments are those that survive the downs: health, entertainment, liquor, and subsistence necessities.

Though the party is over, you can have a ball if you keep your head. The United States is about to go on sale. Be prepared.

Precautions, Patterns, and Profits

- The world economy is about to correct. Expect bank failures, bankruptcies, and confiscation of wealth.

- Order and orthodoxy will dominate the thinking of the populace.

- The materialist economy is in decline. Humanistic values are replacing materialistic ones.

- The coming New World Order will be international, technological, collective, and information oriented.

- Think global. We are inhabitants of planet Earth. We will establish our identities on our expertise and on behalf of those with whom we unite.

GLOSSARY

AIR The element associated with communication, travel, humanistic concerns, immaterial thought processes, and ideas. Intelligence.

ANGLE The four corners of the chart, the power points. On a circle in order of power: noon position, MC, the 10th house cusp, and culminating point; nine o'clock, Ascendant, 1st house cusp, and rising point; three o'clock, the Descendent, 7th house cusp and setting point; and six o'clock, the IC and 4th house cusp.

ARBITRAGE The simultaneous purchase and sale of stocks or commodities in two different markets either to offset a loss in one, whichever way the market goes, or profit on both if the anticipated and hoped for prices materialize. Playing both sides against the middle.

ASCENDANT The sign rising on the horizon at the moment of inception or birth, the 1st house cusp. Also called the *rising sign.*

ASPECT The number of degrees between planets and points. Certain degree configurations have specific interpretations and impact: conjunctions, oppositions, squares, trines, sextiles, etc.

ASTROLOGY A symbolic system that correlates celestial patterns with matters of human concern.

BEAR MARKET A condition of falling price levels.

BULL MARKET A condition of rising price levels.

CARDINAL The mode associated with action, speed, and implementation.

CHART See *horoscope.*

COMBUST A situation where the impact of a planet is blocked by its approaching conjunction with the Sun. For Mercury and Venus, this occurs when they go behind the Sun or pass in front, an orb of 10° operates. For other planets, up to 17°.

CONJUNCTION (☌) Planets or points approaching 0° separation.

CONVERSE A technique that goes backward in time from the natal chart.

CULMINATION The approach of a planet to the Midheaven, the highest point, noon position, on the chart.

CUSP The dividing lines between houses, the twelve segments of the chart, as opposed to the space between the lines. The cusp is the most powerful and active point.

CYCLE Any observable equally spaced repetition of data.

DEGREE One of the 360 divisions of the circle, as commonly used in mathematics, navigation, and astronomy.

DESCENDANT The sign setting at the moment of birth, the 7th house cusp.

DETRIMENT A planet in the sign opposite the sign it rules. This is its weakest place.

DIRECT A planet is direct in motion when it is moving forward in the Zodiac, its natural movement.

DIRECTION A technique that moves all planets and points the same increment to forecast events and changes. Directions are not used in this work.

EARTH The element associated with concrete and material matters. Things.

ECLIPSE A condition where one celestial body aligns closely with another celestial body, to block it from view. See also solar eclipse and lunar eclipse.

EVENING STAR If a planet rises, and therefore sets, after the Sun, it will be seen in the early evening skies as the sky is already dark when it approaches its own setting position.

EXALTATION A planet in a sign of its greatest strength, other than the sign it rules. Every planet, except Mercury, has a sign of exaltation. The exaltations of the outer planets are tentative.

FALL A planet is in the sign of its fall when in the sign opposite its exaltation. A weak and debilitating position.

FIRE The element associated with energy, spirit, impulse, and aggressive force. Power.

FIXED The mode connected with stability, control, stubbornness, accumulation, and resistance to change.

FIXED STARS What we commonly recognize as stars, excluding the Sun. Certain of these are considered to have an impact on charts. They are not covered in this work.

FOCAL POINTS Configurations that draw attention or give power to a planet: head of a T-square; singleton; cutting, handle, and trigger planets in pattern shapes; and chart dispositors.

HARMONIC Any equal division of the circle or astrological chart. The standard Zodiac is the 12th harmonic. The Mutation degree harmonic is the 24th.

HOROSCOPE A chart or map of the heavens from an Earth perspective for any given moment in time.

HOUSE The sector of a chart that represents the materialization or earthly context of planets and signs. The 12 houses are Earth-centered. The 12 signs are ecliptic, and therefore, Sun-centered.

IC The Imum Coeli, the 4th house cusp.

INCEPTION CHART The natal chart of an event that has long term implications. Birth charts of countries are inception charts.

INCONJUNCT (⚻) An aspect of 150°, also called quincunx.

LIGHTS The Sun and Moon.

LUNAR ECLIPSE A condition at Full Moon, where the Earth's shadow blocks the light of the Moon somewhere on Earth. This happens when the Sun is in the area of the nodes.

MC Medium Coeli, the point of culmination, the 10th house cusp. Also called Midheaven.

MEAN NODE An average of the track of the nodes, always retrograde in motion. These values are the most commonly used.

MIDHEAVEN See *MC*.

MODE The nature of a sign as an expression rather than as a material. Cardinal, Fixed, and Mutable are the three modes. Also modality.

MORNING STAR If a planet rises before the Sun, it will be visible in the morning just before sunrise but not in the evening because it goes below the horizon while the Sun is still shining.

MUNDANE Having to do with worldly affairs. Mundane aspects are the same as mutual aspects, current planetary relationships.

MUTABLE The mode associated with flexibility, thought, connections, travel, change, and communication.

MUTATION Any conjunction of Jupiter and Saturn.

MUTATION, GREAT The first conjunction of Jupiter and Saturn in an element that will remain constant for several centuries.

MUTATION CHART A chart drawn for the moment of a Jupiter-Saturn conjunction. The location used to draw this chart illuminates social, political, and economic events for the region.

NATAL CHART A horoscope drawn for the moment of birth.

NODES **(North Node** ☊**, South Node** ☋**)** The points at which the path of the Moon crosses the ecliptic.

OPPOSITION (☍) Planets or points approaching 180° separation.

ORB The amount of separation an aspect can tolerate and still be operative. Depending on the planets and aspects involved orbs can range from 17° for a conjunction with the Sun to 0° for certain techniques.

PARTILE An aspect that is exact, 0° orb.

PLANET The celestial bodies as they are astronomically defined. In astrology, the Sun and Moon are also called planets, even though one is a star and one is a satellite.

POINTS Important degrees on a chart, other than those in which a planet resides: angles, cusps, nodes, etc.

PROGRAM TRADING Using software programs to time stock buying and selling.

PROGRESSION A technique that correlates days before and after birth to years of life to represent potential events and changes.

QUINCUNX (⊼) See *inconjunct*.

RADIX Appearing on the natal or inception chart. Also *radical*.

RECURRENCE The repetition of a previous aspect. Cycles of recurrence are usually periods when a conjunction between two planets, such as Jupiter and Saturn, repeat or when a planet repeats its conjunction with the Sun. The cycles of Mercury and Venus in the Solar Field are cycles of recurrence.

RETROGRADE (℞) A condition where a planet appears to be moving backward in the sky. This happens when Venus and Mercury move between the Sun and the Earth or when the Earth because of its smaller orbit overtakes the planets beyond it.

RULER, RULERSHIP Every sign is associated with a planet. This planet is its ruler. The ruler of a house is the ruler of the sign on the cusp of the house. These are important in interpreting how various departments and functions in life interact.

SCIENCE A mathematical system that equates proof with replicable and consensus observations.

SEMI-SEXTILE (⩢) An aspect of 30°.

SEMI-SQUARE (∟) An aspect of 45°.

SESQUARE See *sesquiquadrate*.

SESQUIQUADRATE (⬓) An aspect of 135°.

SEXTILE (⚹) An aspect of 60°.

SHORT SELLING A technique in which a market speculator borrows a stock to sell at a high price in order to buy it back later at a lower price.

SIDEREAL Data relative to the stars. The sidereal Zodiac is based on the constellations rather than the ecliptic and equinox.

SIGN One of the classic 12 divisions of astrology.

SOLAR ECLIPSE A condition at New Moon, when the Moon is between the Sun and the Earth and blocking a view of the Sun somewhere on the Earth. This happens when the Sun is in the area of the nodes.

SOLAR FIELD The section of the sky bounded by the paths of the Sun, nodes, and Earth.

STATION The point at which a planet's apparent movement changes direction.

SQUARE (□) An aspect of 90°.

TRANSIT The movement of a planet over a point or planet or through a house.

TRIGON The three signs, modalities, of any given element. Aries, Leo, and Sagittarius make up the Fire trigon. Also the Grand Trine.

TRINE (△) An aspect of 120°. A Grand Trine is three planets, each 120° from the other.

TROPICAL The division of the ecliptic that puts 0° Aries, at the Vernal Equinox, where the ecliptic and the equator cross. This is the Zodiac most commonly used in the West.

TRUE NODE The tracking of the actual nodal position, which moves direct and retrograde as do most of the planets.

VOID-OF-COURSE A condition in which a planet makes no further aspects before it leaves a sign. Used especially with the Moon.

WANDERING STARS Since all celestial bodies appear as lights in the sky, the planets were called wandering stars because they changed their positions relative to the fixed stars that did not move.

WATER The element associated with emotion, receptivity, sensitivity, impressionability, and time. The flow.

ZODIAC The area 7-1/2° degrees of latitude on either side of the ecliptic, the apparent path of the Sun through the heavens, in which we see almost all of the planetary activity. Only Pluto's latitude occasionally reaches beyond. The constellations of the same name as the signs fill this area of the sky.

ASTROLOGICAL INTERPRETATIONS AND SYMBOLS

Planets

The organization of planetary interpretation is from the fastest moving to the slowest. The more slowly a planet moves the greater its impact in transits. The faster moving planets are personal and idiosyncratic. The slower moving planets are national, international, and generational.

Moon (☽)

Rules: Cancer

Detriment: Capricorn

Exaltation: Taurus

Fall: Scorpio

Core Meaning: Response.

Correlations: Home, mother, emotions, growth, change, habits, moods, likes and dislikes, needs, security, containers, liquids, memory, intuition, the public, impressionability, sensitivity, women, and babies. The right brain.

Economic indications: the consumer, the instincts and basic needs of people *en masse*, short term fluctuations and inclinations, market ups and downs and mindless urges driven by security needs and public propaganda. What it buys disappears.

Commodities: Silver, investments, consumables, foodstuffs, homes.

Mutation Degree: 29° of Cancer. Degree area 29°/14°. Strongest effect at 29° Cardinal and 14° Fixed.

Transit Action: Provides a focus on the houses or planets involved in larger activities. Destabilization. Times the appropriate day of major activity relevant to a specific chart. The Moon has only a slight impact on a planet unless it is an eclipse, New or Full Moon. The New Moon forecasts the major interest or direction of a monthly cycle, a significant event relative to the planet or house involved. The Full Moon is a culmination of activity or a revelation. The lunar eclipse is a significant revelation or implementation of plans and the effect or conclusion of the conditions created by earlier eclipses to the same place. Except for Full and New Moons and contacts with the nodes, the Moon moves too quickly to have any great impact on trading averages and prices relative to the Mutation chart or the Solar Field. It accounts for hourly ups and downs. The progressed Moon is, however, a major timer of significant life events.

Trading Style: Uncertainty. Follows the crowd. Sells at the bottom and buys at the top. Also true of Sun, Moon, or Ascendant in Cancer, Moon in the angles or in points of focus.

Mercury (☿)

Rules: Gemini and Virgo

Detriment: Sagittarius and Pisces

Exaltation: None

Fall: None

Core Meaning: Connection

Correlations: Communication, short distance travel, brothers and sisters, relatives, vehicles, primary education, voice, ability to handle detail, data processing, design, systems, ability to articulate, co-workers, work habits and the job.

Economic Indications: The recorded price. Market statistics. The trader, who records the value of goods and services against the universal standard. The active buyer and seller as opposed to the relatively inactive investor. The process of exchange. Its transactions give us instantaneous feedback on the current state of financial affairs.

Commodities: Paper, currency as the medium of exchange, not the standard. Mercury, the metal. Also grains and vehicles of communication and transportation.

Mutation Degree: 12° of Aquarius. Degree area: 12°/27°. Greatest impact at 12° Fixed and 27° Mutable.

Transit Action: Over a planet, Mercury brings a message or an idea. Through a house it can bring much discussion about, reorganizations of, and adjustments to methods and materials. Over the Mutation degree a small rise in the price level. In the Solar Field, Mercury indicates intermediate ups and downs in Venus bears and bulls.

Trading Style: Facilitates and analyzes trade. The technical trader who breaks even. The arbitrageur who tries to have it both ways. Also true of Sun, Moon, or Ascendant in Gemini or Virgo, Mercury in the angles, or in points of focus.

Venus (♀)

Rules: Taurus and Libra

Detriment: Scorpio and Aries

Exaltation: Pisces

Fall: Virgo

Core Meaning: Completion

Correlations: Ownership, art, beauty, cosmetics, compliments, jewelry, marriage, partnerships, treaties, balance, lawsuits, consultants, clients, litigators, satisfaction, harmony, anything of a complementary nature.

Economic Indications: The barter trade. Savings and banks. Value given and value received. Long term appreciation. Tendency for the market to double and fall by half. Venus is the great stabilizer. Her movement is always towards achieving a price level she has held before.

Commodities: Copper, land, money as an asset, commercial real estate, nonconsumable raw materials, durable goods, sugar, cattle, and objects that give pleasure apart from their cost, such as art and gems.

Mutation Degree: 26° of Capricorn. Degree area: 26°/11° Greatest impact at 26° of Cardinal and 11° of Fixed.

Transit Action: Stability and peace. Venus over a planet can bring a pleasant interaction, the receipt of money or gifts, and a feeling of well-being. Through a house it brings profit, security or pleasure. By progression, Venus can indicate an increase in wealth in the sector through which it transits, and the health of the money supply and banks according to its sign. In the Mutation degree it signals a small rise in the price level. In the Solar Field it is the timer of a normal bull cycle when it rises ahead of the Sun and a normal bear when it rises behind.

Trading Style: The true investor who buys and holds on. Also true of Sun, Moon, or Ascendant in Taurus or Libra, Venus in angles, or in focal points.

Sun (☉)

Rules: Leo

Detriment: Aquarius

Exaltation: Aries

Fall: Libra

Core Meaning: Power

Correlations: Authority, will, ego, spirit, attention, confidence, energy, the King, males, father as sire, children, recreation.

Economic Indications: Substances of intrinsic value. The final authority and limiter of price rises and falls. The standard of exchange. Value of the currency.

Commodities: Gold and tradables. Currency value.

Mutation Degree: 5° of Aquarius. Degree area, 5°/28°. Strongest impact at 5° of Fixed and 20° of Mutable.

Transit Action: Triggers action. Calls attention to the house or planet involved. Increases wealth. Times the month. In a Mutation degree it signals a rise in price. Solar eclipses indicate a reversal of the conditions surrounding the planet they conjunct or oppose. Major change can be good or bad. In progressions, the sign of the Sun's passage indicate attitudes and problems with stability of the currency and the price of gold. Passage through a house can bring an influx of power, attention, and gold.

Trading Style: Gambles on sure things. Follows trends. Buys after the bottom and before the top. Sells at the top or slightly after. Also true Sun, Moon, or Ascendant in Leo, Sun in the angles or in focal points.

Mars (♂)

Rules: Aries and Scorpio

Detriment: Libra and Taurus

Exaltation: Capricorn

Fall: Cancer

Core Meaning: Impulse

Correlations: Anger, irritability, impatience, force, war, attack, aggression, fighting, muscle, risk-taking, initiative, burns, bruises, damage, cuts, excitement, passion, sex, crisis, theft, and revenge.

Economic Indications: The buyer. The quick buck, interest rates, taxes, debt, cuts, losses, speculation, and crisis. It represents the desire to get something for nothing.

Commodities: Iron and steel, all goods dependent on iron for production.

Mutation Degree: 15° of Pisces. Degree area: 15°/0°. Greatest impact is at 15° Mutable and 0° Fixed.

Transit Action: Mars triggers activity. Disputes, accidents, war, and loss. It excites the planet it transits to action, often by creating an irritation or confrontation from outside. Through a house it causes troubles and irritations, arguments, demands, a

loss of assets, or a cut in price. On the Mutation degree it correlates to a drop in the price level. In the Solar Field, it creates a
buying frenzy just before it joins the Sun, followed by a sharp
drop. From that point it indicates rising interest rates, that
peak and drop as it retrogrades and opposes the Sun (crosses
the Earth line).

Trading Style: The wheeler-dealer. The profit taker and the
short-seller. Also Sun, Moon, or Ascendant in Aries and Scorpio,
angular Mars, or Mars in a focal point.

Jupiter (♃)

Rules: Sagittarius and Pisces

Detriment: Gemini and Virgo

Exaltation: Cancer

Fall: Capricorn

Core Meaning: Expansion

Correlations: Good luck, preservation of assets, asset growth,
optimism, opportunity, overseas travel, religion, judges, law,
advertising, belief, confidence, joviality, forgiveness, wealth.

Economic Indications: Increases in price or supply. Import-
export businesses. Mail Order. Interstate distribution and
transportation system.

Commodities: Tin, imports, gambling returns, and horseflesh.

Mutation Degree: 8° of Capricorn. Degree area: 8°/23°. Major
impact is at 8° of Cardinal and 23° of Fixed.

Transit Action: Brings luck, promotion, growth or protection of
assets, publicity, or legal matters. Confidence and optimism
stimulated in the house it transits. Foreign travel is indicated
when crossing an angle or planet. In the Mutation degree it
indicates a rise in price levels. In its annual transit of the Solar
Field it indicates a large price rise just before the solar conjunction, and a smaller price rise at opposition, the contact
with Earth.

Trading Style: The salesman, who profits whether the buyer wins or loses. Spots trends and operates on hunches and tips. Usually does very well.

Saturn (♄)

Rules: Capricorn and Aquarius

Detriment: Cancer and Leo

Exaltation: Libra

Fall: Aries

Core Meaning: Limitation

Correlations: Skin, bones, boundaries, limits, decisions, blockage, loss, discipline, order, regulations, government, achievement, goals, problem solving ability, policy, executives, restriction, and contraction.

Economic Indications: Demand, tops and bottoms, falling supply, shortages. The packaged product. Retail outlets. The market place. Profit and loss.

Commodities: Lead, retail goods, manufactured goods, leather and furs.

Mutation Degree: 8° of Capricorn. Degree area: 8°/23°. Major impact at 8° of Cardinal and 23° of Fixed.

Transit Action: Always produces a restriction relative to the planet it contacts or the house or sign through which it passes. These force difficult decisions and are fundamental learning experiences in the School of Hard Knocks. Saturn rewards hard work, brings people from the past and punishes immaturity or obliviousness. Saturn is also a planet of forced change and adjustment, a confrontation with one's own limitations or the limitations of one's technique and ability. Paying dues.

Saturn raises prices because of short supply or drops prices because of lack of interest or purchasing power.

In a Mutation degree prices rise then fall. In the Solar Field the Saturn transit of the Sun produces a sharp rise in prices followed by an equally sharp drop. These are also indicative of major tops and bottoms and trading ranges.

Trading Style: Trades on fundamentals, holds on through difficult times, misses out on short term leaps, picks the winners overall. Also applies to Sun, Moon, or Ascendant in Capricorn and Aquarius, Saturn in the angles or focal points.

Uranus (♅)

Rules: Aquarius

Detriment: Leo

Exaltation: Virgo*

Fall: Pisces*

Core Meaning: Reversal

Correlations: What beats in harmony or interrupts the flow. The unusual and unexpected, accidents, rebellion, group activity, contrariness, lawbreaking, mass movements and fads, democracy, modern technology, radio, telegraph, telex, sonar, cartels, conglomerates, and mutual funds.

Economic Indications: Unusual price movements and price breaks, breakthroughs in price levels.

Commodities: Electricity, electronics, public utilities, computers, electrical appliances, radios, and communication equipment.

Mutation Degree: 21° of Pisces.   Degree area: 21°/6°. Major impact on 21° of Mutable and 6° of Fixed.

Transit Action: Creates disruption of the activity of a planet or house through which it passes. It creates accidents, excitement, and chaos. It means breakthroughs in design and development of anything it contacts. In the angles of a Mutation chart or its rulers it provokes rebellion, erratic and irresponsible behavior. It tends towards collectivism, group action, and mob rule. In a Mutation degree it signals a major breakthrough of a price level, and a crash. In the Solar Field, it creates great excitement as it joins the Sun, followed by a drop.

Trading Style: Contrarian and erratic. Inclined to electronic programs and computer trades. Also applies to Sun, Moon, or Ascendant in Aquarius, Uranus in an angle or focal point.

---

*Tentative assignment. Not universally agreed upon.

Neptune (Ψ)

Rules: Pisces

Detriment: Virgo

Exaltation: Leo*

Fall: Aquarius*

Core Meaning: Illusion

Correlations: Institutions, such as hospitals and prisons, charity, drugs, personal excesses and self-undoing, the bureaucracy, all substances that are highly refined or concentrated, glamour and romance, movies and television, retirement places, schemes and scams, lies, obliviousness.

Economic Indications: Hysteria, wild upward swings in price movements that cannot be sustained. Distorted perceptions of market realities. Inflation and junk bonds.

Commodities: Oil, plastics, alcohol, drugs, chemicals.

Mutation Degree: 16° of Aquarius. Degree area: 16°/1°. Major impact at 16° of Fixed and 1° of Cardinal.

Transit Action: Creates confusion, self-destruction, mass hysteria, escapism. Encourages lying and propaganda. Possibility of contagion. A strong desire to retire or retreat. The transit of a planet or house creates unreasonable expectations that lead to disappointment. Matters become chaotic and confused. Theft or loss can be the result of foolish or careless decisions. In the Solar Field the transit of the Sun produces a steep rise then a fall.

Trading Style: Subject to unrealistic expectations of profit and wealth. May fall victim to fraud or get involved in shady practices willingly or unwillingly. Boom and bust.

Pluto (♇)

Rules: Scorpio

Detriment: Taurus

Exaltation: Aries*

Fall: Libra*

---

*Tentative assignment. Not universally agreed upon.

Core Meaning: Resurrection

Correlations: Death, rebirth, debt, bankruptcy, taxes, transformation, operations, crises, shared resources, crime, the underworld, atomic energy, total destruction, obsession, compulsion, addiction, venereal disease, matters of life and death, including heroic life-saving techniques.

Economic Indications: Bankruptcies, debt, taxation, leveraged buy-outs, hostile takeovers, restructuring, market bottoms, fear, and despair.

Commodities: Nuclear power, black market goods, prostitution and pornography, organized crime, toxic waste.

Mutation Degree: 19° of Aries. Degree area: 19°/4°. Major impact at 19° of Cardinal and 4° of Fixed.

Transit Action: Brings destruction, crime, murder, violence, coercion, and death. Promotes research projects, and work that revitalizes or restores things considered useless or dead. Increases pressure on matters connected to the planet transited. Heavy demands for payment of loans or need to take out a loan to pay elsewhere. Confiscation of goods. Indicates a possibility for criminal attacks, surgery, and venereal disease. The transit through a house can indicate losses or great pressures and crises through matters connected with that house, a tendency or need to borrow money to manage the affairs of the sector involved. In a Mutation degree it signifies a steep drop and often a market all time low. In the Solar Field, the market rises at the Sun conjunction itself, but falls before and after.

Trading Style: Pluto usually acts as an agent, profiting from other people's profits and losses. Never uses own money. The leverage player, who cuts his losses through bankruptcy.

Points

Ascendant

Also called ASC, Rising Sign, and First House Cusp

Core Meaning: Materialization

Correlation: The physical appearance, environmental conditioning, the self, the name of a country or company, the population.

Economic Indications: Buyers. Attitude of the public towards current economic conditions. The effect of conditions on the country or company as a whole. What individuals have to cope with in their personal lives.

Mutation Degree: 10° of Scorpio. Degree area: 10°/25°. Major impact at 10° of Fixed and 25° of Mutable.*

Transit Activity: Except in the techniques known as progressions and directions, where it has a major impact on materializing the events connected to the planets it transits, the Ascendant does not move. Transits to the Ascendant and its degree area effect the population as a whole, the country, company, or individual.

Descendant

Primarily known as the Seventh House

Core Meaning: The Other

Correlation: Partners, spouses, enemies, competitors, consultants, clients, lawyers, people with whom there is a contractual obligation.

Economic Indications: Sellers. Availability of people willing to sell. Trading partners, cartel obligations, the strength of the competition.

Mutation Degree: 10° of Taurus. Degree area: 10°/25°. Major impact at 10° of Fixed and 25° of Mutable.*

Transit Activity: Except in the techniques known as progressions and directions, where it has a major impact on materializing the events connected to the planets it transits, the

---

*United States and Washington, D.C. only.

Descendant does not move. Transits to the Descendant and its degree area affect sellers and all contractual relationships, personal, public, and corporate.

IC

Also known as Imum Coeli, Fourth House Cusp

Core Meaning: Foundation

Correlation: Home, land, produce, family, heritage, parental influence, living environment, ecological conditions, headquarters as a building, the physical manufacturing plant.

Economic Indications: Bounty or scarcity of land and natural resources. Consumer supply and demand. The product in a transaction.

Mutation Degree: 18° Aquarius. Degree area: 18°/3°. Major impact at 18° of Fixed and 3° of Cardinal.*

Transit Activity: Same stability as other angles. Transits to the IC indicate changes in land productivity and growth, real estate values, and the living conditions of the population.

Midheaven

Also known as MC, Medium Coeli, Tenth House Cusp

Core Meaning: Direction

Correlation: Goals, objectives, government, achievement, parental influence, how the environment assists or frustrates ones ability to achieve, career, reputation.

Economic Indications: Government intervention in the economy. The market place. The price. Market demand. Retail outlets. Manufactured goods.

Mutation Degree: 18° Leo. Degree area: 18°/3°. Major impact at 18° of Fixed and 3° of Cardinal.*

Transit Activity: Same stability as ASC. Transits to the MC indicate changes in government position or market conditions.

---

*United States and Washington, D.C. only.

North Node (☊)

Core Meaning: Support

Correlation: Forward movement, path to release karma. Events beyond one's control and relationships that enable progress.

Economic Indications: The unforeseeable and uncontrollable. Price tops.

Mutation Degree: 18° Leo. Degree Area: 18°/3°. Major impact at 18° of Fixed and 3° of Cardinal.

Transit Activity: Contact with the planet often times the effect of an eclipse or brings an important condition or person into the life to enable progress and growth.

South Node (☋)

Core Meaning: Restitution.

Correlation: Demand for past debts, karmic baggage.

Economic Indications: The unforeseeable and uncontrollable. Price bottoms

Mutation Degree: 18° Aquarius. Degree area 18°/3°. Major impact, 18° of Fixed and 3° of Cardinal.

Transit Activity: Contact with the planet often times the effect of an eclipse or brings an important condition or person into the life to reveal and heal past errors and redeem past debts.

Signs

Signs indicate how underlying conditions are expressed. They
are both functional and descriptive in nature.

Aries (♈)

Ruler: Mars

Element: Fire

Mode: Cardinal

Gender: Masculine

House: First

Core Meaning: Aggressive self-interest and self-defense.

Correlation: Survival of self. Active and initiating impulses.
Movement is fast, impatient, irritable, argumentative, demanding. Conditions demand action that is quick and aggressive. New
and ground-breaking activities. High levels of risk. Courage.

Taurus (♉)

Ruler: Venus

Element: Earth

Mode: Fixed

Gender: Feminine

House: Second

Core Meaning: Materialization.

Correlation: Possessions. Same qualities as the material side of
Venus. Action is slow and cautious. Attitudes are thrifty, saving,
accumulating, with an eye to receive the best value for money
spent. Material goods and money are needed to achieve in Taurus sectors. Peace, prosperity, and wealth are the result.

Gemini (♊)

Ruler: Mercury

Element: Air

Mode: Mutable

Gender: Masculine

House: Third

Core Meaning: Relation.

Correlation: Communication. Brothers, sisters, relatives: human connections one is born with. Elementary school. Short distance travel. Mercurial pursuits in their non-material, rational, and theoretical form. Conditions require reasoning power, education, communication skills, travel, the ability to relate one entity to another.

Cancer (♋)

Ruler: Moon

Element: Water

Mode: Cardinal

Gender: Feminine

House: Fourth

Core Meaning: Protection.

Correlation: Security, home, family, heritage, living conditions. Action is defensive and cautious. Conditions require constant protection and replenishment.

Leo (♌)

Ruler: Sun

Element: Fire

Mode: Fixed

Gender: Masculine

House: Fifth

Core Meaning: Creativity

Correlation: Self-expression, children, talent, recreation, self-confidence and personal power. Leo dramatizes and calls attention to itself. Conditions demand an exercise of power, confidence, and exposure.

Virgo (♍)

Ruler: Mercury

Element: Earth

Mode: Mutable

Gender: Feminine

House: Sixth

Core Meaning: Precision

Correlation: Data. The material expression of Mercury. Matters of health and work where facts and attention to detail are important. The military, police, firemen, and service personnel of the state or municipality. Doctors and health care professionals. The expression is careful, critical, orderly, and meticulous. Conditions require facts, logic, and organization.

Libra (♎)

Ruler: Venus

Element: Air

Mode: Cardinal

Gender: Masculine

House: Seventh

Core Meaning: Equilibrium

Correlation: Balance. The expression is tactful, pleasing, reasonable, poised, and fair. Conditions require partners or good social connections.The intent is to get even, pleasantly or not and to advance through marriage or contractual relationships. Action is also stimulated by competition.

Scorpio (♏)

Ruler: Mars and Pluto

Element: Water

Mode: Fixed

Gender: Feminine

House: Eighth

Core Meaning: Crisis

Correlation: Fear. The action is often secretive, aggressive compulsive and obsessive, driven by a fear of death or destruction. Conditions require heroic measures or a constant battle. They provoke research into things hidden or obscure. Surgery, debt, death and sex as procreation.

Sagittarius (♐)

Ruler: Jupiter

Element: Fire

Mode: Mutable

Gender: Masculine

House: Ninth

Core Meaning: Inspiration

Correlation: Salesmanship. The lucky side of Jupiter. Actions are expressed with confidence, certainty, and enthusiasm. There is generosity and a tendency to overspend. Associated with higher education, conventional religion, the judiciary, and long distance travel. Conditions require travel, confidence in the future, and persuasive abilities.

Capricorn (♑)

Ruler: Saturn

Element: Earth

Mode: Cardinal

Gender: Feminine

House: Tenth

Core Meaning: Experience

Correlation: Discipline. The material manifestations of Saturn. The action is controlled and steady, patient. Action is taken out of necessity and force, rather than inclination. Conditions are unpleasant, lacking in amenities, cold and hard. They are run by the laws of worst possible case scenarios. Perspective is the result and the requirement.

Aquarius (≈)

Ruler: Saturn and Uranus

Element: Air

Mode: Fixed

Gender: Masculine

House: Eleventh

Core Meaning: Consensus

Correlation: Democracy. Corresponds to the human side of Saturn and Uranus. The expression is humanistic and group directed or rebellious and eccentric, an effort to combat peer and mob pressure or attract public attention. Conditions require the cooperation of or a consensus acknowledgment within groups, organizations, or companies, and an ability to capture the public mood, approval, and taste.

Pisces (ℋ)

Ruler: Jupiter and Neptune

Element: Water

Mode: Mutable

Gender: Feminine

House: Twelfth

Core Meaning: Withdrawal.

Correlation: Denial of the material world. Corresponds to the spiritual, other-worldly, reality-rejecting qualities of Jupiter.

Actions express themselves in secretive, confused, chaotic, and unorganized ways on the surface, even when well planned. Pisces represents the attempt to transcend or ignore the law of the material world for higher motives or for unrealistic goals. Conditions require self-sacrifice, retreat, and faith in a higher power. They often prompt secrecy, lying, misrepresentations, or punishment and feelings of guilt and shame.

Houses

Houses generally follow the interpretations of signs as they relate to the fundamental categories of life experience, as opposed to their expression or materialization. In order:

First—Survival. The outward signs of one's unique existence.

Second—Wealth and resources.

Third—Ability to learn and communicate. Domestic travel.

Fourth—Family and home environment. Building a foundation.

Fifth—Pleasure and offspring.

Sixth—Health and Work.

Seventh—Contractual relationships and enemies.

Eighth—Debt, sex, shared resources and death.

Ninth—Ability to teach and judge. Travel abroad.

Tenth—Relationship to authority, achievement, reputation.

Eleventh—Friends and casual acquaintances.

Twelfth—Retirement, retreat, and self-undoing.

Detailed explanations of the houses as nations, corporations, markets and individuals can be found in chapter five on page 92 and in chapter ten on pages 218–225.

Symbols

This table of symbols is given as a reference for non-astrological types and beginning astrologers who wish to study the charts that are included in the book.

Planets		Points	
Moon	☽	Ascendant	ASC
Mercury	☿	IC (4th house cusp)	IC
Venus	♀	Midheaven	MC
Sun	☉	North Node	☊
Mars	♂	South Node	☋
Jupiter	♃		
Saturn	♄		
Uranus	♅		
Neptune	♆		
Pluto	♇		

Signs		Aspects	
Aries	♈	Conjunction	☌
Taurus	♉	Inconjunct	⚻
Gemini	♊	Opposition	☍
Cancer	♋	Quincunx	⚻
Leo	♌	Semi-Sextile	⚺
Virgo	♍	Semi-Square	∟
Libra	♎	Sesquare	⚼
Scorpio	♏	Sesquiquadrate	⚼
Sagittarius	♐	Sextile	⚹
Capricorn	♑	Square	□
Aquarius	♒	Trine	△
Pisces	♓		

Appendix II

NATIONAL AND MUTATION CHARTS

The following pages contain the national and Mutation charts of selected countries throughout the world to enable students and analysts to time events and their impact on various geographic locations.

The following countries are included partly because of their currency in the news and partly to spot a wide variety of geographical locations. If the Mutation or national chart appears in the body of the book, only the missing chart appears here. The page number for all charts in the book is given for easy cross referencing.

*Since it is important to be able to check events against charts, the West German chart should stand until we know the full implications of the events of the past couple of years.

289

*Since it is important to be able to check events against charts, the U.S.S.R. chart should stand until we know the full implications of the events of the past couple of years.

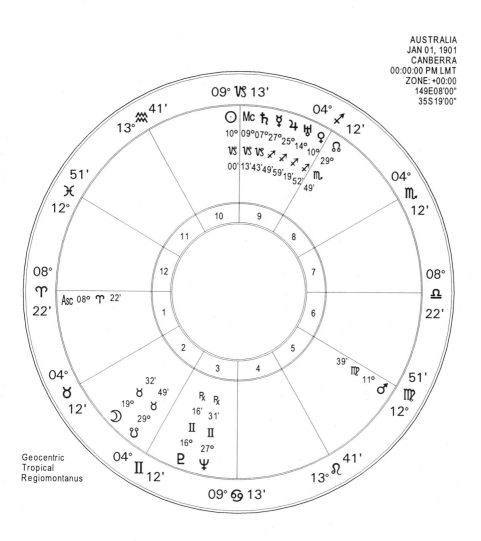

AUSTRALIA
JAN 01, 1901
CANBERRA
00:00:00 PM LMT
ZONE: +00:00
149E08'00"
35S19'00"

Geocentric
Tropical
Regiomontanus

National Chart—Canberra, Australia

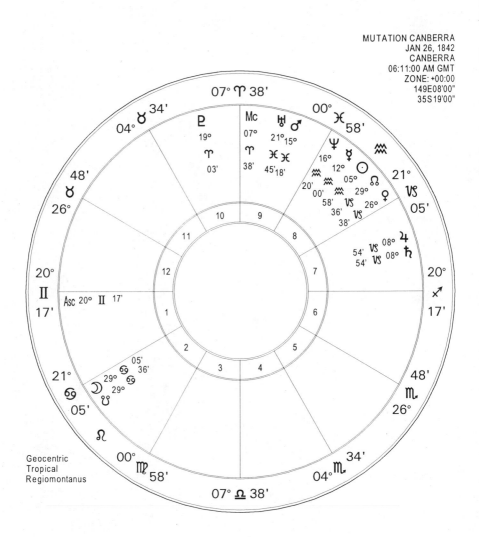

Great Mutation—Canberra, Australia

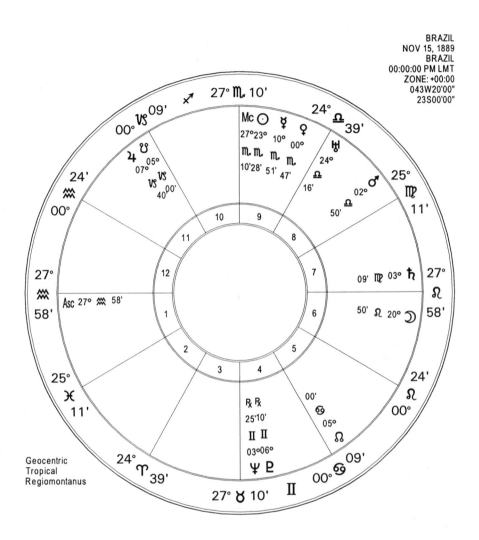

BRAZIL
NOV 15, 1889
BRAZIL
00:00:00 PM LMT
ZONE: +00:00
043W20'00"
23S00'00"

Geocentric
Tropical
Regiomontanus

National Chart—Rio de Janeiro, Brazil

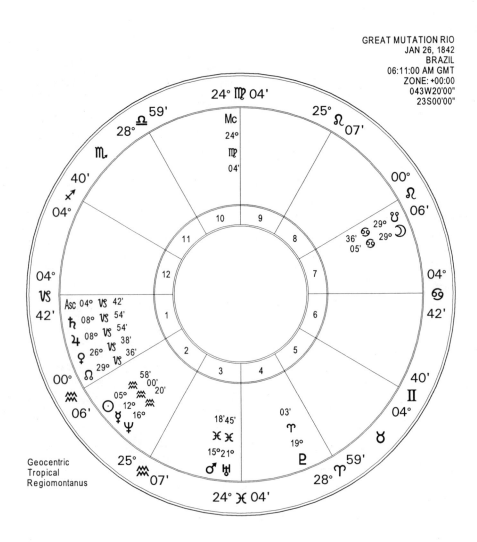

GREAT MUTATION RIO
JAN 26, 1842
BRAZIL
06:11:00 AM GMT
ZONE: +00:00
043W20'00"
23S00'00"

Geocentric
Tropical
Regiomontanus

Great Mutation—Rio de Janeiro, Brazil

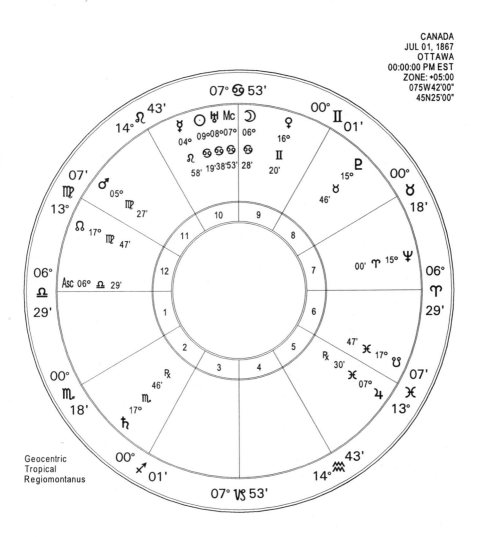

CANADA
JUL 01, 1867
OTTAWA
00:00:00 PM EST
ZONE: +05:00
075W42'00"
45N25'00"

Geocentric
Tropical
Regiomontanus

National Chart—Ottawa, Canada

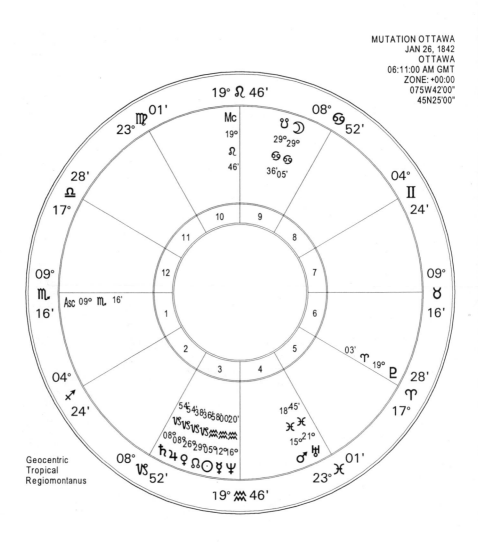

MUTATION OTTAWA
JAN 26, 1842
OTTAWA
06:11:00 AM GMT
ZONE: +00:00
075W42'00"
45N25'00"

Great Mutation—Ottawa, Canada

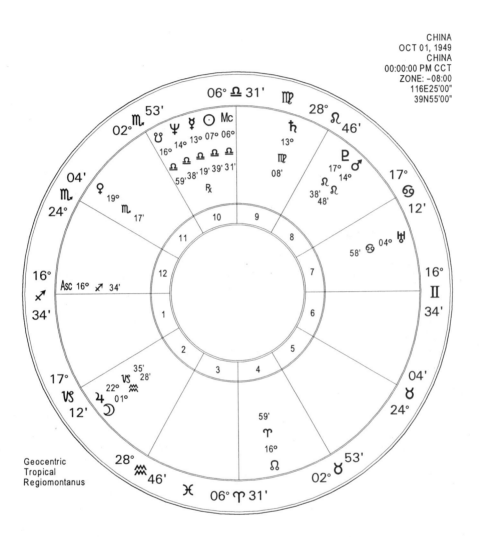

CHINA
OCT 01, 1949
CHINA
00:00:00 PM CCT
ZONE: -08:00
116E25'00"
39N55'00"

06° ♎ 31'   ♍

28° ♌ 46'

02° ♏ 53'

☊ ♆ ☿ ☉ Mc
16° 14° 13° 07° 06°
♎ ♎ ♎ ♎ ♎
59' 38' 19' 39' 31'
℞

♄
13°
♍
08'

♇ ♂
17° 14°
♌
38' ♌
48'

04'
♏
24°   ♀ 19°
♏ 17'

17°
69
12'

58' 69 04° ♅

10   9

11   8

12   7

16°
♐
34'   Asc 16° ♐ 34'

1   6

16°
♊
34'

2   5

17°
♑
12'   35' 28'
♑ ♒
22° 01°
♃
☽

3   4

04'
♉
24°

59'
♈
16°
♌

28° ♒ 46'   ♓   06° ♈ 31'

02° ♉ 53'

Geocentric
Tropical
Regiomontanus

National Chart—Beijing, China

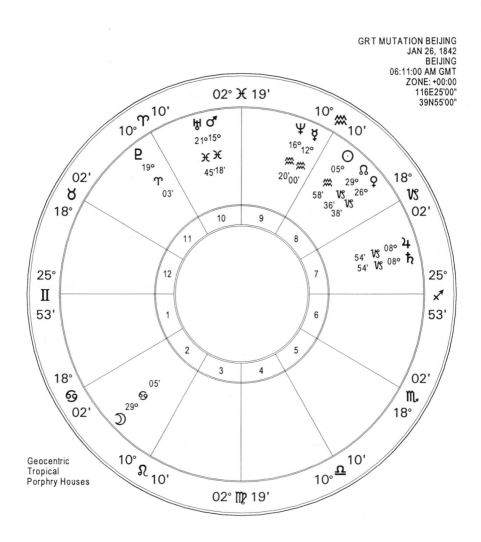

Great Mutation—Beijing, China

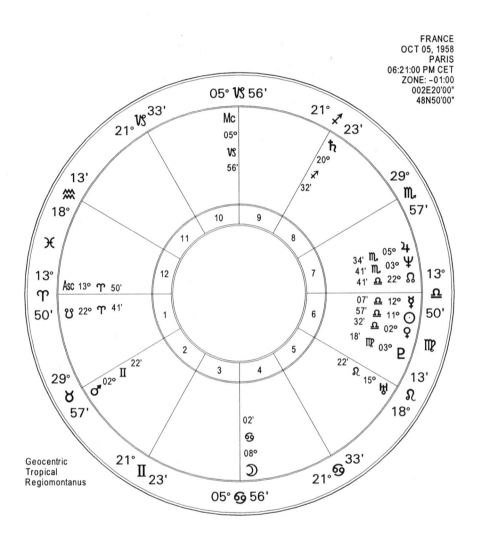

FRANCE
OCT 05, 1958
PARIS
06:21:00 PM CET
ZONE: -01:00
002E20'00"
48N50'00"

Geocentric
Tropical
Regiomontanus

National Chart—Paris, France

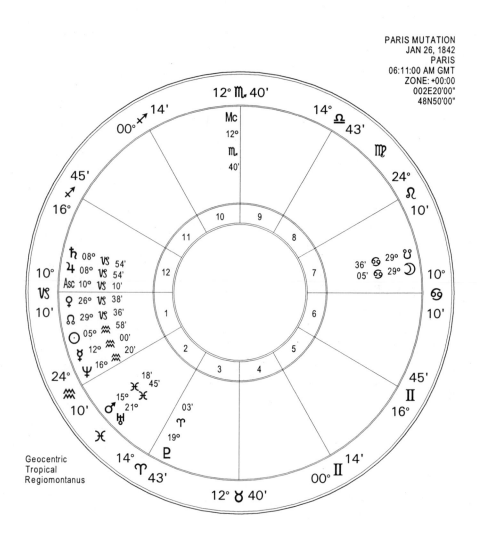

PARIS MUTATION
JAN 26, 1842
PARIS
06:11:00 AM GMT
ZONE: +00:00
002E20'00"
48N50'00"

Geocentric
Tropical
Regiomontanus

Great Mutation—Paris, France

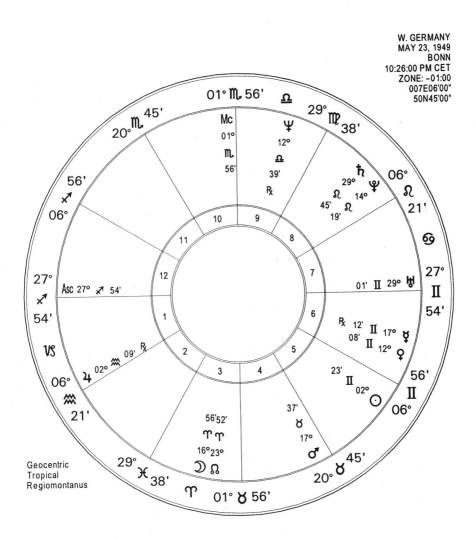

National Chart—Bonn, West Germany*

*Since it is important to be able to check events against charts, the West German chart should stand until we know the full implications of the events of the past couple of years.

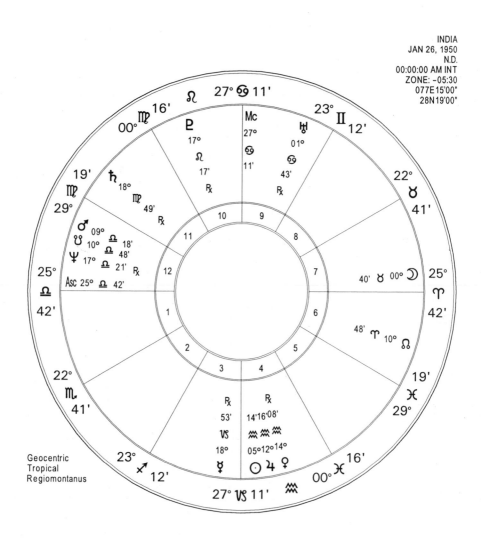

Geocentric
Tropical
Regiomontanus

National Chart—New Dehli, India

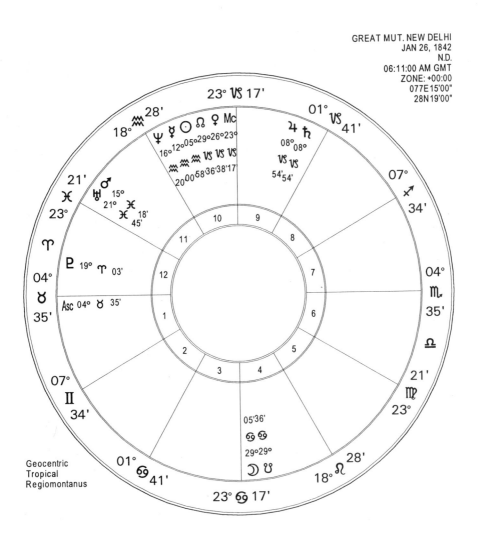

GREAT MUT. NEW DELHI
JAN 26, 1842
N.D.
06:11:00 AM GMT
ZONE: +00:00
077E15'00"
28N19'00"

Geocentric
Tropical
Regiomontanus

Great Mutation—New Dehli, India

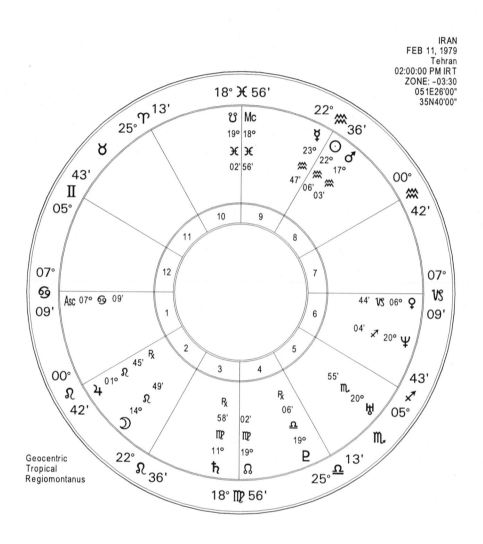

National Chart—Teheran, Iran

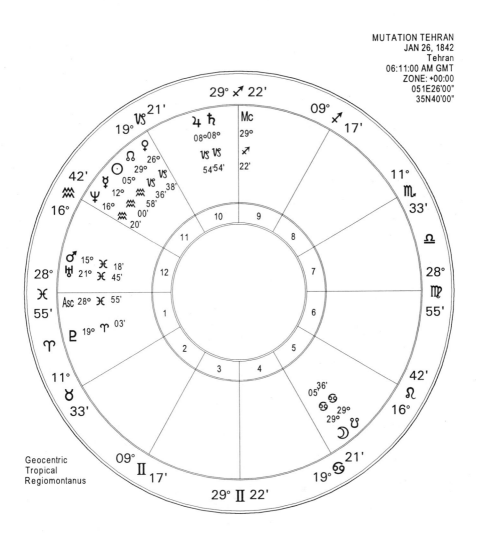

Great Mutation—Teheran, Iran

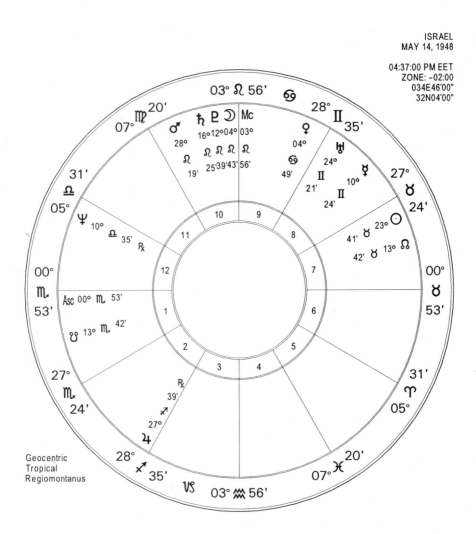

ISRAEL
MAY 14, 1948

04:37:00 PM EET
ZONE: −02:00
034E46'00"
32N04'00"

Geocentric
Tropical
Regiomontanus

National Chart—Israel

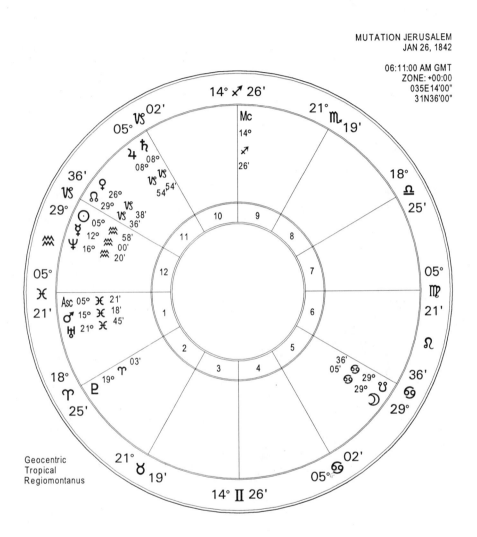

MUTATION JERUSALEM
JAN 26, 1842

06:11:00 AM GMT
ZONE: +00:00
035E14'00"
31N36'00"

Geocentric
Tropical
Regiomontanus

Great Mutation—Jerusalem, Israel

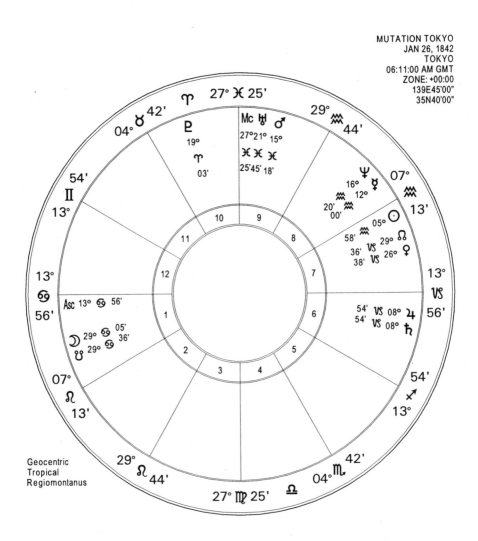

Great Mutation—Tokyo, Japan

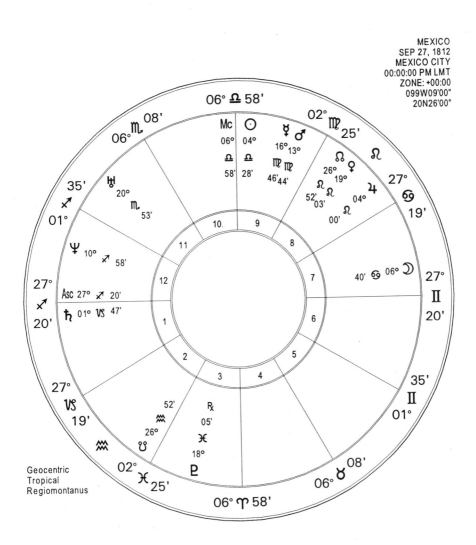

MEXICO
SEP 27, 1812
MEXICO CITY
00:00:00 PM LMT
ZONE: +00:00
099W09'00"
20N26'00"

Geocentric
Tropical
Regiomontanus

National Chart—Mexico City, Mexico

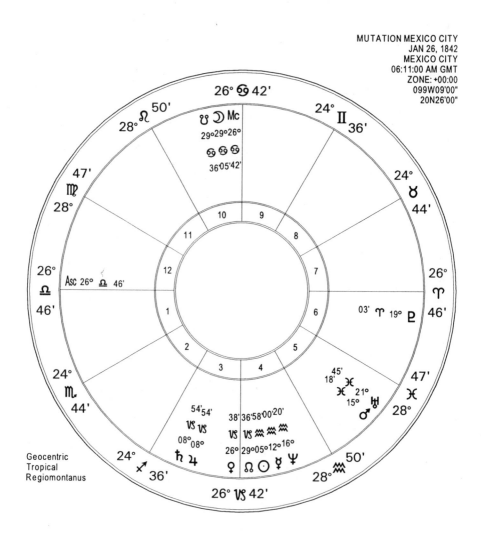

Great Mutation—Mexico City, Mexico

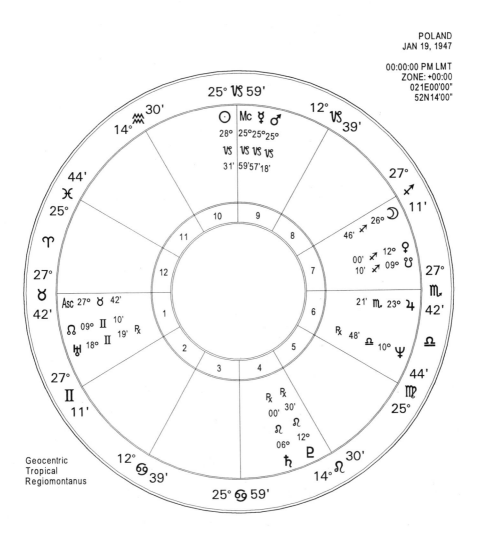

National Chart—Warsaw, Poland

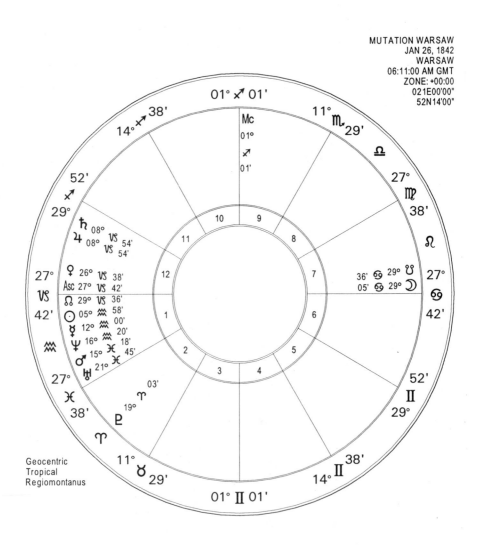

MUTATION WARSAW
JAN 26, 1842
WARSAW
06:11:00 AM GMT
ZONE: +00:00
021E00'00"
52N14'00"

Geocentric
Tropical
Regiomontanus

Great Mutation—Warsaw, Poland

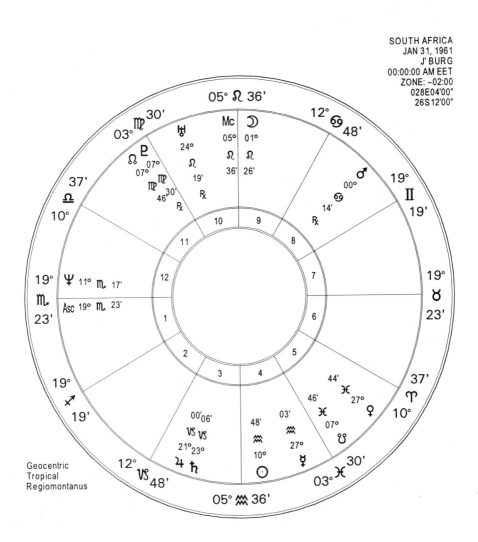

SOUTH AFRICA
JAN 31, 1961
J' BURG
00:00:00 AM EET
ZONE: −02:00
028E04'00"
26S12'00"

05° ♌ 36'

03° ♍ 30'

♅ 24° ♌ 19'

Mc ☽ 05° ♌ 01° ♌ 36' 26'

12° ♋ 48'

♇ 07° ♌ 07°
♊ ♍ ♍ 46° 30'
℞

19°
♊
19'

37'
♎
10°

10 9

♂ 00° ♋ 14' ℞

8

19°
♏︎
23'

Ψ 11° ♏ 17'

Asc 19° ♏ 23'

12

11

7

19°
♉
23'

1

2

6

5

19°
♐
19'

3 4

44' ♓ 27' ♀
46' ♓ 07°
☊

37'
♈
10°

00' 06'
♑ ♑
21° 23'
♃ ♄

48' 03'
♒ ♒
10° 27'
☉ ☿

30'
03° ♓

12° ♑ 48'

Geocentric
Tropical
Regiomontanus

05° ♒ 36'

National Chart—Johannesburg, South Africa

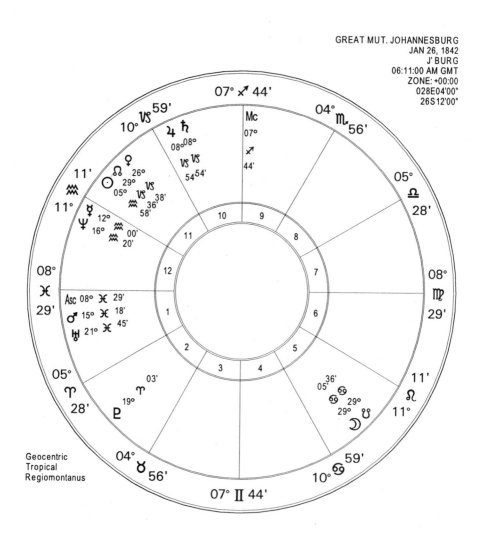

GREAT MUT. JOHANNESBURG
JAN 26, 1842
J'BURG
06:11:00 AM GMT
ZONE: +00:00
028E04'00"
26S12'00"

Geocentric
Tropical
Regiomontanus

Great Mutation—Johannesburg, South Africa

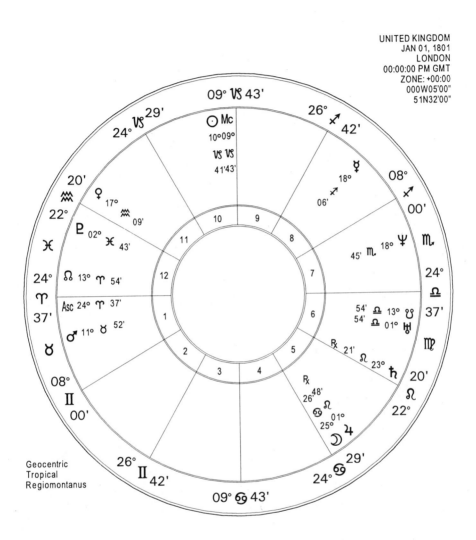

UNITED KINGDOM
JAN 01, 1801
LONDON
00:00:00 PM GMT
ZONE: +00:00
000W05'00"
51N32'00"

Geocentric
Tropical
Regiomontanus

National Chart—London, United Kingdom

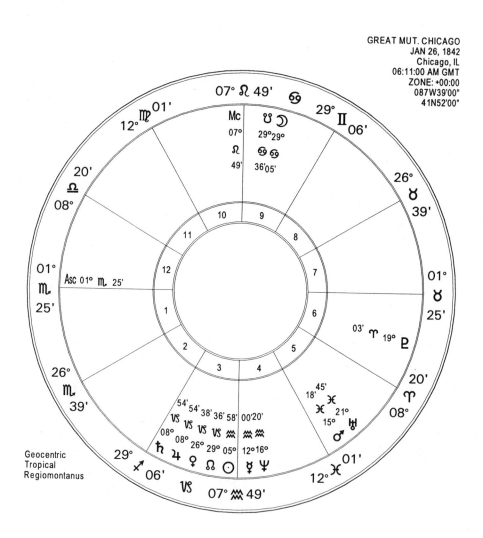

Great Mutation—Chicago

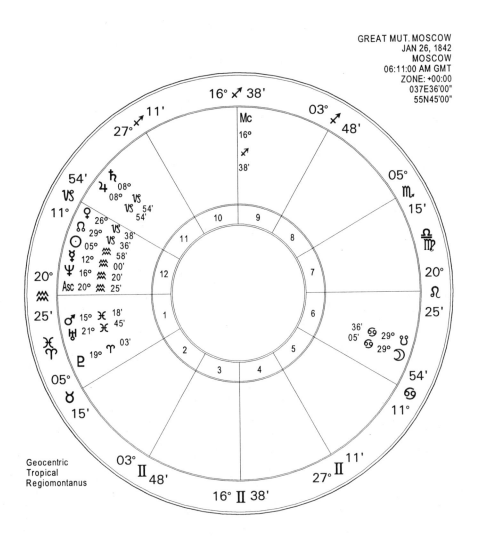

GREAT MUT. MOSCOW
JAN 26, 1842
MOSCOW
06:11:00 AM GMT
ZONE: +00:00
037E36'00"
55N45'00"

Geocentric
Tropical
Regiomontanus

Great Mutation—Moscow, U.S.S.R.*

*Since it is important to be able to check events against charts, the U.S.S.R. chart
should stand until we know the full implications of the events of the past couple of years.

THE UNITED STATES
INCEPTION CHART

Much controversy surrounds the true birth or inception chart of the United States. The following explains the use of the Sagittarius rising July 4th chart in this work.

The Date

Classic horary rules would mandate the signing and actual adoption of the Constitution as the proper date for an inception (natal) chart for a country. Some argument can be made for the signing of the Declaration of Independence, as the the first cohesive and unified action of a communion of men and territory that resulted in a new nation. Neither of those conditions apply to the July 4th birth date. July 4th is the day that the founding fathers (the phrase is significant for Sun in Cancer) determined and agreed on the final wording of the Declaration of Independence. Although not actually signed until August 3rd, that the Declaration materialized in written form on that day is some justification for July 4, 1776 even from a horary point of view.

From a practical and pragmatic stance:

1. The nation celebrates its birth as an independent nation on that date.

2. We have a population consensus for July 4th as the birthday.

3. It is an almost universally accepted date.

Since astrology is a description of the real, not an application of astrological rules, July 4th should stand. The more compelling reason from an astrological point of view, is that the July 4th chart describes the country and fits the events. It works.

The Rising Sign

An equally important controversy is the rising sign. While we like to think of our founding fathers as rushing against the night trying to get consensus and miraculously achieving it at 2 A.M., this neither squares with the facts nor the conditions of history. There was no electricity in 1776. Candles were expensive. The days were long. Most of the attenders were gentlemen farmers who rose and slept with the motions of the Sun. The convention was held in the summer months to give them more daylight time to work and argue. The birth of the United States must have taken place during daylight hours or shortly after dark if it was necessary to hold the meeting over because they were too close to agreement to risk letting any of their members sleep on it.

On July 4th the Declaration was accepted in written form. It was not the end of a hassle, but the beginning of a document. The Sagittarius Rising chart is the only chart that not only meets the conditions of history but describes the realities of the United States as an economic entity.

If you read the Declaration, you see a document not only full of noble ideals as to why the U.S. should break from England, but also a rather boring complaint of taxes and injustices against the mother country: ruling planet, Jupiter, in Cancer conjunct the Sun and Venus in the sign on the 8th of debt and taxes: a protest about being treated like other peoples' property.

The Rising Degree

The rising degree is difficult to ascertain because of the many other important charts that impact the affairs of a nation. Because of the timing of events in general and the economic ones in particular the degree should fall between 5° and 10° of Sagittarius. This degree area is highly charged in the Mutation chart: 10° is the rising sign, 8° is the conjunction of Jupiter and Saturn, 5° is the Sun.

Five degrees of Sagittarius give 22° of Virgo on the MC with Neptune in an exact conjunction. Ten degrees gives 29° of Virgo. Virgo must be on the MC for several reasons.

1. The short terms of the presidency.
2. The stated attempt to keep the ruler weak: Virgo, ruled by a retrograde Mercury.
3. A Virgo/Neptune/retrograde Mercury describe George III, the ruler at the time, considered to be weak and something less than bright.

Because of the high degree of activity in the 5° and 22° areas during economic turns in this country, we will arbitrarily choose 5°. All three work equally well and equally bad when applying primary directions to events. The 5° area puts the ruling planet in the 8th house which perfectly describes a country that functions almost exclusively and highly successfully in debt.

Events Over Time

The progress of Saturn and Jupiter through the national chart also has a major impact on the economy of any country. The chart used for the United States is the Sagittarius rising chart for a very simple reason—the United States *always* has a recession or depression with Saturn in Capricorn, the sign on the 2nd house of money. It always has an economic jolt when Saturn joins, squares or opposes its natal Saturn in Libra, which rules the 2nd house. And it does not, despite Sun, Venus, and Jupiter in Cancer, have a wildly prosperous time with Jupiter in Cancer, because a Jupiter passage through the 8th house is not as likely to bring money as it is to bring debt. If the United States had Sun, Jupiter, and Venus in the 2nd, as on the widely used Gemini Rising chart, not only would we be consistently and persistently wealthy, we would have fabulous prosperity when Jupiter transits Cancer. We do not. We have a wealthy economy that is constantly beset by boom and bust. The only reason we did not have a major bust in the 1950s (apart from some wise government decisions at the time) was that our progressed Sun was in Capricorn passing through the 2nd house. Instead of losing substance, we were raking in almost half of the world's gold. The United States chart is not a matter of calculation or speculation, but simply of observation. Balance sheets do not lie.

BIBLIOGRAPHY

Suggested reading to assist in research, investing, and in understanding astro-economics and astrology.

Appleby and McCann, *Eclipses*. Wellingborough, England: The Aquarian Press, 1989.

Baigent, Campion, Harvey, *Mundane Astrology*. Wellingborough, England: The Aquarian Press, 1984.

Bradley, Donald, A., *Stock Market Prediction*. St. Paul, MN: Llewellyn Publications, 1968.

Donoghue, William E., *Donoghue's Mutual Fund Almanac*. Published annually. Contains starting dates of mutual funds.

Grun, Bernard, *Timetables of History*. New York: Simon and Shuster, New Uork, 1974.

Guarino, Frank J., *Relationship of Stock Market Fluctuations to the Lunar Cycle*. Tempe, AZ: American Federation of Astrologers, 1978.

Long, Jeanne, Editor, *A Traders Astrological Almanac*. Ft. Lauderdale, FL. Annual compilation of astro-economic data.

Matrix Software, *Compact Data System*. Includes Carol Mull's compilation of corporate/stock data.

McEvers, Joan, Editor, *Financial Astrology*. St. Paul, MN: Llewellyn Publications, 1991.

Moody's Handbook of Common Stocks.

Moody's Handbook of OTC Stocks. Both *Moody's* contain start-
     ing dates of many large and medium publicly traded com-
     panies. Published quarterly.

Munkasey, Michael, *The Astrological Thesaurus.* St. Paul, MN:
     Llewellyn Publications, 1992

Reider, Thomas, *Astrological Warnings and the Stock Market.*
     Toronto, Canada: Pagurian Press Limited, 1972.

United States Bureau of the Census, *Statistical History of the
     United States.* New York: Basic Books, 1976

Williams, Lcdr. David, *Astro-Economics.* St. Paul, MN:
     Llewellyn Publications, 1970.

INDEX

C

STAY IN TOUCH

On the following pages you will find listed, with their current prices, some of the books now available on related subjects. Your book dealer stocks most of these and will stock new titles in the Llewellyn series as they become available. We urge your patronage.

To obtain our full catalog, to keep informed about new titles as they are released and to benefit from informative articles and helpful news, you are invited to write for our bimonthly news magazine/catalog, *Llewellyn's New Worlds of Mind and Spirit*. A sample copy is free, and it will continue coming to you at no cost as long as you are an active mail customer. Or you may subscribe for just $7.00 in the U.S.A. and Canada ($20.00 overseas, first class mail). Many bookstores also have *New Worlds* available to their customers. Ask for it.

Stay in touch! In *New Worlds'* pages you will find news and features about new books, tapes and services, announcements of meetings and seminars, articles helpful to our readers, news of authors, products and services, special money-making opportunities, and much more.

Llewellyn's New Worlds of Mind and Spirit
P.O. Box 64383-364, St. Paul, MN 55164-0383, U.S.A.

TO ORDER BOOKS AND TAPES

If your book dealer does not have the books described on the following pages readily available, you may order them direct from the publisher by sending full price in U.S. funds, plus $3.00 for postage and handling for orders *under* $10.00; $4.00 for orders *over* $10.00. There are no postage and handling charges for orders over $50.00. Postage and handling rates are subject to change. UPS Delivery: We ship UPS whenever possible. Delivery guaranteed. Provide your street address as UPS does not deliver to P.O. Boxes. UPS to Canada requires a $50.00 minimum order. Allow 4-6 weeks for delivery. Orders outside the U.S.A. and Canada: Airmail—add retail price of book; add $5.00 for each non-book item (tapes, etc.); add $1.00 per item for surface mail.

FOR GROUP STUDY AND PURCHASE

Because there is a great deal of interest in group discussion and study of the subject matter of this book, we feel that we should encourage the adoption and use of this particular book by such groups by offering a special quantity price to group leaders or agents.

Our special quantity price for a minimum order of five copies of *Time & Money* is $38.85 cash-with-order. This price includes postage and handling within the United States. Minnesota residents must add 6.5% sales tax. For additional quantities, please order in multiples of five. For Canadian and foreign orders, add postage and handling charges as above. Credit card (VISA, MasterCard, American Express) orders are accepted. Charge card orders only ($15.00 minimum order) may be phoned in free within the U.S.A. or Canada by dialing 1-800-THE-MOON. For customer service, call 1-612-291-1970. Mail orders to:

LLEWELLYN PUBLICATIONS
P.O. Box 64383-364, St. Paul, MN 55164-0383, U.S.A.

COMPUTERIZED ASTROLOGY REPORTS

Simple Natal APS03-119: Your chart calculated by computer in the Tropical/Placidus House system or the House system of your choice. It has all of the trimmings, including aspects, midpoints, Chiron and a glossary of symbols, plus a free booklet! **$5.00**

Personality Profile Horoscope APS03-503: Our most popular reading! This ten-part reading gives you a complete look at how the planets affect you. Learn about your general characteristics and life patterns. Look into your imagination and emotional needs. It is an excellent way to become acquainted with astrology and to learn about yourself. Very reasonable price!........**$20.00**

Transit Forecasts: These reports keep you abreast of positive trends and challenging periods. Transit Forecasts can be a helpful aid for timing your actions and decision making. Reports begin the first day of the month you specify.

  3-month Transit Forecast APS03-500 ....**$15.00**
  6-month Transit Forecast APS03-501..**$30.00**
  1-year Transit Forecast APS03-502 ....**$50.00**

READINGS BY PROFESSIONAL ASTROLOGERS

These chart readings are done by experienced, professional astrologers who focus on your particular concerns. Include descriptive letter along with your birth data.

Detailed Natal APS03-102: Complete natal chart plus interpretation with the focus on one specific question as stated by you. Learn about aspects of your chart and what they mean to you. **$65.00**

Complete Natal APS03-101: Our most thorough reading. It not only gives you the computer chart and detailed reading, but also interpretation of the trends shown in your chart for the coming year. It is activated by transits and focuses on any issue you specify. Include full birth data and a descriptive letter.**$125.00**

Compatibility Reading APS03-114: Determines the compatibility of two people in any type of relationship. Two natal charts plus an interpretation are included. Give birth data for both..**$75.00**

Progressed Chart with Transits APS03-105: Your birth chart is progressed by techniques to determine what it says about you now. Use this reading to understand the evolution of your personal power. Provides interpretation of present and future conditions for a year's time with a special focus as stated by you..**$85.00**

Horary Chart APS03-110: Gives the answer to any specific questions. This is divination at its best. Should you marry? Will you get a new job soon? Give precise time and day of writing letter...**$50.00**

PREDICTION IN ASTROLOGY
A Master Volume of Technique and Practice
by Noel Tyl

No matter how much you know about astrology already, you'll be fascinated by *Prediction in Astrology*. Using the Solar Arc theory and methods he describes in this book, the author was able to accurately predict the Gulf War, including the actual date it would begin and the timetable of tactics, two months *before* it began. He also predicted the overturning of Communist rule in the Eastern bloc nations nine months in advance of its actual occurrence.

  Tyl teaches through example. You learn by doing astrology. Tyl introduces Solar Arc theory in terms of "rapport" measurements, which you begin to do immediately, without paper, pencil, or computer, dials, or wheels. Just with your eyes! You will never look at a horoscope the same way again!

  Tyl also gets personal. He presents 30 Aphorisms, the keenest of maxims, the most practical of techniques, to create predictions from any horoscope, and 20 Aphorisms for Counseling. Look for Tyl's "Quick-Glance" Transit Table, 1940-2040, to which you can refer more quickly than a computer. The busy astrologer will use this Appendix every day for many years to come.

0-87542-814-2, 360 pgs., 6 x 9, softcover **$14.95**

HOW TO USE VOCATIONAL ASTROLOGY FOR SUCCESS IN THE WORKPLACE
edited by Noel Tyl

Announcing the most practical examination of Vocational Astrology in five decades! Improve your astrological skills with these revolutionary NEW tools for vocational and business analysis! Now, in *How to Use Vocational Astrology for Success in the Workplace,* edited by Noel Tyl, seven respected astrologers provide their well-seasoned modern views on that great issue of personal life— Work. Their expert advice will prepare you well for those tricky questions clients often ask: "Am I in the right job?" "Will I get promoted?" or "When is the best time to make a career move?"

With an introduction by Noel Tyl, discussing the startling research of the Gauquelins, this ninth volume in Llewellyn's New World Astrology Series features enlightening counsel from these experts:

- Jayj Jacobs: The Transits of Experience/Career Cycles, Job Changes and Rewards
- Gina Ceaglio: Money Patterns in the Horoscope
- Donna Cunningham: Attitudes and Aptitudes in the Chart
- Anthony Louis: Void-of-Course Moon Strategies for Doing Business, Retrograde Planets, and Electional Astrology
- Noel Tyl: Special Measurements for Vocational Guidance, and How to Evaluate Personnel for Profit
- Henry Weingarten: 12 Principles of Modern Astro-Vocational Guidance, Planetary Rulership and Career Guidance, and The 21st Century Astrologer
- Bob Mulligan: How to Advance *Your Own* Career as a Professional Astrologer!

Read *How to Use Vocational Astrology* today, and add "Vocational Counselor" to *your* resume tomorrow! Includes the complete 1942 classic by Charles E. Luntz *Vocational Guidance by Astrology*

0-87542-387-6, 384 pgs., 6 x 9, illus., softcover..................................$14.95

FINANCIAL ASTROLOGY
Edited by Joan McEvers

Money . . . investment . . . finance . . . speculation. The contributors to this popular book in Llewellyn's New World Astrology Series have vast financial and astrological experience and are well-known in the field. Did you know that new tools such as the 360 dial and the graphic ephemeris can help you spot impending market changes? Learn about the various types of analysis and how astrology fine-tunes these methods. Covered cycles include the Lunar Cycle, the Mars/Vesta Cycle, the 4-1/2-year Martian Cycle, the 500-year Civilization Cycle used by Nostradamus, the Kondratieff Wave and the Elliot Wave.

- Michael Munkasey: A Primer on Market Forecasting
- Pat Esclavon Hardy: Charting the United States and the NYSE
- Jeanne Long: New Concepts for Commodities Trading Combining Astrology and Technical Analysis
- Georgia Stathis: The Real Estate Process
- Mary B. Downing: An Investor's Guide to Financial Astrology
- Judy Johns: The Gann Technique
- Carol S. Mull: Predicting the Dow
- Bill Meridian: The Effect of Planetary Stations on U.S. Stock Prices
- Georgia Stathis: Delineating the Corporation
- Robert Cole: The Predictable Economy

0-87542-382-5, 368 pgs., 5-1/4 x 8, illus., softcover............................$14.95

THE ASTROLOGY OF THE MACROCOSM
New Directions in Mundane Astrology
Edited by Joan McEvers

Explains various mundane, transpersonal and worldly events through astrology. The perfect introduction to understanding the fate of nations, weather patterns and other global movements.

- Jimm Erickson: A Philosophy of Mundane Astrology
- Judy Johns: The Ingress Chart
- Jim Lewis: Astro*Carto*Graphy—Bringing Mundane Astrology Down to Earth
- Richard Nolle: The SuperMoon Alignment
- Chris McRae: The Geodetic Equivalent Method of Prediction
- Nicholas Campion: The Age of Aquarius—A Modern Myth
- Nancy Soller: Weather Watching with an Ephemeris
- Marc Penfield: The Mystery of the Romanovs
- Steve Cozzi: The Astrological Quatrains of Michel Nostradamus
- Diana K. Rosenberg: Stalking the Wild Earthquake
- Caroline W. Casey: Dreams and Disasters—Patterns of Cultural and Mythological Evolution into the 21st Century

0-87542-384-1, 420 pgs., 5-1/4 x 8, charts, softcover **$19.95**

THE LLEWELLYN ANNUALS

Llewellyn's MOON SIGN BOOK: Approximately 400 pages of valuable information on gardening, fishing, weather, stock market forecasts, personal horoscopes, good planting dates, and general instructions for finding the best date to do just about anything! Articles by prominent forecasters and writers in the fields of gardening, astrology, politics, economics and cycles. This special almanac, different from any other, has been published annually since 1906. It's fun, informative and has been a great help to millions in their daily planning. ....**State year $4.95**

Llewellyn's SUN SIGN BOOK: Your personal horoscope for the entire year! All 12 signs are included in one handy book. Also included are forecasts, special feature articles, and an action guide for each sign. Monthly horoscopes are written by Gloria Star, author of *Optimum Child*, for your personal Sun Sign and there are articles on a variety of subjects written by well-known astrologers from around the country. Much more than just a horoscope guide! Entertaining and fun the year around. ....**State year $4.95**

Llewellyn's DAILY PLANETARY GUIDE: Includes all of the major daily aspects plus their exact times in Eastern and Pacific time zones, lunar phases, signs and voids plus their times, planetary motion, a monthly ephemeris, sunrise and sunset tables, special articles on the planets, signs, aspects, a business guide, planetary hours, rulerships, and much more. Large 5-1/4 x 8 format for more writing space, spiral bound to lay flat, address and phone listings, time-zone conversion chart and blank horoscope chart. **State year $6.95**

Llewellyn's ASTROLOGICAL CALENDAR: Large wall calendar of 48 pages. Beautiful full-color cover and full-color paintings inside. Includes special feature articles by famous astrologers, and complete introductory information on astrology. It also contains a Lunar Gardening Guide, celestial phenomena, a blank horoscope chart, and monthly date pages which include aspects, Moon phases, signs and voids, planetary motion, an ephemeris, personal forecasts, lucky dates, planting and fishing dates, and more. 10 x 13 size. Set in Central time, with fold-down conversion table for other time zones worldwide. ....**State year $9.95**